We Never Expected That

We Never Expected That

A Comparative Study of Failures in National and Business Intelligence

Avner Barnea

LEXINGTON BOOKS
Lanham • Boulder • New York • London

Published by Lexington Books
An imprint of The Rowman & Littlefield Publishing Group, Inc.
4501 Forbes Boulevard, Suite 200, Lanham, Maryland 20706
www.rowman.com

6 Tinworth Street, London SE11 5AL, United Kingdom

British Library Cataloguing in Publication Information Available

Library of Congress Cataloging-in-Publication Data

Names: Barnea, Avner, author.
Title: We never expected that : a comparative study of failures in national and business intelligence / Avner Barnea.
Description: Lanham : Lexington Books, [2021] | Includes bibliographical references and index. | Summary: "The basic premise of this book is that in both fields, national and business, intelligence gathered about adversaries or competitors regarding changes in the external environment support the decision-making process. In both fields the subject has been studied within its own framework without comparative analysis or mutual learning"—Provided by publisher.
Identifiers: LCCN 2021027581 (print) | LCCN 2021027582 (ebook) | ISBN 9781793619884 (cloth) | ISBN 9781793619891 (ebook) Subjects:
LCSH: Business intelligence. | Intelligence service. | Decision making.
Classification: LCC HD38.7 .B3675 2021 (print) | LCC HD38.7 (ebook) | DDC 658.4/72—dc3
LC record available at https://lccn.loc.gov/2021027581
LC ebook record available at https://lccn.loc.gov/2021027582

Contents

List of Tables

Preface

We Never Expected That: A Comparative Study of Failures in National and Business Intelligence

By Avner Barnea

The disciplines of strategic intelligence at the governmental level and competitive intelligence constitute accepted methods of decision-supporting to prevent mistakes and strategic surprise. Through my research, I discovered that many researchers in the intelligence field feel that intelligence methodology in both contexts has reached a "glass ceiling." In addition, research has focused separately on national intelligence and intelligence in business, without any attempt to benchmark from one field to the other. In this book, I show that it is possible to use experience gained in the business field to improve intelligence practices in national security, and vice versa through mutual learning. This book focuses on a comparison between how states, through their intelligence organizations, cope with strategic surprises, and how business organizations deal with unexpected movement in their field. Based on this comparison, I propose a new model that distinguishes between *concentrated* and *diffused* surprises; this will provide a breakthrough in the intelligence field, and facilitate better prediction of the surprise development. This, I think, is the book's main innovation.

I believe that this book can contribute significantly to the study of intelligence, which hopefully will become more influential in the coming years.

The basic premise of this book is that in both fields, national and business, intelligence gathered about adversaries or competitors regarding changes in the external environment support the decision-making process. In both fields, the subject has been studied only within its own framework without comparative analysis or mutual learning. Thus, both fields need improvement, which can be achieved through cross-organizational research. This is especially important, given that it is the decision makers who receive and process information and who tend to make mistakes; however, errors are investigated more efficiently in business organizations than in intelligence entities.

I would like to extend my special thanks to Professor Uri Bar-Joseph, my thesis advisor from the University of Haifa, in Israel, for helping me formulate my hypotheses and turning them into a comprehensive model, which provides a different perspective on strategic surprises. I also give special thanks to my good friends, Professor Avraham Meshulach, in the Business School, of the Hebrew University of Jerusalem, and to Professor Avraham Sela, in the Department of Internal Relations, at the Hebrew University of Jerusalem, for their advice and support. This book would not be published without Elizabeth Yuval's dedicated translation from Hebrew.

Finally, I want to specially thank my wife Hani, and my children Nir, Gal, Lior, and Rotem, whose great support has helped me to write this book.

Acknowledgments

This book is based on the author's PhD thesis, and the Hebrew book called *We Did Not Anticipate That: A Comparative Study of Failures in National and Business Intelligence*, which was launched in Israel in 2019. Based on the feedback received on my Hebrew book, the author was encouraged to share his ideas with larger audiences in English. The process of translating and editing this book was quite challenging and especially so in the time of the CORONA 19 virus. It took longer than expected.

The author thanks his PhD tutor Professor Uri Bar-Joseph, from the Department of International Relations, the University of Haifa. Professor Bar-Joseph had such a significant input into the process of deciding what will be researched and later during the process of the research and writing. As the issue that was researched was a comparative study of intelligence failures in National Intelligence and in Business, the author had the opportunity to receive a great support and valuable feedback from Professor Avi Meshulach, the former dean of the Business School in the Hebrew University of Jerusalem. A special acknowledgment goes to Professor Avraham Sela from the Department of International Relations of the Hebrew University of Jerusalem. Finally, the author would like to thank numerous readers who came across with my book in Hebrew and also participants in various workshops where he presents his ideas and gave incredible feedback.

The task that the writer took upon himself to write a comparative study that had never been done before put a lot of pressure while the expectations were high and there was a risk that it will be hard to fulfill them. Hope that the readers, practitioners, scholars and students will find the content of this book challenging and encouraging in further thinking and discussion.

Avner Barnea

Introduction

The failure of intelligence to provide warnings, in the realms of both national security and business, is the subject of ongoing research, especially regarding warnings of sudden attacks. It has been the main topic of strategic studies since Roberta Wohlstetter published a groundbreaking book in the early 1960s about the Japanese attack on Pearl Harbor. In the world of business, the lack of warning about developing threats, such as the economic crisis of September 2008 or the collapse of global conglomerates, reflects problems similar to those of national security and have not been sufficiently investigated. So far, national and economic threats have been studied separately, without mutually identifying and implementing the lessons learned. This book will show how a joint research can enrich the understanding of intelligence failures, and will separate strategic surprises into two types contributes to explain these failures. This understanding can help improve our preparation for strategic surprises.

So far, almost every study of strategic surprises and national intelligence failures has focused on a certain type of strategic surprise, usually a surprise attack (Handel 2003), which can be described as a *deliberate* or *concentrated attack*. Concentrated attacks are planned by one actor to prevent a rival actor from carrying out plans (Singer 1958) through concealment and disinformation, thereby achieving a unilateral advantage. Familiar examples are Operation Barbarossa, Pearl Harbor, and the Yom Kippur War. However, no serious attention has been paid to another kind of surprise attack, one which is *spontaneous* and *unplanned*, that is, a *diffused attack* that has not been orchestrated by organizations and cannot be predicted. Thus, it is difficult for countermeasures to be taken, because the objective of the attack is less well-defined since it is being the result of spontaneous social and political processes, such as popular uprisings. Examples are the Iranian Islamic Revolution in 1979, the First and Second Palestinian Intifadas, in 1987 and

2000, respectively, and the so-called Arab Spring in 2011. In effect, there are now two types of surprise attacks that occur, rather than one, yet the study of intelligence failures has not changed.

In the past, the analysis of intelligence failures was based on events that had already occurred, which were, generally speaking, concentrated attacks. Theoretically, at least, much can be learned from events in other fields, such as business, to improve prediction capabilities to prevent intelligence surprises. Intelligence failure and strategic surprise are also studied in the field of business, not only to prevent concentrated attacks by rivals but also to predict broad marketing changes and consumer preferences to prevent, insofar as is possible, unpredictable events. National intelligence, which finds it difficult to deal with unpredictable attacks, can learn from the world of business.

This book focuses on two types of surprises, concentrated and diffused, in two realms, national and business, and presents an attempt to understand why both are subject to intelligence failures. The four types of surprises are compared depending on the environments in which they occur (national intelligence or business) and whether they are concentrated or diffused. These four types of surprises were not taken into consideration in the past, examining them reveals new aspects of intelligence failures. This book intends to present a new model for preventing prediction errors based on the distinction between concentrated and diffused surprises. At its core are three hypotheses: one, that the causes of intelligence failures in the national and business realms are similar; two, that lessons learned from one realm can improve the understanding of surprises in the others; and three, such an understanding can improve coping with intelligence failures by providing early warnings in both realms.

Until now, the focus of research has been on examining the failures of the intelligence target assessor, but this book examines the issues from the viewpoint of the assessed intelligence target, through an analysis of the difficulties experienced in preventing diffused surprises. Issues that leak from the business to the national realm and vice versa will be noted to show how they contribute to the theoretical aspects of improving intelligence work. The problem is that, in practice, the theoretical models encounter difficulties, which will be dealt with below.

Four strategic intelligence failures are presented as test cases, each of which illustrates one type of surprise in each realm and provides a framework for studying the others. The four illustrate the common problems confronting national and business intelligence and can help formulate ways to better deal with strategic surprises and prevent intelligence failures in the future. The examples are in no way exceptional and were chosen from a long list of strategic surprises that had proved to be intelligence failures.

The first test case is the First Palestinian Intifada, which broke out in December 1987 and was a *diffused national security surprise*. The second is the 9/11 terrorist attack, which was a *concentrated national security surprise*. The third test case is the 2008 Recession in the United States, which was a *diffused strategic surprise*, and the fourth is the 1993 collapse of IBM, which was a *concentrated strategic surprise*.

As this book was put into final form during the COVID-19 pandemic, it is also possible to ask if the model presented here could have been useful in giving an early warning for its outbreak. We are aware of how challenging it is to recognize early warnings, but had there been one for COVID-19, it would have been a great benefit for the world.

One possibility is that COVID-19 was an example of a "diffused surprise," my newly recognized type of attack, which develops over time, is spontaneous and unplanned attack, and is not orchestrated by rivals. That is why it is difficult to predict and warn against. Perceiving COVID-19 as diffused attack could be relevant to an analysis of the difficulties in issuing a timely warning for the pandemic. When the first outbreak occurred in Wuhan, China, in December 2019, the world at large ignored the potential threat by relating to it as far away, like the SARS epidemic in 2002–2003. Understanding it as a diffused attack or threat could have led to more effective research from the early signals. Governments, businesses, and NGOs are struggling with the rapid disruption to institutional, corporate, and political life. Based on diffused and spontaneous attacks, it would have been possible to act differently and predict more accurately. It is important to note that apparently there had been an American intelligence unit that had issued an early warning, only to be rebuffed by the decision makers, who did not respond immediately and make preparations to deal with a pandemic.

Chapter 1

Surprise and Intelligence Failure

Studies of strategic surprise and intelligence failure have dealt, for the most part, with military surprises which, generally speaking, have been failures of intelligence organizations that have erred in assessing the enemy's intentions or capabilities. Monitoring such threats has been the responsibility of military intelligence and intelligence organizations dealing with foreign countries. There also have been cases of strategic surprises related to internal security, such as the 9/11 attacks or popular uprisings, the First and Second Palestinian Intifadas, the so-called Arab Spring, and events of the type generally monitored by internal security organizations, known as counterintelligence organizations. Organizations monitoring foreign countries also have been expected to participate in events occurring in their respective provinces, yet the CIA failed to issue an alert for Khomeini's Iranian Islamic Revolution or the Arab Spring, in Egypt.

In the world of commerce, intelligence has been active in assessing threats from competitors, and companies have shown themselves to be extremely competent in identifying customers and clients who had been liable to have left them for a different company, which could have hurt them financially.

Comprehensive studies of national intelligence failures and strategic surprises have been carried out for the past fifty years. They have successfully isolated military-security intelligence failures from other relevant failures, making it possible to focus on their causes in the hopes of preventing recurrences in the future. In the world of commerce, on the other hand, studies of intelligence surprises and failures have found it difficult to distinguish between the various types of failures and to isolate intelligence as a standalone topic. However, according to the literature, it is important for companies to monitor the competitive environment where intelligence threats often develop; this is part of business strategy and is a key business concept.

This book presents a theoretical research framework that divides, for the first time, strategic surprises and national and business intelligence failures into two categories, concentrated surprise and diffused surprise. By doing so it raises the question of the extent to which intelligence research has to think, from the beginning, not only in terms of concentrated surprise, which has been the usual procedure, but also in terms of diffused surprise, or in terms of both. As the test cases will show, awareness apparently has been low. In addition, this study relates to an important issue, namely the assessed intelligence target. In cases of diffused surprise, it has been difficult to identify the threat posed by the assessed intelligence target, because of the habit of regarding issues only as concentrated surprises. When intelligence does not have a clear target, it cannot focus its collection efforts. That has led to a failure in the "intelligence cycle" process, which has ended with the final production of an intelligence report which has not successfully identified the threat because it had not focused on the correct target. This is another innovation in the theoretical concept presented here: normally, when failure has occurred, it has been the decisions made by the analyst (the intelligence researcher or competitive intelligence practitioner) that have been examined, and attempts to improve his capabilities and skills have been based on an analysis of the events. However, there have been instances in which the assessed intelligence target had to be identified and verified, in order to have explained the failure.

The book presents two major innovations:

It separates the surprise into two categories, concentrated and diffused, and then it explains the areas of the intelligence failures, national intelligence and business. Until now, explanations characterizing most intelligence surprises have been of the concentrated surprise type, although they were not recognized as such. With concentrated surprises, the assessed intelligence target usually has been a known organization that has been identified as a threat. On the other hand, it has been difficult to identify the intelligence target in diffused surprises, which has increased the risk of their occurrence.

The concept of the diffused surprise has two aspects. One is that it is a specific type of strategic surprise, which in the past usually has been analyzed as a concentrated surprise, but the explanations given for it were unconvincing. Since intuitively there has been a tendency to look for explanations for a concentrated surprise, it sometimes has been difficult to understand that the specific case has been a different type of surprise. Another aspect of the diffused surprise is that, generally speaking, analysis usually has dealt with mistakes and difficulties on the part of the assessors, but it will be argued in this book that failure also has been the result of an assessment of the target instead of the assessor. That means that when an intelligence failure has been exposed, the type of surprise must be identified, and when a mistake has been made in predicting the surprise, part of the reason has been a failure in assessing the intelligence target which, in retrospect, has been the surprise factor. That error has had long-term consequences. When the surprise actually has occurred, collecting information about the wrong intelligence target has produced irrelevant information, the conclusions drawn have been incorrect, and so it had been difficult to formulate an alert. This also has occurred in the world of business. However, as business and marketing have operated together and have been more aware of the possibility of surprise, they have not focused only on the targets (their competitors), but also have been aware of the need to monitor their target audiences, usually their customers. Their objective has been to attain insights to help them make decisions, even if they have not been aware of the distinction between concentrated and diffused surprises. According to Chart 1, failure to distinguish between concentrated and diffused surprises leads to two sources of error in prediction, focused and diffused key intelligence topics, making it even more difficult to identify the threat.

Daniel Kahneman says the following: "The ability to be surprised is an essential aspect of our mental lives and the surprise itself is the most sensitive indicator of how we understand our world and our expectations from it" (Kahneman 2013, 85–86). He has divided surprise into two categories, active and passive. An active surprise is when you actively expect a certain event to take place, and you are surprised if it does not occur. However, there is a much broader category of event you expect passively. While you do not wait for it to occur, you are surprised if it does not materialize. Passive surprises are normal events which, while they are uncertain, make you actively anticipate them.

In the field of intelligence, some surprises can be categorized according to Kahneman's second type: information is continually monitored passively, events are expected to occur because they are part of the intelligence routine, but it is uncertain whether they will take place. If an intelligence analyst does not actively expect events to occur, he will find it difficult to prevent a surprise. Under certain circumstances, passive expectations become active, which increases the possibility of preventing a surprise. According to Kahneman, an error in assessing an intelligence target, which can be shown to be a diffused surprise is, to a certain extent, a passive surprise. Since intelligence analysts have been used to active surprises (called "concentrated surprises" in this book), the chances of a passive (or "diffused") surprise occurring have increased (chart 1).

To examine the theoretical model at the foundation of the study, four test cases have been chosen, two in the field of national intelligence failures (one concentrated and one diffused) and two in the field of business intelligence failures (one concentrated and one diffused). The four will be compared here, according to environment and type of surprise (chart 2).

Chart 1 The Distinction between Concentrated Surprise and Diffused Surprise

Concentrated Surprise	*Diffused Surprise*
Focused key intelligence topics	Diffused key intelligence topics
↓	↓
New information Intelligence cycle	New information Intelligence cycle
↓	↓
Error in prediction Failure explained (concentrated surprise)	Error in prediction Failure explained (diffused surprise)

Source: Avner Barnea, 2020.

The test cases are representative of intelligence failures and comparing them makes them easier to understand. We'll examine how well each performed in predicting the surprise, which will enable us to expand our explanations for prediction failures. Comparing these four test cases also provides us with the possibility of using the experience gained in intelligence activities in the business field to improve intelligence in the national field, and vice versa. That means that in the future, in the case of a strategic surprise, the question asked will be what type it is. Raising the awareness of the intelligence community to the existence of two types of surprises will help focus on the key intelligence target, which is the key to dealing with information which is supposed to indicate an approaching threat in time.

The theoretical development of the research presented, here, about diffused surprises and distinguishing them from concentrated surprises can, to a certain extent, be credited to the *grounded theory* (Glaser & Strauss 1967).

In my review of the literature on national and business intelligence, I have concluded that the phenomenon of a diffused surprise is a threat that has developed over time, in which an organization, intelligence agencies, and decision makers have been surprised by a diffused external threat coming from many organizations and/or broad populations that have not necessarily coordinated among themselves.

Chart 2 Test Studies According to the Type of Surprise and Its Environment

	Concentrated Surprise	*Diffused Surprise*
National Intelligence	Palestinian Intifada	9/11
Business Intelligence	2008	IBM

Source: Avner Barnea, 2020.

The research method that I have employed in the research, for each of the test cases, was a comparative analysis of the assessment of intelligence groups and decision makers before the event and any changes in assessment following information received; in addition, I have examined the reasons for changes or the absence of change. In other words, I have wanted to determine to what extent the assessment reflected the new information, and what caused the intelligence failure.

Chapter 2

National Intelligence Failures

The field of intelligence failures is broad and is covered by literature that has examined it from several directions. This book focuses on an analysis of intelligence failures along two axes: the national/business axis on the one hand, and the concentrated/diffused axis on the other.

Intelligence and its failures have been studied for the past fifty years and include national security and military operations, which have been examined using a realistic approach, focusing on the conflicts between states and the use of force (Khan 2009; Lawson 2003). At the end of the Second World War, the importance of intelligence rose, and it has come a long way since Clausewitz, who had said that it was unimportant (Ferris and Handel 1995). Sherman Kent (1949) was responsible for an important change when he analyzed strategic intelligence rather than espionage and carrying out missions, as had been the formerly accepted approach. Since Wohlstetter's study on the attack on Pearl Harbor (Wohlstetter 1962), intelligence research has looked at various issues, including collection and assessment, with the interface between the decision-making process and intelligence, difficulties in implementation, and the need to ensure independent intelligence assessments.

One of the main fields in intelligence research is strategic surprise and intelligence failures. Academic research into intelligence, which has dealt mainly with the analysis of past events, developed because of the release of previously classified materials, including from the era of the Cold War. Since 9/11, research has turned to the field of terrorism, because non-state threats have threatened national security (Turbiville 2005). More research attention has been paid to studies of individual events, rather than to development of new research approaches, especially in the field of intelligence failures in current global conditions. The difficulty inherent, for example, in the report of the commission that investigated 9/11, is that very little attention was paid to the need for the improvements necessary in intelligence research methodology (Schmitt 2005).

As was noted, according to Schmitt's above-cited study, most of the intelligence failures have been concentrated surprises, and only a minority have been diffused surprises. Other studies have examined the reasons for failures and have tried to suggest various improvements to prevent future failures. During the Cold War, intelligence had developed in the field of long-term prediction and warning (Davis 2007, 143-165) and there was an improvement in capabilities for collecting intelligence (Fingar 2011). Later, however, especially since 9/11, the intelligence community has had to adapt itself to new situations and has had to focus on tactical warnings and coping with non-state organizations, which have posed a different kind of threat from the ones previously known (European Union 2003). Despite the criticism of the effectiveness and relevance of the main model in intelligence work—that is, the intelligence cycle—for the new, post-9/11 world (Hulnick 2006; Lowenthal 2013), it has continued as the main basis for intelligence work.

This book has aspired to present a new theoretical direction which has not been discussed in the literature about intelligence failures but is appropriate for the post-9/11 era—namely, a direction that goes beyond an empirical analysis of the various factors behind failure, such as structural/organizational, psychological, and political factors. To that end, the two types of surprises will be compared and the possibility of taking conclusions from one field and will be examined and implementing to another field.

NATIONAL INTELLIGENCE FAILURES—CHARACTERISTICS AND CAUSES

The academic research has dealt with the organizational problems of intelligence agencies, among them the culture of excessive compartmentalization, failures resulting from group thinking, structural complexity and intra- and interagency competition, which have had an adverse effect on cooperation and have influenced the usage of intelligence material. Despite the attempts made by intelligence agencies to reduce collective influences, promoting sharing information and work methods encouraging the presentation of a variety of assessments, they apparently have found it difficult to adapt and instead have focused more on attempts to improve intelligence products. Proposals for changing the situation generally have been based on lessons learned from concentrated surprises. However, it has been possible, in cases of diffused surprises, which have been rarer and depend on processes rather than events, to include other factors within intelligence and even beyond it. Research in the fields of business and the social sciences have significantly contributed to improving intelligence, as it has been possible to rely less on information from secret sources. The findings that will be presented below stress the central factors leading to intelligence failures, especially in five main areas:

Intelligence Collection Capabilities

The greatest concern in a surprise attack has been that there will be a change in the intentions without the other side's (i.e., rival, competitor, enemy) having noticed it. The information to be gained from intelligence collection through indicators can serve as a foundation for analysis and assessment and, if necessary, the product can be an early warning. These indicators may relate to preparations that have been made by the enemy and his long-term plans and also to his tactical activity for a coming attack. The attacker can conceal some of the indicators or deliberately feed disinformation, but he cannot conceal all his preparations over time. Responsibility for formulating an alert has belonged to the analysts and they have been judged accordingly (Davis 2002; Kam 1990, 81). The central role of intelligence has continued to be providing the warning in time, to prevent a strategic surprise.

The failure of intelligence collection has only infrequently been the main reason for intelligence failure (Betts 1980; Kam 1990; Wohlstetter, 1962). In 2011, United States senators Wyden and Udall raised doubts about the ability to derive any benefit from the massive quantities of information that had been collected by the NSA (Harris 2013). However, directing intelligence collection, through the key intelligence topics, causes focus to be put on the collection targets. Technological advances in collecting information from signals intelligence (SIGINT) have provided so much raw intelligence, of such a high quality, that 75% of the President's Daily Brief can be based on these sources (Riley 2013; Wheaton 2001). British intelligence also has relied greatly on SIGINT (Traywick 2013). Capabilities in the field of collection and methodical handling through dynamic key intelligence topics, updated indicators for new fields, and overt intelligence have all developed greatly. As a result, improvement in information collection has little significance without an improvement in research (Cordesman 2002, 440).

Collection generally has focused on preventing a concentrated surprise by covering known targets—which have been countries and military organizations. However, when collection has been aware of the possibility of a diffused surprise, there has been the understanding that the intelligence that will be received will be irrelevant to the developing threat; and collection also has realized that there will be a slim chance of receiving an alert to the threat. Since the Arab Spring, greater emphasis has been put on preventing a diffused surprise. Such a course of action usually has been an ongoing process and not an event, and the target covered sometimes has been unclear or not easy to identify. In a diffused surprise, the probability of making a mistake in assessing the intelligence target (the rival) which had not been identified has increased the chances of an unpredicted surprise.

A Noisy Intelligence Environment

A noisy intelligence environment has been characterized by large volumes of information from covert and overt sources of various levels of reliability, which has delayed the process of categorizing and absorbing intelligence before it has been assessed (Kam 1990, 80; Latimer 1979). When information has come in, a distinction has had to have been made between the relevant material, material which has been incorrect because of its nature or sources, and material that has been the result of disinformation, which had been received either actively or passively (Handel 1987, 385-430). The difficulty in distinguishing between signals and noises has been worsened by the amount of information and the necessity to identify contradictory and often ambiguous information, or information that has seemed unreliable. Studies have dealt to a great extent with information that had been influenced by objective difficulties and concepts and biases of intelligence agents (Kam 1990, 222). Jarvis describes unclear situations as situations those in which there has been a difficulty in understanding the importance of signals after different interpretations by different analysts, as well as situations that have had a lack of clear information, the influence from the immediate environment or organizational failures and the influence from the decision makers or due to organizational failures (Jervis 1986, 113-138; Kam 1987, 321-338).

One reason for intelligence failure has been the difficulty of intelligence analysts to categorize and absorb information, before it has been assessed, because of the large volume of information or because it has been unclear and partially contradictory. New, significant information needs to receive the attention it deserves and to be passed along through the intelligence cycle. Support from advanced information systems has been one solution for the initial process of assessing information, along with focusing on the key intelligence topic and improving the capabilities of intelligence analysts. Currently, the analysts have seemed to be directed more toward preventing a concentrated surprise of the more familiar type and related to specific information regarding a threat that they have looked for intuitively. However, while in the case of a diffused surprise, the process has been ongoing and an isolated item of information may be less clear and therefore may be given less attention as the process is ongoing. Another mistake has been in focusing on the key intelligence topic, which has followed from a problem in assessing the intelligence target. While this approach has been characteristic used for a concentrated surprise following a problem in assessing the intelligence target, the information that has arrived has been irrelevant and has made issuing a warning difficult.

Failures Due to Human Error

Identifying threats in time has been a main reason for the existence of intelligence agencies, because they have learned from past events and have used the information for future developments (Herman 1996). The analytic foundation has been an examination of intentions and capabilities which had developed in the intelligence community in the 1950s (NSC 1950) and has not changed, even though, since 2001 there have been fewer well-defined enemies and it has been more difficult to identify them (Kahn 2006). Failures resulting from human error have been investigated, more frequently, in cases of concentrated surprises, in order to improve the situation, and less frequently, in cases of diffused surprises, where the information has been ambiguous, creating difficulties in analyzing the intentions and capabilities in a familiar fashion.

The Difficulties of the Intelligence Analyst

How an intelligence analyst works has not changed despite the massive use of information systems, and the problems that have been identified in the past exist to this day. Most of the intelligence failures have been concentrated surprises: the analysts had incorrectly assessed the measures taken by the other side even though they had been identified and known. In a diffused surprise, the mistake has not only been in identifying the intelligence targets but also in interpreting events over time, after having focused on incorrect targets, and the difficulty of having had to define who the enemy was, and therefore the risk of mistake has been greater. In both types of surprises, the analysts' failures have been significant in producing incorrect assessments.

The literature regarding the difficulties of intelligence analyst has made no distinction between preventing a concentrated surprise and preventing a diffused surprise. The human factor has had weight in mistakes in assessing the threat and the intentions and capabilities of potential enemies. Analysis and human assessment have been regarded as an important factor in intelligence work (Herman 1996) and also in intelligence failures (Church Committee 1976; Johnson 1985; Oron 1988; Sinclair 2010), especially in the wake of the analysts' difficulties and cognitive failures (de Franco and Meyer 2011).

The intelligence analyst usually has had more than one way to explain the enemy's intentions and behavior. In cases of failure, it was obvious that the investigators had tended to choose the assumption that seemed best to them under pressure. They had not always chosen the same assessment later on and sometimes it had become fixed (Heuer 1980). In conflict situations between states, the analysts have had a strong tendency to support existing concepts and avoid predicting change; they have looked for information that had corresponded to trusted assessments (Maddrell 2016), they have rejected information that did not agree with the assessment, or they have changed the information to make it correspond to what they did trust (Baron 2000; Frey 2009; Petersen 2001; Tversky & Kahneman 1974; Zegart 2000). According to Kunda, Tversky and Kahneman (1982), information that had corresponded to preferences had been accepted as is, while information that did not generally was received critically, with a tendency to having been rejected. Wohlstetter showed that certain information could have been viewed from different angles, and the analysts had chosen explanations that corresponded to accepted assumptions (Wohlstetter 1962, 386). Cooper (2005, 26) described a wrong puzzle in which, consciously or not, the analyst arrived at what he wanted to know and not what he should have known, and items of information which had been relevant remained outside the picture, as they had not corresponded to his view.

One of the analyst's difficulties is that he has been under pressure to reach a rapid cognitive closing, that is, to put an end to the intellectual and psychological distress created by vagueness, uncertainty, and doubt (Kruglanski et al., 1993). In 1973, before the Yom Kippur War, Eli Zeira, the head of Israel's military intelligence, had been in a situation Bar-Yoseph (2011) and Kruglanski (2003) had called "cognitive closure": he had been overly confident and not receptive to new information that had contradicted his beliefs. In instances of diffused surprises, that has not been a problem, because the information received had seemed reasonable and analysts had been unaware that it was irrelevant. That is because the key intelligence topic had been incorrect and the information collected had not been what was needed or because monitoring the events had necessitated a rapid cognitive closure.

An additional problem for the investigator has been the source of the information. The way that the investigator has related to information has been influenced by his knowledge and opinion of the source; and therefore there are analysts who have put more faith in information from a covert source than from open-source intelligence (OSINT). Sometimes the reliability of the source has been more important than the content of the information provided, and that has led to bias which has influenced the assessment (Jervis 1976).

Heuer sums up the cognitive challenges facing the analyst. In uncertain situations, where the picture has been fuzzy, the brain has ignored vague information, which has made it difficult to identify deliberately misleading information (Heuer 1999). While there have been concentrated strategic surprises in which disinformation had made it difficult for investigators to grasp the true nature of the situation, such as in Pearl Harbor, Operation Barbarossa and the Yom Kippur War, generally speaking, disinformation has not been a central factor in achieving surprise.

According to Graham and Nussbaum (2008), analytical problems and difficulties have been some of the reasons contributing to intelligence failures. They continue by saying that there also have been the difficulties of understanding changes in the global situation, of the intelligence community's inability to have drawn a clear strategic picture, of defining priorities for intelligence activity, and of recruiting suitable manpower. Thus, it can be seen analysts have confronted many problems when they have examined national intelligence events, and when they had not distinguished between the types of surprises present, various problems arose.

Solutions and explanations are possible. In cases of intelligence failures, the analysts' difficulties have resulted from the complexity of treating information, the influence of bias, and insufficient professional competence. An analysis of intelligence failures and post–Cold War changes has led to conclusions similar to those proposed in the past, namely that it has been necessary to improve analytical capabilities, to increase sensitivity to problematic information and to improve the use of information systems. Despite the changes in a world based on a state system which has become less defined and more diffuse, the analytic base, which began in the United States with a need for alerts regarding the Soviet Union, has not changed and continues to be based on an analysis of the enemy's capabilities and on an early warning of his intentions (Cabinet Office 2009; Cavelty & Mauer 2009; Weiner 2009). A relatively new lesson to be learned has been the need for an increase in the sharing of information, but there have been difficulties in implementing it mainly because of the organizational culture of exaggerated compartmentalization.

Intelligence studies have not changed much since the end of the Cold War and continue to be based on the dual analysis of intent and capability expressed in intelligence products. No improvement has been made in sharing information in intelligence analysis, which was the main recommendation of the 9/11 Commission, and compartmentalization has continued to block it (Treverton 2011). In addition, the use of advanced analytical tools, such as specific computer programs, has not significantly aided in improving the field of analysis. Others have been of the opinion that using information systems has not improved analysis (DeRosa 2004). Warnings of terrorist threats have been different from strategic warnings and general stress tactical and operational aspects, as there has been the need for immediate responses (Davis 2003). Preparing research for terrorism has been faster, but the emphasis has been on an operational response and not on an innovative, theoretical approach (Berkowitz 2003). Attempts have been made to find an alternative research method to replace traditional analysis, in order to provide timely alerts, especially with regard to terrorist attacks, but the solutions proposed have been, generally speaking, an improvement in the practical dealing with the information and not in its theoretical aspects (Hollywood et al. 2004). No tools have been developed for evaluating intelligence products beyond analyses of intelligence failures, which have been thoroughly analyzed, because of their political and social consequences (Dahl 2010).

Treverton is doubtful about the possibility of creating a significant improvement in the analysts' word without the participation of those who need the intelligence who, in turn, would have to define their needs and provide feedback (Treverton 2001). The problem lies not only with the analysts but also with the influence that has been exerted on them by internal and external factors, which has led to lessening the quality of intelligence analysis (Bar-Joseph & McDermoth 2008; Betts 2004; Nisbitt & Ross 1980). The literature has focused on the need for improvement to prevent concentrated surprises in national intelligence and not on the development of a new analytic approach that would, for example, cope with both terrorism and NGOs. Less attention has been paid to the development of analytic capabilities for preventing diffused surprises, since intelligence has had no interest in it. An intelligence analyst has not been aware of diffused concepts, as he has not dealt with them. Apparently, the literature has focused on assessment and offers solutions which have been more of the same, instead of having focused on the assessed, which has been the object of attention for a diffused surprise, and which also has made both assessment and identification difficult.

Organizational Difficulties and Faulty Collaboration

Difficulties in creating good intelligence assessments also have arisen from the organizational aspects of intelligence work. There have been organizational barriers between senior and junior-level operatives that have damaged not only the process of preparing intelligence assessments but also their distribution to various levels. Intelligence organizations have been large and hierarchical and operated according to procedure, and barriers have been liable to influence the quality of the intelligence product (Betts 1980; Wilensky 1967). In addition, the organizations have competed with one another and there also has been intramural competition. The changes that occurred after 2001 have necessitated greater flexibility and rapidity that have made it possible to react more quickly to threats from non-state organizations, but no special effort in that direction seems to have been made, despite the recommendations of the 9/11 Commission and the 2003 invasion of Iraq.

The academic research has dealt with the organizational difficulties of intelligence organizations, among them the culture of excessive compartmentalization, failures caused by group thinking, the complexity of intelligence organizations and inter- and intra-organizational competition, all of which have harmed cooperation and influence and have made it impossible to fully exploit the intelligence. Despite the organizations' limiting collective influence and dealing with sharing intelligence and organizing work in a way that encourages presenting a variety of analyses (which can lead to an improvement in intelligence), intelligence organizations apparently have found it difficult to adapt to the new situation and have focused more on attempts to improve the intelligence product. Suggestions to change the situation usually have been based on lessons learned from concentrated surprises. What has been possible, in instances of diffused surprises, which have been less frequent and have depended on processes and not events, has been including other individuals within and even outside intelligence. Experts from business and social fields have significantly contributed to improving the intelligence, as this has decreased the need to rely on intelligence from secret sources.

Difficulties Arise from the Following

There has been a problem of unshared information. The lack of shared information, especially regarding assessment, also has been part of the intelligence culture (Davis 2006), meaning that there has been no shared assessing and distributing of information. Davis makes an interesting observation about the weight of the "intelligence culture" on intelligence failures in the United States and Britain: for example, there has been a lack of shared intelligence because of the concern of a baseless alert (also see Mouton & Troy 2002). That was the case when China was about to invade South Korea, and the information was rejected because it opposed conventional assessment and never reached the highest ranks (Janis 1972).

There has been a problem of group thinking. An intelligence analyst usually has been one of a small group of experts whose deliberations have been crucial to the assessment process. However, the situation also has been problematic because of group dynamics, which have been liable to reject opinions or prevent them from reaching the decision makers. Difficulties caused by group thinking have had a negative effect on assessment and decision-making, and on intelligence activity (Janis 1982; Janis & Mann, 1980, 1997; Mintz & DeRouen 2010). When an intelligence analyst has worked within a small, isolated group, he or she has aspired to conform to the others in the group, so that different opinions have been likely to have remained unuttered. Having one collective opinion and preserving unity has made the members of the group sure of their assessment, but has been known to damage its quality. At times, then, it has become an organizational problem preventing the formulation of more than one opinion (Huges-Wilson 1999; Mellers et al. 2001).

There has been a problem of learning from others. To improve organizational functioning in intelligence organizations, one possibility has been to collaborate with external experts to learn about other fields, such as business. The Fischhoff committee report examined the subject and came to the conclusion that the approach of intelligence organizations has to change to improve their capabilities and that they have to open themselves up to what is occurring in relevant fields outside the intelligence community. However, these ideas have not been tried, because of opposition from the intelligence organizations, and their opinions often have not been accepted (Fischhoff 2011; Hackman 2001; Martin 2002).

Interaction between Intelligence and Decision Makers

The senior government decision makers have made their decisions based on information from the intelligence community; they have wanted the best information possible, but they also have suffered from bias and constraints and have found it difficult to deal with vague, uncertain reports (Dror 2004). Political leaders can either accept or reject intelligence reports. If they ignore or reject certain information, they will not be able to make the correct decision to prevent a surprise attack. They have paid less attention to reports in cases where it has been difficult to locate a coming surprise attack, or when changes have occurred whose nature has been unclear, which is what has characterized diffused surprise.

The government decision makers have tended to believe their horizons have been wider than those of the intelligence community, because they also have examined the internal situation and have received information from the government (Baumfeld 2014) and from other influential factors, such as the business sector. They have not only relied on intelligence assessments (*Butler Report* 2004), but have made their own (Petersen 2011), and have been liable to search for conclusions that have been politically convenient, while having rejected those from intelligence (Bar-Joseph 2004; Szanton & Allison 1976). When an assessment has been formulated, it has been difficult for the decision makers to accept and internalize intelligence that may have cast doubt on the policies that they have reached (George & Smoke 1974), and sometimes focus has been lacking that could have helped them reach their decisions (Dahl 2013). There has been concern lest the decision makers influence intelligence and, on the other hand, that a direct line may have been required from intelligence to the decision makers to better understand their needs (Colby 1980).

THE CONNECTION BETWEEN INTELLIGENCE AND LEADERSHIP

Intelligence has been responsible for collecting and assessing information and has been expected to be objective and divorced from political considerations. The proximity of intelligence analysts to decision makers can have an adverse effect on their professionality, and the concern has been that the decision makers will attempt to force their own opinions and beliefs on the intelligence community, and influence intelligence processes, which is potentially damaging. In instances such as Pearl Harbor and the German invasion of Russia, the assessments of the intelligence community were precise, but the generals and politicians refused to listen or to read their bulletins (Hilsman 1956).

The question of the connection between statesmanship and intelligence can be argued, and there has been no unequivocal approach. Huntington (Huntington 1957) representatives from this professional school reject close contact between the political leadership and intelligence, claiming that correct relations between political and military leadership have to be based on a clear division; there also has been the recognition that the military as an institution has been subordinate to the political leadership, but Huntington has a different opinion. Harkabi also calls for a separation of state and intelligence, in which intelligence provides the decision makers with a picture of the situation and they decide on policy (Harkabi, 1984, 1987). Handel and Wirtz are of the same opinion (Handel 1987; Wirtz 2007), as are other intelligence analysts. The interactions between an intelligence analyst and the decision makers have been complex. According to the professional school, intelligence has to be divorced from politics to ensure that it will not be influenced, while according to the realist school, the involvement of intelligence is a legitimate means of influencing the process of making decisions. According to another approach, intelligence analysts have to work closely with decision makers and help them by making intelligence products more relevant to their needs (Betts 1980; Church Committee 1976; Colby 1980; Gates 1987).

The changes in the American intelligence community after 9/11 and the lessons learned from the invasion of Iraq in 2003 have been carried out partially to improve collaboration between the intelligence community and the decision makers, since apparently such improvements have been made only after failures (Pillar 2004). The intention has been for the intelligence community to be less subject to external influences, for example, from governmental leadership (Armstrong 1989; Gates 1969; Jervis 2006). One objective of dialogue between intelligence and leadership in any country has been for the leadership to clarify its position, regarding targets, long-term policy, and intent. Therefore, leadership has had to present its key intelligence topic even though it generally has not done so of its own accord, and has not created expectations for the desired conclusions (Colby 1978; Pillar 2006; Wasserman 1960). In Israel, as well, the decision makers have not tended to indicate their demands to intelligence (Meridor 2013).

The literature has dealt with the link between the governmental leadership and intelligence, primarily in the realm of concentrated surprise, where there have been developments which have appeared threatening and the leaders have had to make a decision, as opposed to a diffused surprise, where they often have not been required to make operative decisions, because of the difficulty in recognizing the difference.

THE INFLUENCE OF THE LEADERSHIP ON INTELLIGENCE ASSESSMENTS

The leadership has been liable to be influenced, directly or indirectly, deliberately or not, by the analysis of intelligence when it has expressed opinions that have biased the intelligence process. The political leaders have been able to influence the content of intelligence assessment; however, it is they who have been responsible for taking measures to prevent surprise attacks, not the intelligence community.

It has been difficult to find specific examples because of censorship, which may have been the situation in Israel before the Yom Kippur War, when the heads of the Israeli government had claimed that Israel's strategic situation was very good. They had assured the public that there was no war on the horizon in the coming years, and Israeli intelligence had gotten in line behind the political leadership (Gilboa 2012). The same thing had happened during the war in Vietnam (Wirtz, 1991, 1994), where intelligence assessments had been influenced by the government's expectations of a victory (Pike Papers 1976). There had been analysts who had argued that the information on the ground about "successes" was biased and deceptive, but their assessments had been rejected or ignored (Hiam 2006).

The situation had been similar in 2003, when the American administration decided to invade Iraq, and the political leadership had influenced the intelligence assessments (Betts 2007). Intelligence assessments regarding Iraq could have been politicized (Treverton 2011). Political influence, overt or covert, direct or indirect (Glees & Davis 2008), had been strong before Iraq was invaded (Betts 2003, 2004, 2007; Pillar 2006), and in other instances as well (Bar-Joseph & McDermoth 2010; McGravey 1973). The decision makers have formulated independent assessments appropriate for their political needs and the Office of Special Plans (OSP) was established to convince public opinion that Iraq had possessed weapons of mass destruction (Diamond 2008; Gordon & Trainer 2006).

Intelligence assessments also have been influenced by the armed forces, not only by the political leadership. That was the case in November 1950 before China invaded Korea, which had been influenced by the positions taken by General MacArthur (Halberstam 2007), and the assessments of General Willoughby, chief intelligence for the UN forces, who had coordinated his assessments according to those of MacArthur (Haynes 2009). The Tet offensive in Vietnam in 1968 was a surprise and an intelligence failure because no warning had been given (Andrew 1995; Oberdorfer 2001). The DIA analysts had in fact seen signs indicating a coming attack, but they had withdrawn their opinions in favor of those of the senior American military leadership (Kam 1988).

As far as the Second Palestinian Intifada (2000) is concerned, Lavi noted, during "Arik Sharon and the Second Intifada," a television program had aired on Israeli Channel 10 TV on February 11, 2013, that the intelligence assessments had been rewritten to accommodate the decision makers (Lavi 2008). Matti Steinberg, who had been an advisor to the Shabak (the Israel Security Agency), agreed with Lavi, stating that military intelligence had refused to listen to assessments that were inconsistent with the prime minister's position (Adler 2009; Steinberg 2013). According to Emmanuel Sivan, conditions for intelligence analysis failures have included distorting intelligence, the need to justify a concept, stubborn adherence to concepts consistent with the policies of the decision makers, and disregarding the need for regular examination of the reliability of the information (Sivan 2004).

Examples in which the position of the political leadership influenced intelligence analysts in instances of intelligence failures usually have been concentrated surprises. This was because they were instances in which doubts arose regarding the intelligence assessment following the receipt of information, and a conflict could have been created between the policies desired by the leadership and what was indicated by the intelligence assessments. The result has been that the assessments could have been altered or possibly not even transmitted. Since internal security has been a very sensitive public issue, the leadership may have tended to ignore uncertain alerts of diffused surprises, such as warnings of war, as had happened in the cases of the First and Second Palestinian Intifadas, or the Arab Spring, as they had been the product of ongoing processes. In such cases, the decision makers have had less influence on intelligence assessments than in instances of concentrated surprises.

EXAMPLES OF SURPRISES ACCORDING TO THE SURPRISE ENVIRONMENT AND THE TYPE OF SURPRISE

Examples of concentrated surprises have been Operation Barbarossa (1940), the attack on Pearl Harbor (1941), the Japanese invasion of Singapore (1942), the invasion of Normandy (1944), the revolt against the British in Malay (1948), the Algerian revolution (1954), the construction of the Berlin Wall (1961), the Bay of Pigs fiasco (1961), the Cuban missile crisis (1962), the Tet offensive in Vietnam (1968), the murder of the Israeli athletes in Munich (1972), the Argentinian invasion of the Falkland Islands (1982), Iraq's invasion of Kuwait (1990), the first attack on the World Trade Center (1993), and 9/11 (2001).

Examples of diffused surprises have been the Arab Revolt in Palestine (1936), the Hungarian Uprising (1956), the Polish Uprising (1956), the Prague Spring (1968), the Vietnam War (mainly between 1969 and 1971), the Iranian Islamic Revolution (1979), the First Palestinian Intifada (1987), collapse of the Soviet Union (1991), the Second Palestinian Intifada (2000), and the so-called Arab Spring (2011).

Chapter 3

Intelligence Failures in Business

The research literature on business has dealt with competition between companies, and globalization has made competition more dynamic (Chan Kim & Mauborgne 2007; Grant 2005). Business strategy literature, which has dealt with the early identification of the intentions of the competition (Fellman & Post 2010) and of the main measures taken by competitors and their strategies, targets, strengths, and weaknesses, as well as marketing trends (Hughes et al. 2013), notes that they all have been critical for a company's success. A study done of 800 organizations showed that the most important factor for the success of a company is recognition of customer demands and the measures taken by competitors (Nunes & Breene 2011). The importance of monitoring the external environment has been very important because of the rapid development of technology (Grant 2005, 507-508). It has been impossible to win a strategic competition without having had a familiarity with the competitors, receiving warning of threats (Henderson 1981) and an analysis of the information regarding the competitive environment (Benssousan & Fleisher 2008, 19, 23-24; Chernev & Kotler 2012, 67-70) As in national intelligence, in business there have been diffused surprises, and often the causes have been a combination of factors: for example, when it has been a case of measures taken by the competition (a concentrated surprise) and the conduct of customers or changes in the competitive environment, such as technological changes (a diffused surprise).

Research into intelligence failures in business has found it hard to isolate the factors in the competitive environment causing intelligence failures; it also has not distinguished between the types of failures. The research has analyzed the types of failures, and financial, organizational, and psychological factors have been examined, as have the relations between workers and management. In addition, research has examined the failing measures in the competitive environment that have been based on a great deal of information, and which have increased since the technical revolution. Generally speaking, not enough advanced research has been done into the issue of intelligence failure as a central cause of business failure, usually because of insufficient awareness. Sometimes a comparison of successful companies and failing companies shows that the latter had not correctly read the competitive map. Competitive intelligence has attempted to improve its capabilities in both types of surprises at the same time, despite the fact that the concepts and methods used in this book have been unknown to them. That is, they have not known about preventing concentrated surprises, by using the methodology of business management and national intelligence, and also using analyses of the customers' needs and expectations, which is in the field of preventing diffused surprises.

THE PLACE OF INTELLIGENCE IN BUSINESS FAILURES

Most of the research into intelligence failure and the study of concentrated surprises has dealt with concentrated surprises that had occurred following measures taken by competitors that had led to their gaining significant advantages. Intelligence failure has been a significant surprise for a business (Porter 2000, 79-97) and it has stemmed from an incorrect assessment of the competitive environment and its risks; it has caused financial damage and commercial difficulties (Chussil 2005, 26-33; Feder 2001; Kaplan & Mikes 2012). Such a failure usually has been implicit in information about business failures and has been difficult to isolate. It has been expected that companies would identify threats in time (Horn et al. 2005). Known intelligence failures have occurred in companies such as Motorola, Xerox, Nortel Networks, Lucent, Johnson & Johnson, IBM, Kodak, Polaroid, Compaq, Mattel, Swissair, Levi Strauss & Co., and Barco Medical Displays, as well as in the American automotive industry.

Tsitoura and Stephens (2012) discuss failures in competitive intelligence as errors in one of the stages of the intelligence cycle, which could have caused financial loss or the loss of a commercial opportunity. They focus on errors in intelligence activity in companies and less on the use of intelligence made by the decision makers. In their opinion, business intelligence failure, similar to national intelligence failure, can occur when a company lacks an intelligence unit and when the company fails to identify threats and has not sufficiently prepared itself to make changes.

Several researchers (Day & Reibstein 1997, 1-18; Montgomery, Moore & Urbany 2005) relate the aforementioned failures to the functioning of company directors and to employees who do not support intelligence activity, while others (Evangelista 2005; Gilad 1998; Straus & du Toit 2010) add the lack of communication between intelligence and senior management. Most of the research deals with concentrated surprises.

The discipline of business intelligence has been based on the intelligence cycle of national intelligence (Fuld 1995; Herring 2008; Miller 2007; Waters 2010). The definition of key intelligence topic, which has been the first stage of the intelligence cycle, has been integrated into the discipline (Herring 1999; McGonagle & Vella 1999). Researchers have highlighted the need for an intelligence base in business to help businesses succeed and to prevent surprises in their organizational activity, but they have noted the difficulties in implementation, which apparently have arisen from the lack of management's familiarity with the discipline of intelligence and with psychological and organizational failures (Hedin et al. 2011).

At the beginning of the millennium, competitive intelligence became formalized, as a discipline, and now has collaborated with market research, focusing more on strategy. Especially in the field of preventing surprises, competitive intelligence has become more valuable to management (Gainor & Bouthillier 2014).

Despite the great amount of academic information about intelligence failures in business, studies have found it difficult to isolate the influence of factors in the competitive environment, for which intelligence has been responsible, from other business factors operating within the company. The research has dealt with analyzing company failures relating mainly to factors noted above. Competitive intelligence has attempted to prevent both types of surprise: concentrated surprise, by using the methods of business management and national intelligence, and diffused surprise, by analyzing customers and their expectations.

FACTORS FOR INTELLIGENCE FAILURES IN BUSINESS

Collection Capabilities

In business, only open-source information has been collected and dealt with. The information revolution has enabled easier and more rapid access to information, mainly through the Internet. Automatic tools also have been available, such as alerts, allowing the user direct access to new information, according to key intelligence topics. Extensive use of the Internet has made it possible for companies to improve the surveillance of competitors and to focus on those that have been relevant (Baum & Korn 1996). Of seventeen parameters examined, competitive intelligence was in second place for influencing the effectiveness of a company (Nelson et al. 2008). The focus has been on preventing a concentrated surprise, but since the social media explosion, the possibility of preventing a diffused surprise has improved, although it still has been difficult because of the large number of factors that have to be monitored.

Using Key Intelligence Topics to Focus Collection

In the digital world, there has been no lack of information. The problems have been collecting it, according to the current key intelligence topic (the first stage of the intelligence cycle) and recognizing changes in the business environment, in order to be alerted to and to identify threats. Mistakes, which sometimes have occurred, later, as a result in having hit blind spots, generally have not been the result of lack of skill in monitoring the external environment, but rather of not having focused correctly on important subjects (Gilad 1998; Holtzman 2005; Zajac & Bazerman 1991).

Skill in Recognizing Indicators

Indicators have been the product of focused intelligence collection. The intelligence failure generally has not taken place because of lack of monitoring of the competition, but of not having identified indicators in time and of the failure of the decision makers to act appropriately (Finkelstein 2004; Gilad, 1989, 2004).

A Noisy Information Environment

A company collects information from a large number of varied sources. Most of the information has come from external sources and less from internal sources, which have included employees, and has been of higher quality. The first challenge of the intelligence analyst has been to classify, synchronize, absorb, and distribute the information according to the intelligence cycle, which also has been used in business (Wilson 2008). The correct organization of information has been very important (Kahaner 1996, 94; Porter 1991, 83). It also is important to distinguish between signals (which can be significant), and noise (which is not), as mistakes can be critical.

Other reasons for intelligence failures have been lack of attention paid to important information, because of the volume of data received, lack of resources, the difficulty in distinguishing between misinformation and disinformation, and the need to focus on new, relevant information even if it has been contradictory or at odds with information that the organization already possesses. Advanced information systems tools can be used, which have helped treat the information. Greater awareness has been needed on the part of intelligence analysts and managers, both in preventing a concentrated surprise, generally from competitors, and in preventing a concentrated surprise, generally from many customers. Intelligence analysts and managers also have needed to be open to receiving support from tools from various fields, to prevent surprises.

Failure Caused by Human Error

Mistakes in assessment in a competitive environment have been caused when intelligence analysts and management have relied too closely on existing assessments and have ignored new information, even though they have had advanced tools for identification and analysis and capabilities from external research factors. Despite the progress made in information sharing within an organization, wrong analyses have been made and companies have not been prepared or have not reacted in time to threats in the sales environment. As mentioned above, attention paid to preventing concentrated surprises needs to be the same as that paid to preventing diffused surprises, and the analysis is carried out as a combination of the two.

Cooperation between Intelligence Analysts and Managers

In the era of the information revolution, managers have been regarded as being responsible for information in the organization (Mintzberg 2009), but that has yet to be absorbed. The result has been a lack of identifying of the intentions of competitors and of changes in the competitive environment (Amit et al. 1988, 431-442; Dishman & Calof 2008; Fleisher & Wright 2010, 717-730; Montgomery & Weinberg 1979; Zajac & Bazerman 1991).

Failures Caused by Bounded Awareness

Intelligence failures have not been sudden occurrences. They have been processes that have developed over time (Barnea 2010). Bazerman and Chugh (2002, 88-97) relate to the bounded awareness of management to threats as an important factor in a company's intelligence failure. Intelligence has to help management see beyond its bounded awareness. There has been a difficulty in absorbing and processing new information, which has caused vulnerability to surprises (Bazerman & Watkins, 2003, 2004, 153-224).

Ignoring Competitors or Incorrect Assessment of Their Capabilities and Intentions

Another explanation for failures has been ignoring competitors, and blame for that has belonged to executives who have disregarded them. Kahneman argues that the competition is not consciously ignored, but that cognitive biases play an important role in the process (Kahneman 2013, 290-291).

Cognitive biases and group thinking have raised the question of how critical information can be brought to the attention of people making decisions, when there are political and internal organizational difficulties (Fahey 1998). Sometimes, intelligence failures have been caused when competitors have been ignored or there has been an incorrect assessment of their capabilities and intentions (Montgomery et al. 2005).

Additional Biases and Cognitive Failures

A study done of about 1,000 investment companies showed that a decrease in the information of bias in decision-making improved business results (Lovallo & Sibony 2010). Collins investigated 60 model companies, whose financial performance had been weakened, and noted that one of the five reasons for the fall of the companies was their denial of danger and incorrect deployment in the face of the threat (Collins 2009).

Organizational Difficulties and Faulty Collaboration

One role of intelligence in a company has been to provide management with updated information. Management has needed to interpret a sudden move made by a competitor; it has had to know about competitors' strengths and weaknesses; and, when the company has been weighing a move, management has needed to discuss what the competitor's expected response would be (Cotler & Hornik 2000, 271). According to the Arthur D. Little consulting firm, intelligence management improves the decision-making process and leads to better performance (Johansson et al. 2010). While a company's need for an intelligence unit and its methodical activity have been understood, implementation sometimes has been faulty. To overcome difficulties in dealing with information and to formulate an intelligence picture, experts employed by the company have had to collaborate with external factors specialists. The existence of a designated intelligence unit has increased the chance of preventing both concentrated and diffused surprises, since the unit will integrate the information.

Implementing Intelligence in Business Faces Organizational Problems: The Need for a Dedicated Intelligence Unit

According to Fuld (2013) and Prescott (2001), a company's intelligence unit has to identify threats, and Herring (1990) claims that the number one role of a company's head of intelligence is to create actionable intelligence which is responsible and unbiased. However, Fahey, Gilad, and Reger note that it is sufficient to develop the awareness of management; there is no need for a specific intelligence function, as that is the role of everyone in the company (Fahey 1998; Gilad 2004, 129; Reger 1990).

Exploiting Information about the Competitive Environment around an Organization

In business, there is a unique situation in which company employees have important information about the competitive environment, which they receive from outside sources, such as suppliers, clients, competitors, and business partners. Drucker (1993 42) calls it the only meaningful resource. Such information must reach the intelligence analysts and decision makers of the company (Calof 2008, 39-42; Moran 2005). Problems of internal cooperation in organizations make it difficult to understand the external environment (Fleisher & Wright, 2010).

Organizing Intelligence Analysis in a Company

As opposed to national intelligence, in a business the intelligence unit is usually a small unit in the organization. Its role is not to issue an alert but rather to create a situation in which management gives the organization the attention it deserves (McMullen et al. 2009). Lower management has to be exposed to information, especially to threats, and must pass the information along to upper management (Pascale 1984), according to Andrew Grove, former CEO and Chairman of Intel Corporation (Grove 1996).

Giving Accessibility to Information to Many Individuals in an Organization

In the business sector, internal information sharing has been developed, which has been the primary tool for improving the company's capabilities. In organizations where a great deal of information has been amassed, tools should be developed that will enable many employees to access information and use it with the information-sharing tool (Nonaka 1991), known as knowledge management.

Relations between Intelligence and the Decision Makers

In companies, the issue of intelligence usually has not been at the core of their activities, as it has been in national intelligence. The competitive intelligence units usually have been small and have not had interactions with senior management, to the detriment of both sides. Intelligence has received neither instructions nor feedback, and management has not made the best use of the intelligence that it has received. Intelligence has not received the importance it should have, and management has been able to ignore alerts, especially when they have been ambiguous. Management can only be concerned about threats to their business if they are aware that there are concentrated and diffused surprises. The tendency to be concerned about intelligence work has come into play when management has defined its needs.

Grove (1996) discusses the problem and suggests to senior executives to maintain contact with middle management, who receive competitive information from subordinates, who are also more objective. Others, including Weick and Sutcliffe (2001) and Calof and Wright (2008), support that position.

The tendency of management not to have delved deeply into intelligence analysis also has been manifested by the fact that managers have not customarily defined their intelligence needs, which has made it difficult for the intelligence unit to function. Coyne and Horn (2009) explain management's dismissal of information about the measures taken by competitors, by saying that this dismissal is the result of norms, biases, and patterns of behavior characteristic of company directors, leading to intelligence failures.

Examples of Surprises According to Environment and Type in the Business-Economy Field

Concentrated surprises: the collapse of Kodak, the fall of IBM (1993); the fall of Levi Strauss (1996); the appearance of Ford Model T vehicles (1908), the collapse of Compaq (2001); the launch of the DVD by Sony (1997); the launching of the LCD monitor by Hitachi and NEC (2005); the Swiss Air's declaration of bankruptcy (2002); Hoover vacuum cleaner lost its global leadership (2005); the collapse of Blockbuster (2010); the ending of Digital Equipment Corporation (DEC) activities (1998); the loss of the Barbie Doll market to Bratz (2001); the entrance of Japanese cars into the American market (1970s); the fall of Crown Cork and Seal (the world's largest manufacturer of food packaging: 2002)), the launch of the iPhone (2007); the collapse of Nortel Networks (2009); the collapse of Nokia (2011); the collapse of Netscape (2003).

Diffused surprises: the 2008 financial crisis; the failure of New Coke to enter the market (1985); the Great Depression of 1929–1939; the failure of the Daimler-Chrysler merger (2007); Polaroid's declaration of bankruptcy (2001); the fall of Novell (1999); the collapse of Palm (makers of the Palm Pilot) (2009); the fall of Lego (2003); the fall of Blackberry (2012); the end of the *Encyclopedia Britannica* (2012); the closing of the Iridium telephone project (2000); the collapse of Gateway Computers (2007).

Chapter 4

Test Case

The First Palestinian Intifada

OVERVIEW

The First Palestinian Intifada began on December 9, 1987, after a serious clash between residents of the Jabalia refugee camp in the Gaza Strip and the IDF on December 8; it was a strategic surprise for the Israeli Ministry of Defense and, importantly, to the Israel Security Agency (ISA), better known by its Hebrew acronym, "Shabak." The first Intifada can be considered a diffused surprise because it was not the result of organized Palestinian Liberation Organization (PLO) activity, as the defense establishment initially thought, and it continued on and off until 1993. It turned into a comprehensive confrontation of large riots and attacks on IDF forces, first with cold weapons (stones, rocks, and Molotov cocktails) and later with guns, first in the Gaza Strip and later in Judea and Samaria. It paralyzed life in the Palestinian territories, with long general strikes, mass demonstrations and riots, a complete shutdown of the Palestinian educational system for a year and a half, and far longer for colleges and universities, and a general resignation of Palestinian employees from the Israeli civilian administration.

The Intifada began as an unarmed popular uprising (hence its name, "The Intifada of Stones"), and later was carried out under PLO aegis and oversight. Local popular committees, which had been organized by the PLO years previously, acted spontaneously to sever relations with the Israeli administration. A boycott of Israeli-made goods was announced and scores of people suspected of collaborating with Israel were murdered. The leaders' intention was to separate the Palestinian economy from the Israeli, but it was not implemented for a number of reasons, one of which was that a significant part of the Palestinian workforce was employed by Israel. Following the Intifada, there was a kind of autonomy in many villages, in which the local residents managed their own affairs and IDF forces did not enter, mainly because they were occupied with dealing with mass riots (Lustick 1993).

According to a survey of the events in the IDF archives, until the outbreak of the Intifada, terrorist activity against IDF forces and civilian targets in Judea, Samaria, and the Gaza Strip was "routine," and maintained the same profile it had had for the 20 years, since the end of the Six Day War, in 1967. The PLO tried, on the one hand, to win international recognition, and on the other, it continued organizing terrorist attacks against Israel. The PLO did win legitimacy and recognition, while Israel came to be regarded as a foreign regime. Furthermore, the PLO was seen as successfully fighting terrorist organizations, and the terrorism was considered to be arising from foreign, Israeli targets. The PLO was seen as a weak organization standing up to a strong military state; Israel's actions were strongly criticized and condemned by the entire world, but not in a way that threatened its continued presence in the territories. At the core of the first months of the Intifada was an attempt to deal with the Israeli occupation in a new way, different from the past: the hope was that it would be more effective, while also continuing to receive international support.

At the end of the 1970s, Israel had tried to construct a different framework for the territories. To weaken the power of the PLO, Israel (the military administration) had established village associations (Mishal and Aharoni 1989, 26) that were supposed to replace the PLO as local leadership. This failed for a number of reasons, among them, the associations were seen as collaborating with Israel, and both Jordan and the PLO opposed them. At the outbreak of the Intifada, about 830,000 people were living in Judea and Samaria, 540,000 in the Gaza Strip and 130,000 in east Jerusalem (Levenberg 2011).

THE SITUATION ON THE GROUND AS SEEN BY THE ISRAEL DEFENSE ESTABLISHMENT

In Judea, Samaria, and the Gaza Strip, according to the monthly IDF reports in 1987, until the outbreak of the Intifada (according to information from the IDF archive), the security situation on the ground was routine and there were no indicators of a coming change. The intelligence collection targeted PLO activity in Tunisia. After December 9, 1987, there were reports of "a wave of riots." Apparently, the IDF continued thinking in terms of what was true before the Intifada, although even after it broke out, the military-security establishment continued broadcasting "business as usual." The PLO represented itself as in control of events in the territories, despite the fact that it had been completely surprised by the events.

THE SITUATION ON THE GROUND IN THE TERRITORIES, AS REFLECTED IN THE ISRAELI MEDIA

Before the outbreak of the Intifada, events in the territories did not particularly interest the Israeli public or its politicians. Interest generally peaked in the wake of specific incidents and not part of a concept for a political solution. For example, on October 13, 1987, Defense Minister Yitzhak Rabin said that, as a result of a visit from the American secretary of state Schultz, a worsening of the situation in the territories could be expected (Ben-Yishai 1988). In the middle of the year (1987), Shmuel Goren, the Israeli coordinator of Government Activities in the Territories (COGAT), said (interview by author, October 2013) that the problem of the territories was not Israel's top priority. A few days before the outbreak of the Intifada, Goren gave a speech saying that Israel's policies in the territories were very successful, had brought a sense of calmness, and only minimal measures were needed to be taken for Israel's continued control (Ben-Yishai1988).

According to the newspapers, by the end of November through the beginning of December, the IDF and the Israeli public, as well, were dealing with the failure of the IDF to prevent a terrorist attack by Ahmed Jibril's Popular Front for the Liberation of Palestine—General Command (PFLP-GC). The PFLP-GC had attacked an IDF base in Israel's extreme north and six IDF soldiers were killed. The attack was nicknamed "The night of the hang-gliders," because the terrorists had used them to infiltrate Israeli territory. An increase in the number of stones and Molotov cocktails was attributed to the date, November 29, which was the anniversary of the acceptance of the UN Partition Plan.

On December 10, Eitan Rabin, who had covered security matters for the Israeli daily newspaper, *Haaretz*, reported on riots in the Jabalia refugee camp. The riots were attributed to two causes: the first was the expulsion of the leader of the Palestinian Islamic Jihad from the Gaza Strip. The second was suspicion that a traffic accident, which had occurred on December 9, involving an Israeli vehicle and resulting in the deaths of four Jabalia residents, had been deliberate and was a reprisal for the killing of an Israeli, in Gaza, on December 6.

Newspaper reporting changed shortly afterward. Beginning on December 11, *Haaretz* headlines referred to the situation in the territories. On December 11, the front-page headline read (in Hebrew) "The IDF will take a hard line to counter the riots in the territories." The article continued, "The IDF does not relate the recent wave of riots to any political development. They are a violent uprising following clashes with IDF soldiers in the Gaza Strip and the West Bank" (Nir 1987). According to an article by Eitan Rabin, who quoted an IDF source, Israel had destroyed the Palestinian Islamic Jihad, after arresting thirty of the organization's leaders (an event that took place before the Intifada) (Rabin, 1987). Yitzhak Mordechai, the head of the Southern Command, was quoted as saying (Rabin, 1987) that the IDF was not worried Israel would become entangled in the Gaza Strip. At that point, military assessment was that the events were routine and of the sort familiar from the past, as noted in the summary of the meeting with the COGAT, on December 10.

It seems that the media was aware of the change before the IDF. On December 13, Yehuda Litani, writing for the *Jerusalem Post*, reported that the events of December 9 were a turning point from civil uprising to a genuine revolt (Litani 1987). *Haaretz* reported that according to senior IDF sources, the riots in the territories had reached the proportions of a full-scale rebellion. The riots, claimed the sources, would not end any time soon, and the IDF expected them to increase as Fatah Day, January 1. On December 14, Ori Nir wrote in *Haaretz* that the IDF was trying to limit the riots in the territories (Nir 1987), and in an article about the weekly government meeting, Akiva Eldar reported, also in *Haaretz*, that Prime Minister Shamir had denied the existence of a civil uprising. It was, he said, young men acting up and getting out of hand here and there (Eldar 1987). The government ministers accused the media of exaggerating protests that they claimed had never gotten out of control. The government had apparently regarded the events as a passing wave, in spite of a period of demonstrations and riots, throughout the West Bank and the Gaza Strip, which had reached a level that had not been seen in the past.

While some of the media seemed to have understood, from the beginning, that the situation was different this time, the Israeli defense establishment—the ISA, the IDF and the COGAT—all insisted that the events were routine, not planned or orchestrated, and that the IDF was in control of the situation, and that the riots would die down after a few days—this was the opinion presented at the weekly government meeting on December 13 (Ben-Yishai 1988). When asked by one of the ministers, IDF Chief of Staff Dan Shomron repeated that calm would be restored within a few days (Markus 2013). Shomron claimed that the events were not serious and could easily be put to an end. Contrary to Shomron's claim, Ze'ev Shiff wrote, in *Haaretz,* on December 20, that the riots were the worst since 1967 (Shiff 1987), After a month, when the riots had not ended, large IDF forces were deployed to Judea, Samaria, and the Gaza Strip, and the IDF responded strongly to suppress them.

THE OUTBREAK OF THE INTIFADA: A DIFFUSED SURPRISE

The outbreak of the Intifada surprised not only the IDF and the ISA, as will be seen below, but also the Israeli public, which was virtually apathetic regarding the territories. During the first few weeks, the defense establishment issued messages of calm assuring the public that the situation in the territories was under control. Only after several weeks did it become generally understood that this time things were different and that instead of networks organized to carry out terrorist attacks and political activity directed by the PLO, Israel was facing a spontaneous popular uprising against its rule in Judea, Samaria, and the Gaza Strip.

Israel had been controlling the Palestinian Authority-administered territories since the Six Day War (1967). The territories were under Israeli military rule, and the military administration—later to be replaced by the civilian administration, was responsible for regulating the Palestinians' daily lives. As soon as the Six Day War ended, the Shabak entered the area and was responsible for preventing terrorist attacks and political subversion, in collaboration with the IDF and the Israeli police. The Shabak's preventive intelligence successfully kept the number of terrorist attacks low. Most of its activities targeted Fatah, which was not only the main perpetrator of terrorist attacks but the organization that also carried out political activities in the territories.

Until that point, the territories had been relatively quiet. The Shabak usually had managed to prevent attacks while they were still in the planning stage and, in other instances, had detained the perpetrators a short time after the attack. For twenty years, a status quo existed; the Shabak had constructed an intelligence force, and the local population was aware of its capabilities. The Shabak acquired comprehensive knowledge of what occurred in the territories, and the IDF and government consulted and coordinated with it regarding every measure taken there. That was the routine activity in headquarters—that is, the Ministry of Defense and COGAT—and in the areas themselves, in the Palestinian cities and the countryside.

The Intifada was both an intelligence surprise and an intelligence failure. An analysis of the data indicates that it was a diffused strategic surprise for the State of Israel. According to Yaakov Peri, who had headed the Shabak from 1989 to 1994, and who was, at the time, second in command to Shabak director Joseph Harmelin, no intelligence organization that had existed, then, would have been able to predict or detect spontaneous events. He said that intelligence organizations far larger than the Shabak had not predicted the fall of the Berlin Wall. He said that, officially, the Shabak should have been able to predict it, but that almost all the large intelligence organizations failed to predict great historical events (Moreh 2014). Dichter made the same claim (Moreh 2014). "For months, the Shabak had reported about the sentiments of the Arab street and the direction the local leadership was taking. The situation was explosive and bound to blow up as soon as someone lit the fuse, but the Shabak did not know exactly when that would happen" (Peri 1999,159).

According to Shmuel Goren (interview by author, 2013), the COGAT at the time, the Intifada was a shock for the Shabak, not only in terms of the extent of the riots, but for weeks after it began, no one knew who was organizing the riots or who was behind the uprising. He said that at the weekly Ministry of Defense meetings, no one had voiced a warning that the territories had undergone a radical change. Nahman Tal, head of the Shabak's Arab division, agreed with Goren that the Shabak had hundreds and thousands of detainees and had not managed to identify the heads of the Intifada (Tal 2011). Hundreds and thousands of Palestinians had been detained, but the leaders of the Intifada were never identified; there was no commander and no headquarters (Levenberg 2011).

When the Intifada broke out in the Gaza Strip, Avi Dichter, who had headed the Shabak from 2000 to 2005, told the Israeli TV program *The Gatekeepers* (Moreh 2014) that they did not know what to do, as such massive events had never been seen before. Hundreds and thousands marched and could only be stopped by live fire (Lahav 2005). He said that the local populations were no longer blindly obedient, that that era had ended. According to Nahman Tal, who had headed the Shabak's Arab desk during the Intifada, and to Haim Levenberg , who wrote a study of the Intifada for the IDF's historical department, apparently it was Yitzhak Mordechai, the head of the Southern Command, who was the first person to notice that events were of a different type (Tal 2011; Levenberg 2011).

Peri claimed "that the first Intifada spontaneously ignited the territories, with the intention of driving Israel out, that it was a genuine grassroots protest—a broad protest, a protest of the villages, a protest of the youth, against the occupation" (Moreh 2014, 99-108). The PLO, said Peri, "was no less surprised than Israel by the wave of riots that washed over the country" (Peri 1999,159).

The civilian administration in Judea and Samaria had been highly convinced that the situation in the territories was calm and under control; this is clear from an interview with Brigadier General Ephraim Sneh, who had ended his term as head of the civilian administration a month before the Intifada began (Argaman 1987). Sneh said that the great majority of the population recognized the need to live alongside Israel in peace. He said COGAT was attuned to the atmosphere but mainly what the various strata of society were saying. At the time, he said, it seemed that senior Palestinian figures expressed independent opinions and even criticized the PLO, and that slowly but surely the Palestinians were becoming more realistic. When asked, in the middle of 1987, when a revolt in the territories would begin, the COGAT said, "Never. No revolt" (Ben-Yishai 1988).

However, according to General (Res.) Shlomo Gazit, former head of military intelligence,

> the Intifada broke out after there had been early signs, in 1986 and 1987, that something exceptional was going to happen in the territories, but there had been no specific alert. He said that no attempt had been made to examine the overall situation or to analyze the common denominator of all the clashes. In addition, of the three systems involved in or responsible for the territories—the IDF, the Shabak, and the civilian administration—not one assessed or gave the alert that such a large popular uprising was about to occur. (Gazit 1999, 254)

Shabak officer Nahman Tal said that by November, the Shabak was aware of the uprising, but that the riots were not very severe (Tal 1998). Tal described the period before the Intifada as a systematic failure for several reasons: first, not one of the agencies responsible for the territories had foreseen that thousands of Palestinians would take to the streets to demonstrate and riot. Second, there had been no misconception among all of the Israeli factors responsible for control of the territory, but there was a general feeling that any disturbance that occurred could be quelled, as had been possible before the Intifada. Third, after two or three weeks, when the Intifada had spread from Gaza to Judea and Samaria, it was clear that there were new aspects to the conflict, which the Shabak had only begun to comprehend (Haim Levenberg, formerly ISA official, interview by author, October 2013; Reuven Paz, formerly head of Research unit, ISA, interview by author, March 2013). Fourth, intelligence failed because such an outbreak had never been considered. Israel was prepared for war on the ground and the war on terrorism, but not for coping with a popular uprising. It could have been possible to have learned from other countries, such as France's experience in Algeria. Fifth, one of the lessons learned from the Intifada was setting up a Palestinian research department in the Shabak, responsible for strategic political assessment and operational research. Last, no difficulty had existed in collecting information about events in the Intifada, as they were overt and perfectly obvious.

According to announcements issued by the joint national headquarters and Hamas, the objective of the uprising was to found a Palestinian state and weaken Israel's governing apparatus in the territories, through a civilian rebellion leading to Israel's eventual expulsion. The announcements were not issued by the familiar professional politicians and there had been no fixed leadership. The detentions and expulsions were temporary setbacks, but the announcements continued. The instructions, both violent and nonviolent, issued by the joint headquarters, were greater in number and more detailed than those of Hamas, and the number of violent instructions grew over time. From the beginning it was clear that they came from people on the ground, and they put emphasis on the local activity of popular committees set up before and during the Intifada (Mishal and Aharoni 1989).

Paz, who had been with Shabak, added that IDF intelligence kept saying that events were being guided only by the PLO headquarters in Tunisia; they refused to accept the concept of local initiatives. However, more and more attacks were being carried out by individuals not necessarily receiving instructions from Fatah (Paz 2013). Even before the Intifada, there were signs that local initiatives were increasing and that not every occurrence was a decision of PLO headquarters, as had been customary.

The first Intifada broke out more than a year after the founding of the IDF intelligence Palestinian terrorism division, which exposed the problems in designating responsibility for researching and collecting information on the Palestinian issue. The terrorism unit investigated the Palestinian organizations beyond the territories, especially the PLO in Tunisia, and the Shabak dealt mainly with preventing terrorist attacks in the territories. It did not see its role extending to the investigation of the dynamics of Palestinian society. The civilian administration was fully aware of events as they developed but did not have investigative powers. Gadi Zohar, who then headed the terrorism branch in military intelligence, had assessed, in the middle of 1987, that an unprecedented type of outbreak could be expected in the territories; the Intifada did, in fact, begin a few months later. However, the heads of the IDF intelligence research division did not accept the prediction, claiming that the terrorism unit did not have the capabilities of IDF intelligence and was not, in fact, responsible for investigating the Palestinians in the territories. The head of the IDF intelligence research division, at that time, said that the reports of the intelligence unit were general and that no attempt had been made to convince IDF intelligence that there was any particular substance to them. There was no assessment that the Intifada was on the horizon, no discussions were held to deal specifically with the possibility, and the Shabak did not discuss the issue (Rothschild 2013). According to Paz, two or three months before the Intifada broke out, the IDF discussed the situation in the Gaza Strip, where more and more stones were being thrown (Paz 2013), but civilian administration and the COGAT did not attend the meetings. Paz goes on to say that, later on, the unrest in the Gaza Strip was discussed, where IDF soldiers on the ground were finding the situation more difficult to control, with more stones, more backtalk, and less obeying of orders.

Anat Kurtz argued that in 1987, the number of disturbances and riots in the Gaza Strip and Judea and Samaria was greater than in previous years, and it was possible to sense a trend of independent actions unrelated to the terrorist organizations. The general IDF assessment was that PLO was worried because more activities were taking place in the territories without its direction (Kurtz 2008). Mishal and Aharoni agree with Paz, from the Shabak, who also claimed that the IDF had made a similar assessment (Mishal and Aharoni 1989; Paz 2013). Rothschild (2013) did not agree, claiming that there had been no indications of an uprising. Kurtz (2008) and Paz (2013) claimed that the PLO had been completely surprised.

Ben-Yishai was of a different opinion, warning, at the beginning of December, that in the near future large-scale riots would break out in the territories; however, he said nothing about a general popular uprising (Ben-Yishai 1988). He added that a month before the Intifada, the IDF had appointed a team to examine procedures and standing orders in the territories, to adapt them to a situation in which IDF soldiers would have to deal with riots, but no written references for its existence could be found.

There were vast discrepancies between the Israeli concept of the situation, the Palestinian Authority's concept, and the situation on the ground (Ahikam 2013). The Israeli and Palestinian leaderships separately regarded the events as riots, and only later began to understand the change and adapt their policies to the situation. It can be assumed that both sides were thinking in terms of concentrated surprise and looked for the organization behind the uprising, not understanding they were facing a different kind of surprise—a diffused surprise. The IDF's mistake was in misidentifying the assessed key intelligence target—it was not the PLO, but rather unorganized groups that were directed and handled, on the ground, by volunteers. Before the Intifada, there was a small Analysis and Production department in the Shabak that had been established at the beginning of the 1980s, on the recommendation of the Israel National Defense College. Avraham Shalom, then head of the Shabak, was not enthusiastic, claiming his organization was the operational aspect of preventive intelligence, but that notwithstanding, the department was established and headed by Reuven Paz (2013). According to Nahman Tal, before the Intifada, the subject of the territories had not been investigated from an intelligence perspective beyond the monitoring of terrorist attacks (Tal 1998). Rothschild agreed, saying that the issued slipped between their military intelligence and the Shabak (Rothschild 2013).

According to the Palestinians, the factors behind the popular uprising were (1) a response to Israel's detentions, expulsions, destruction of homes and closing of Palestinian educational institutions; (2) a protest against taking possession of lands, the problems of daily life and employment, and the lack of local industry; and (3) demographic trends, especially the growth of the Palestinian population and the lack of employment for university graduates (Gazit 1999, 255).

Other reasons for the Intifada were an ongoing sense of oppression and humiliation, the despair and hopelessness of the population after twenty years of Israeli occupation, and disappointment with the support from the Arab states (Tal 1998). The issue of the economy may have been secondary, since about 100,000 Gazans left the Gaza Strip to work in Israel every day. Paz agreed with him (2013).

According to Adnan Damiri's PhD thesis for al-Najah University in 1985, the opinions of the younger generation were characterized by determination and the lack of desire to rely on the Arab states for a solution to the problem. What they wanted was to participate in ending the occupation (Ben-Yishai 1988). Dr. Mubarak Awad, a Palestinian who had studied and lives and in the United States, had the theory of rebelling against the Israeli regime nonviolently, and began to preach a Gandhi-like nonviolent rebellion. He referred to an economic boycott and strikes (Awad 1984, 22-26). He was expelled from the Palestinian territories in 1988.

An incident in the Balata refugee camp near Nablus in May 1987 may be considered the beginning of the Intifada. Leaders of the Shabiba, Fatah's youth movement, began attacking people they had suspected of collaborating with Israel. They forcibly prevented residents from going to work in Israel on Palestinian holidays and prevented IDF forces from entering the camp, significantly reducing their presence. The situation peaked on May 31, when an IDF force was attacked while detaining Palestinians, and the commander, Amram Mitzna, who was present at the time, decided to stop the operation (Mitzna 2011). In September 1987, Defense Minister Rabin wanted to visit the Balata refugee camp, but the civilian administration prevented him from doing so on the grounds that the Shabiba controlled the camp. In fact, the issue of the Balata refugee camp had never been formally discussed, as it was viewed as a local, isolated problem.

Israel could not identify the leadership of the Intifada as known PLO representatives in the territories. Before the Intifada had broken out, a new, local, leadership had arisen, made up of young Palestinians, most of whom had been imprisoned in Israel, at one time or another, had been well known to the local residents, and had been perceived as representing them. Popular support turned them into celebrities. For the first time since the Six Day War, a new, young cadre of leaders arose, who represented a political alternative to the traditional, familiar faces of the old guard, threatening the PLO leadership that had been exiled to Tunisia. Those social processes had existed for a long time. The Shabiba, which took over and controlled the Balata refugee camp for several months until the Intifada broke out, was an example of an authentic grassroots leadership with popular support.

Based on past experience, the Israeli defense establishment, especially the Shabak, geared up to monitor the terrorist organizations and terrorist operatives in order to prevent a concentrated surprise. The main intelligence target was PLO headquarters in Tunisia, which conducted the terrorist and political activities in the territories. The IDF and the Shabak monitored them to prevent terrorist attacks orchestrated by the PLO and its affiliated organizations. Intelligence information collection focused on the wrong key intelligence target and on irrelevant data and thus failed to warn of the diffused surprise, characteristic of instances where preparations are made, based on the habit of dealing with concentrated surprises.

THE PERIOD IMMEDIATELY PRECEDING THE OUTBREAK OF THE FIRST INTIFADA

The defense establishment focused on the PLO's activities, as it had been perceived as controlling events in the territories from Tunisia. Therefore, to a great extent, it focused on the organization's political activities in Judea, Samaria, and the Gaza Strip. Even after the deliberations held on August 12, 1987, the general assessment was that the Arab street was quiet, if not apathetic. Most of the discussions centered on the daily agenda. No comprehensive deliberations were held concerning trends or processes, and certainly not on the big picture, that is, the sea of changes occurring beneath the surface, and no change was perceived on the horizon. Even when the Palestinian Islamic Jihad was recognized as becoming more powerful, no follow-up deliberations were held. Riots and terrorist attacks were background noise and no one paid attention to them.

Among the signs of the approaching Intifada were the events, in May, in the Balata refugee camp, but these were not discussed, and the possible implications were not taken into account, especially for Judea and Samaria. No one thought about the broader, long-term consequences of the fact that, for months, IDF forces had been prevented from entering one of the largest refugee camps in the West Bank. Paz claimed a document had been written on the issue, but he admitted that it did not relate to the broader, long-term implications of a situation in which the IDF was prevented from entering a large refugee camp for a long period of time (Paz 2013).

RESERVE BRIGADIER GENERAL SEGEV GIVES THE ALERT

One of the very few who predicted the Intifada and warned of its coming was Brigadier General (Res.) Yitzhak Segev, who served as the governor of the Gaza Strip from 1979 to 1981, and IDF attaché in Iran from 1977 to 1978, until Khomeini rose to power. After 1981, he remained in contact with public figures in the Gaza Strip and was an informal advisor to IDF Chief of Staff Dan Shomron regarding the territories. Segev (interview by author, September 2013) claimed that, in November 1987, about a month before the outbreak of the Intifada, he reported what he believed would happen to Shomron. Shomron, in turn, said at a meeting that an "explosion" could be expected in the territories. Asked by Defense Minister Rabin where his information had come from, Shomron said he was his own source and in constant communication with people in the Gaza Strip. Rabin asked for more information, which Segev provided the following week; although the information was not focused and precise, it was mainly about the despair and hopelessness of the younger generation. Shmuel Goren, the COGAT, dismissed this report, saying that examinations that had been conducted in the territories, by the Shabak, which indicated that Segev's information was incorrect. Rabin accepted the COGAT's opinion, which was passed along to the decision makers in the government.

On December 13, 1987, the *Jerusalem Post* published an op-ed piece by Yehuda Litani, who wrote about Arab affairs for the paper entitled "Analysis," stating that the events that began on December 9 indicated a turning point in the civilian uprising, which was now a revolt. According to the author, the following day he received a phone call from Segev, who had said that within a short time, when the truth came out, the author would see that he had been right. The IDF, claimed Segev, was panicking, and its commanders could see no further than the tip of their noses (Litani 1998). Segev was the first to understand, as soon as the Intifada broke out, that it would continue for a long time.

ANOTHER WARNING THAT WAS IGNORED

Even if there had been no warnings about the changes in the territories, they could have been seen as important, or at least unusual, and there were, in fact, people who sensed that the situation was changing for the worse and could end in an uprising. Ehud Ilan (Interview by author. Kfar Sava, May 2013), a former senior Shabak official, said that, in March 1987, the annual meeting of the unit responsible for Judea and Samaria was attended by all the district heads, and each was asked to report on the situation in his area (Ilan 2013). He was asked for his opinion of what was happening in the territories; he reported that according to talks he had held with Palestinians detained for interrogation, very few of the attacks had been carried out by operatives of the established terrorist organizations, but most had been done by local networks. He added that the economic situation in the territories was bad: he knew of many people who were hungry, and of people who had attacked in order to be caught and be sent to an Israeli jail, where they would eat regularly. It was also easier for the Shabak to recruit informers because everyone needed money. At the time, the Shabiba, the youth organizations of the Popular and Democratic Fronts for the Liberation of Palestine, had increased their activities, as did Fatah. To a certain extent, Israel turned a blind eye, assuming the

Palestinians would be busy with educational and social activities and would carry out fewer terrorist attacks. However, one dissenting opinion was that within a year there would be a popular revolt in the territories that would make what happened in Algeria look like a walk in the park. He was ignored and the meeting chairman had his opinion kept out of the minutes (Ilan, 2013). According to Ilan, in August 1987, about half a year after the meeting, he had said that the uprising in the Balata refugee camp was going to develop into a situation in the territories that would be far worse than Algeria had been and that the IDF would not be able to cope with it. The senior Shabak executives said nothing.

THE SURPRISE

The Intifada was a double surprise. One was the fact that the riots broke out spontaneously, without PLO direction (Nasser and Heacock 1990; Mishal and Aharoni 1989; Levenberg 2011; Friedman, 1990, 313). The other was that the Intifada organizers had been unknown to the Shabak and the IDF and had not belonged to any organization. In January 1988, according to COGAT headquarters, they still did not know who the leaders were (IDF Archive, 382-1185-1932; Summary of Deliberations, January 20, 1987).

The degree to which the defense establishment did not understand the significance of the outbreak of the riots in December 1987 was reflected in the minutes of the meeting held in the COGAT's office on December 10. None of those present understood what the developments in the territories meant. The atmosphere was business as usual, the riots in the Gaza Strip were considered routine, and there was no mention of their extent. No thought was given to what might happen next. The COGAT authorized the assessments of those present and did not realize that events in the territories pointed to an essential change (Goren 2013).

On the evening of December 10, 1987, Defense Minister Yitzhak Rabin was about to leave Israel to visit the United States. Deliberations held the same day did not mention the possibility of cancelling it. The general assessment was that the wave of riots would end quickly, as they had in the past (Schiff and Yaari 1990). The Shabak and IDF intelligence had been surprised by the riots and did not understand their significance and therefore did not recommend changes in Rabin's plans. Rabin hoped that the IDF would quell the riots; otherwise, he said, they could create anarchy, and Israel would not be able to put the genie back into the lamp (Levenberg 2011).

Rabin was away from Israel for the first ten critical days of the Intifada, returning on December 21. While away, he asked if he ought to return earlier than planned; the IDF chief of staff told him that there was no need for him to cut the visit short, because the riots were of a familiar type and could be quelled (Shiffer 2011). It was confirmed by Eitan Haber, Rabin's senior assistant, interview by author. Tel Aviv, 2013.

As soon as he returned to Israel, Rabin held a press conference, accusing Syria and Iran of inciting the uprising; his office quickly issued a retraction, saying that Rabin had been mistaken (Erlich 2008; Shiff and Yaari 1990; Litani, 1998). Nonetheless, this was the first time that Rabin mentioned the change in the territories (Goren 2013). Yitzhak Shamir, who had been acting defense minister while Rabin was in the United States, accused the PLO of inciting the riots; but he had been wrong—the PLO had been as surprised as Israel. Shamir refused to accept the fact that there was a new situation in the territories and, as far as he was concerned, all that was necessary to stop the riots was to deploy more soldiers.

On December 14, while Rabin was still abroad, high-ranking IDF officers held a meeting about the riots. Ehud Barak, the deputy chief of staff, was of the opinion that the territories were on the brink of a civilian rebellion but, except for the head of IDF intelligence, his opinion was rejected. The position of the Shabak was that the riots would continue for a few weeks, as they had in the past, and then gradually wane after Fatah Day on January 1, 1988 (Goren 2013).

During the first month of the Intifada, Israel expected the riots to end of their own accord, but they did not (Mishal and Aharoni 1989). The first government meeting to discuss the issue was held in January 1988, when the deputy chief of staff said it would be a long confrontation, not one of days or weeks: it could last years (Caspit and Kfir 1998, 225).

SURPRISE FOR THE SHABAK AND THE DEFENSE ESTABLISHMENT

The defense establishment, especially the Shabak, as well as the PLO leadership in Tunisia, had not expected the Intifada and had not understood that it was a comprehensive popular uprising; rather, they had believed that it was just another wave of riots (Schiff and Yaari 1990). IDF intelligence had intercepted calls made from the PLO in Tunisia to their affiliates in the territories, and it was clear that the PLO had had no idea, but was trying to understand what was happening, who was leading the uprising, and who were the main actors.

The IDF had had no way of dealing with the situation (Levenberg 2011). Anti-Israel activities usually had been of two types: the first was nonviolent events, which included large demonstrations, cutting off commercial ties with Israel, civil disobedience, shows of solidarity, and not going to work in Israel.

The second was violence, which included the throwing of stones and Molotov cocktails, erecting barriers, burning tires, using knives, clashing with IDF forces, and violence against Palestinians perceived as collaborators.

On January 25, 1988, after a month and a half, Rabin recognized that the situation had completely changed and that they were faced with a rebellion of the entire Palestinian population (Levenberg 2011). It was the first time that the clashes were led by the local residents, and the defense establishment was unprepared. Dichter, former head of Shabak, said that no such uprising had ever been seen. Hundreds and thousands of Palestinians marched and could only be halted by live fire (Moreh 2014). The riots snowballed to unprecedented proportions, and it was difficult to believe that it was a popular phenomenon without a core leadership (Melman and Raviv 2012, 377). Israel had had no response, and the Shabak could not identify the leaders and therefore could not break the back of the Intifada (Schiff and Yaari 1990, 230). The main reason for the surprise was that the intelligence establishment had not believed that there would ever be a mass Palestinian uprising, because no such thing had happened before (Melman and Raviv 2012, 380). Peri agreed that there were tens of thousands of attacks and the number of wanted Palestinians was the largest that any intelligence organization had ever had to deal with— hundreds, if not thousands, in every district (Moreh 2014). The Shabak did not have a designated research department or even basic information. Its research had always dealt with operational aspects, that is, terrorist attacks, and not with in-depth research (Gazit 2003; Paz 2013).

Danny Rothschild, the head of the analysis division in IDF intelligence, had suggested, in 1987, that there might be unrest in the territories, directed by PLO headquarters in Tunisia (Rothschild 2013). That assessment had not been prominently noted because it was not within the province of military intelligence responsibility. Rothschild added that it had contradicted the COGAT, who had been of the opinion that the situation was expected to remain calm, because the economic situation was good, and that the uprising was a minor problem. A bulletin was issued with that message a few weeks before the outbreak of the Intifada. According to Amnon Lipkin Shahak, who had been the director of IDF intelligence, if someone or some group had been behind the uprising, it would have been exposed at some stage of the planning. In hindsight, no one had planned it (Abramowitz 2013).

According to Matti Steinberg, special advisor to the head of the ISA (interview by author, July 2013), it had been a surprise mainly for the Shabak, but not only for them (Steinberg 2008), and also by Goren (interview by author 2013). The last time Israel had had such a significant intelligence surprise was in October 1973, with the slight exception of Sadat's visit to Israel in 1977 and the peace process with Egypt. Yoel Ben-Porat, commander of Unit 8200, which deals with SIGINT, said the Intifada should be considered a failure, because no intelligence warning had been given (Ben-Porat 1988). The Shabak was not alone, because PLO leadership in Tunisia also had been surprised (Rubinstein 2001, 103; Peri 1999, 159; Melman and Raviv 2012, 376; Rothschild 2013). According to Peri, the Palestinian masses had not consulted the PLO about whether or not to riot (Rubinstein 2001,103). They had not received instructions as to how to demonstrate or riot. Arafat claimed, although only in retrospect, that he had commanded the Palestinians to rebel and launch an Intifada. At first, the Intifada had no local leadership but, after several weeks, the PLO jumped on the wagon and led the Intifada with other Palestinian organizations (Klein 1991).

At the beginning of January 1988, Shabak informed the Israeli government that the Intifada was not a routine development (Peri 1999,160). Prime Minister Shamir agreed that the situation in the territories was worrying and had to be dealt with, but he had not claimed, unambiguously, that the army had to be sent in. Apparently the Shabak and the IDF were still slaves to the concepts that one, there would be no rebellion in the territories and that nothing significant would happen without the initiative, coordination and oversight of the PLO; two, that as long as the Palestinian organizations quarreled with one another, there would be no change in the status quo in the territories; three, that the Palestinians had become accustomed to the situation, their economic circumstances were good, and they had no reason to look for a change; and four, as long as Israel's battle against the Palestinian groups and organizations was successful, especially the prevention of terrorist attacks, there would be no change on the ground.

The Intifada turned everything upside down. Before the Intifada, the PLO had led the Palestinian struggle, but in the Intifada, local residents began to spearhead the conflict. Thus, it was no longer a struggle between two armed forces and organizations, but clashes between civilians and an army (Klein 1991, 11). The Intifada took over the entire Palestinian population and, at the beginning, there was a new unified, national leadership (Klein 1991,12). The Intifada represented a generation born and brought up in the shadow of the Israeli occupation, with all of its internal contradictions—contradictions between the "enlightened occupation" and the Jewish settlement project, which threatened Palestinian lands. Some Palestinians adopted the idea of nonviolence, which had charted the path of the uprising when it began, but the idea collapsed under violence and counterviolence activities (Sela 2012).

According to certain assessments, Hamas had been behind the Intifada. Hamas had claimed it began in October 1987, when four Palestinian Islamic Jihad operatives, who had escaped from an Israeli jail, were killed in Jabalia. Paz was of the opinion that, in all probability, Hamas was not behind the Intifada; nonetheless, as soon as it broke out, Hamas became an important factor, because it had an organizational network in the Gaza Strip. However, about a week after the Intifada had begun, Hamas was formally established as a terrorist organization (Paz 2013). As far as the Shabak was concerned, many Hamas operatives were unknown because, until then, the organization had operated at the social level and was not given high priority by the Shabak.

As the Intifada continued, Hamas integrated into the events and became an important Islamist trend in Palestinian politics (Tal 1995, 92; Hacham 2006), especially after establishing its military-terrorist wing (Shaked and Shaabi 1994). Sheikh Ahmed Yassin told David Hacham, advisor for Arab affairs in the Gaza Strip, that he had supported joining the Intifada with operatives from the Muslim Brotherhood in the Gaza Strip, and thus Hamas was founded; previously, it had not supported violence but focused on religious education and social welfare (Hacham 2006, 20). Yassin ordered the establishment of "shock groups," whose role was to go to the Israeli roadblocks and throw stones, write slogans, and make sure the populace followed the Intifada's orders, such as holding general strikes and preventing Palestinian workers from going to work in Israel (Hacham 2006, 23).

The PLO, as noted, had been taken completely by surprise. The events had been spontaneous, and before notices were distributed instructions had been passed by word of mouth. The PLO's first reaction to the Intifada came a month later. It issued its first notice on January 1, 1988, which had not yet borne the stamp of the United Headquarters, but rather of the Palestinian Forces (Mishal and Aharoni, 1989). It mentioned the PLO only once, and not in the headline. It did not mention the establishment of a headquarters but had rather been a call for a joint organization (Inbari 1994). On January 10, 1988, the first notice of the United Headquarters was issued, which began issuing its notices alongside those of the Palestinian Islamic Jihad and Hamas. On January 16, 1988, Fatah and its affiliated organizations established the United National Leadership and began distributing its own notices. In effect, there were two blocs active on the ground: the secular block, headed by Fatah, and the Islamist block, led by Hamas and the Palestinian Islamic Jihad (Kahana 2010, 281-283). Only after the third notice was Fatah included in the United Headquarters (Inbari 1994; Shiff and Yaari, 1990). To ride the wave of the Intifada's success, the PLO's Abu Jihad called it the result of the determined struggle that the PLO had waged in the past, as well as its ongoing activities (Kahana 2010, 283). Initially, the PLO adhered to its position that the solution would come from the muzzle of a rifle, and therefore the Intifada, given the direction it was taking, would not bring results (Schiff and Yaari 1990, 25).

The PLO, which had worked for years to create a local leadership in the territories, had no choice, in retrospect, but to give its agreement to the establishment of the national headquarters (Firsch 1992, 61). The pressure exerted on the PLO to take control of the Intifada events was also a function of the rise of Islamist power, especially Hamas and the Palestinian Islamic Jihad. During the first stage of the Intifada, Palestinians had thrown stones and Molotov cocktails, and later had carried out "commando attacks" (Kahana 2010, 284). In 2007, when the Palestinian Authority marked the 20th anniversary of the first Intifada, Fatah announced it had been the spine of the 1987 Intifada (Jerusalem Center for Public Affairs 2007), which was an unprecedented event and resounded throughout the territories and the world. There are claims that its influence had gone far beyond the territories—and rebellions, such as those in Algeria (1988), Myanmar (1988), the Baltic states (1989), and other countries in Eastern Europe and later in China, South Africa, Kenya and even the Soviet Union—had been influenced by the Intifada, which had expressed a mass popular uprising for the sake of democratic, economic rights, and had fought against oppression (Lustick 1993, 561).

One of the key questions is, why had the Intifada not broken out previously? The events that had preceded it had lasted only for a few weeks. Why, in the past, had not large swaths of the population been enlisted? In 1929 and especially in 1936 (Gelber 1992), the local Arab populations had successfully organized revolts. One reason might have been geography: the Intifada took place within a relatively small, limited area, in which very effective counterterrorist activities had been carried out by Israel for many years (Lustick 1993, 563). In addition, Israel's carrot and stick policies (which included opening the bridges over the Jordan River for commercial and pedestrian and car traffic), instituted by Moshe Dayan in 1967, had proved themselves effective, and there was a feeling that a modus vivendi had been created between Israel and the territories.

Before the Intifada, terrorist activity had been generally directed by the Fatah and other organization headquarters from abroad. Beginning in 1982, terrorist activity was directed by the Fatah headquarters in Tunisia. The attacks were carried out intermittently, generally by individual terrorists or small cells, with almost no active participation of the general population. However, the number of attacks carried out by local initiatives and not by the PLO began rising, in the middle of the 1980s. The Intifada was the turning point. A relatively long time passed before the Israeli defense establishment had internalized the fact that something critical had changed in the territories. The Palestinians who had joined the Intifada were not combatants, and it was hard to distinguish between those who took to the streets and the rest of the population. The question was how to limit the protests, as the usual measures were not proving effective. At the beginning, there had been no good intelligence about the new operatives, which had made it difficult to prevent their activities. The Shabak was the entity that was most familiar with the local residents, having interrogated many of them for rioting and throwing stones, but the Shabak had not taken an interest. Even when the Intifada broke out, Shabak interrogators were not enthusiastic about interrogating rioters, claiming that the main problem was terrorism, not riots (Paz 2013; Ilan 2013; Moran 2013).

In view of the lack of warning, the IDF had not had the appropriate means to cope with the mass riots. Months passed before suitable forces were sent to deal with the riots, only then receiving crowd-dispersal equipment for a violent, or actually, semi-violent uprising (Meir-Roth 2007). Hence, at the beginning of the Intifada, Israel's response was not effective.

The approach of the Shabak had been to investigate what was happening in PLO headquarters in Tunisia, and then, according to its intelligence, which was good, to study the extent to which the PLO was directing the activities on the ground. In addition, there had been intelligence surveillance of terrorist attack targets in the territories before and immediately after the Intifada broke out. It clearly showed that the PLO was not involved, and therefore the Shabak assumed that no change could be expected on the ground (table 4.1).

The Intifada had been a strategic surprise for Israel intelligence, especially the Shabak and the political establishment, and in retrospect it is clear that both the Shabak and IDF had been mistaken in their identification of the key intelligence targets. Instead of looking inward, to occurrences on the ground, they had looked outward, as was their custom, to PLO headquarters in Tunisia, from which instructions came for terrorist attacks and other activities in the territories. They had relied on past experience, which indicated that no significant event occurred on the ground without PLO direction, and thus they deployed for a concentrated surprise, as usual. However, the Intifada was a diffused surprise, the result of a spontaneous development of many people who had not been significantly organized by a known factor, and therefore it could not have been identified as having been caused by a known factor. During the first days of the Intifada, it had become clear that the PLO was not leading it and, that being the case, it was considered unimportant and transitory. The Shabak had not realized

Table 4.1 Intifada, Data from 1987 to 1993

Number	*Data*
66	IDF soldiers killed by Palestinians
4,918	IDF soldiers wounded by Palestinians
157	Israeli civilians killed by Palestinians
4,915	Israeli civilians wounded by Palestinians
808	Palestinians killed by the Israeli security forces
16,824	Palestinians wounded by the Israeli security forces
985	Palestinians killed by Palestinians
940	Shooting attacks
43,520	Public disturbances (riots, demonstrations, instances of stones thrown)

Source: IDF 1987-1993.

that this time it was a completely different type of event. It was a diffused surprise and therefore monitoring the activities of the PLO not only would not lead to the PLO, but the PLO's actual participation had been misleading. This had been a broad, diffused surprise, unknown from past events. Since the key intelligence target had been wrong, the information received was irrelevant. The information that had been received before December 9, 1987, had been interpreted incorrectly, and thus the situation in the territories was considered stable, with ups and downs that were being caused by incitement from afar.

THE REASONS FOR INTELLIGENCE FAILURE IN THE INTIFADA

Intelligence Collection Capabilities

The test case of the Intifada shows that the problem had not been a lack of information, but rather a focus on irrelevant intelligence targets and a mistaken order of priorities in collecting information; the outbreak of the Intifada had been a diffused surprise for the IDF and the Israeli political leadership. Two groups had covered events in Judea, Samaria, and the Gaza Strip: the Shabak and the COGAT. The Shabak had focused on preventing terrorist attacks, and the COGAT had dealt with regulating daily life in the territories but had a unit of advisors for Arab affairs that had operated on the ground, whose function had been to maintain a connection with the local residents, in order to see to their needs and to gain a sense of what the Arab street was thinking.

The Shabak, which gave political subversion a low priority, had not suspected a popular uprising. The COGAT had agreed and had maintained contact with only specific sectors of the population, usually those in whose interest it was to maintain contact with Israel: such as the old-guard leadership, the elite, public figures, mayors, and businessmen. Thus, they had believed that they could influence the Palestinian public, calm the situation and prevent an overt revolt. The younger generation had not interested the advisors for Arab affairs in the least, and there had been practical difficulties in creating contacts with them because they were militant and opposed the continuing Israeli occupation. Intelligence coverage of the Palestinian territories was very good, especially from the viewpoint of preventing terrorist attacks, but the issue of political subversion slipped between the fingers of Israeli intelligence and no one had been designated to be specifically responsible for it. In the absence of a Shabak department to deal with general public opinion, no one was genuinely familiar with it.

The concept that had been popular with IDF intelligence was that the Palestinians had no reason to change the status quo, and if there had been a change or a political awakening, it would come from the familiar organizations, especially the PLO leadership in Tunisia. It took weeks before the PLO took control of the activities in the territories. The initial lack of organization was one factor that had made it difficult to halt the riots. Unable to identify the leaders, the Shabak detained a great many rioters but, in most cases, they were merely participants. Despite the detentions and expulsions, the events lasted until the Oslo Accords in 1993. During the Intifada, terrorist attacks against Israel continued, and the Shabak and the IDF paid most of their attention to them.

The conclusion to be drawn is that the problem was not lack of information but rather a focus on terrorism instead of political subversion, and therefore the information flowing through the intelligence cycle was irrelevant to the developing threat. In addition, there was a lack of basic research into the events taking place in the territories, because there had been no cadre of intelligence professionals whose job had been to be focused on political subversion.

The Noisy Work Environment

The intensive intelligence coverage of the territories, primarily carried out by the Shabak and the COGAT, meant that from 1967 on there was no lack of information. However, until the Intifada, the information was partially contradictory. On the one hand, familiar types of terrorist attacks were being carried out; on the other hand, there had been a rise in the number of riots and of local networks throwing stones and Molotov cocktails for months before the Intifada began. When the Intifada broke out, the riots were of a scope that never had been seen before. In addition to throwing stones, rocks, and Molotov cocktails, Palestinians erected road blocks, burned tires, used knives and axes, clashed with IDF forces and carried out activities against those whom the Palestinians had considered to be collaborators. Also, at the beginning of the Intifada, the continuous monitoring of ties between PLO headquarters in Tunisia and organizations and individuals in the territories was intensive. It was clear that the PLO did not understand what was happening on the ground or who was in charge and was very worried that, for the first time since 1967, it was not in charge.

Apparently, all the information that had been possessed by the defense establishment indicated that the routine of the situation on the ground was not about to change. Certain events perhaps hinted at a change, but IDF intelligence did not interpret them correctly. The events in the Balata refugee camp, in May 1987, when IDF forces had to withdraw and control of the camp passed into the hands of the Shabiba (which stayed there for months), should have sounded a tocsin, but they did not. Rabin's communication advisor Eitan Haber said (interview by author, in 2013, that the defense establishment had not regarded Balata as anything extraordinary, or as having any particular consequences. The escape of the Palestinian Islamic Jihad terrorists, from an Israeli jail, in the Gaza Strip, and their overt appearances in the refugee camps in Gaza during the months before the Intifada should have been proof that Israel's deterrence was on the wane. The clash between IDF forces and Bir Zeit University students in 1986 may also have been an early sign. Three students were killed in the clash, sending the West Bank and Gaza Strip into an uproar until calm was gradually restored, which took ten days. The organizing of Shabiba networks in every village had constructed an infrastructure for the future which also should have caught the attention of the defense establishment. The Shabiba was preparing the groundwork (Mishal and Aharoni 1989, 13-15), as well as Palestinian hearts and minds, for the outbreak of the Intifada; it had been operating under the Shabak's radar, which had focused on preventing terrorist attacks. While the British Foreign Office argued in its annual report that, for the first time, the Palestinian issue was not discussed at the Arab League Summit (held in Amman in October 1987), the Summit was another catalyst for the outbreak of the Intifada (The National Archives 1989). In the Gaza Strip, the Islamist student networks were very strong and had forged ties with the local population as part of their community activities.

The assessment of the defense establishment was that the Palestinian populace was passive and worried about day-to-day affairs; nothing had changed in the PLO's modus operandi and it was not fomenting a change in the status quo. There was a certain change, however, due to local organizations, especially of the younger generation, that might have indicated frustration and a decline in the PLO's power. The Shabak's focus on preventing a concentrated surprise (uprising initiated by the PLO) deflected its attention from the possibility of a diffused surprise (a popular revolt initiated by the crowds). In a concentrated surprise, a single item of intelligence can be critical and can help to identify the intentions of rival, but in a diffused surprise which is an ongoing process, there are many pieces of information, which are unclear and can be easily overlooked. Because of the mistake in locating the key intelligence topic, the intelligence that had been collected was irrelevant to the surprise.

Human Error

The security establishment had believed that the situation in the territories was static and that there were no changes on the horizon. It had been generally assumed for years that the local population had no desire for change, that they were interested in making a living and leading their routine lives, and that if there were a change or a rebellion, it would come from the familiar organizations and known activists and would be led and pushed forward by PLO headquarters in Tunisia. Thus, Israel would have had forewarning from its intelligence monitoring of the target in Tunisia. Even the events in the Balata refugee camp had been regarded as a local, limited anomaly of little significance, simply because they had not been orchestrated from Tunisia. No one had thought differently or had expressed a different opinion, and if someone had raised the issue, as Yitzhak Segev did, it was rejected out of hand. When the Intifada finally did break out, it was generally assumed that it would be over in two or three weeks. The lightbulbs began to go on only when Rabin returned from the United States on December 21, 1987. The defense establishment was confused and could not grasp that a popular rebellion was taking place. Rabin, after consulting with the heads of the defense establishment, held a press conference when he landed in Israel and announced that Syria and Iran were behind the uprising. The Shabak and the COGAT stuck to their original story of a wave of riots that would soon die down and did not recommend using stricter measures against the rioters. In addition, there was no intelligence analysis and production department to assess the situation since, at that time, neither the Shabak nor IDF intelligence had dealt or even had been familiar with the issue of popular uprisings. No one had understood or had fathomed the importance of what turned out to be special circumstances.

Organizational Difficulties and Poor Cooperation

Before the Intifada, cooperation within the defense establishment, between the Shabak and the COGAT, had been weak. The Shabak had focused wholly on preventing terrorist attacks and customarily reported only raw statistics with no attempt to analyze or interpret them. It had dealt with political subversion, but only superficially. It had not held regular meetings with the COGAT, and the Shabak representatives at the weekly COGAT meetings usually sat in silence without presenting reports. According to Goren, he had served as the COGAT for six years and had never seen an intelligence report from the Shabak. The Shabak had, however, contributed to the meetings held by the Minister of Defense every week, which had begun at the end of 1986. The Shabak had had a great deal of material about political subversion collected through its extensive prevention of terrorist attacks, but the information had not been considered important; rather, it was a by-product, and never reached a desk where it could be analyzed, processed and turned into an intelligence report. The Shabak's intelligence product had consisted of weekly statistical summaries of the numbers of terrorist attacks, the number of attackers apprehended, the amounts of weapons confiscated, the number of riots, of stones and Molotov cocktails thrown and of PLO flags waved. Thus, their contribution, for the most part, had been negligible, especially since the IDF had produced very similar summaries. Apparently the Shabak had not considered it necessary to share sensitive intelligence with the COGAT (Paz 2013), regarding the COGAT as supporting the Shabak's activities and nothing more. That also had been the feeling among the advisors for Arab affairs, like Brig. General Res. Shalom Harari (interview by author February 2013), whose ties to the Shabak had been based more on personal relationships and less on the cooperation that should have been inherent between the two organizations.

Thus, the general conclusion that can be drawn is that the Shabak had cooperated only slightly with the COGAT, who had not regarded the Shabak's input as particularly important. There had been no professional ties with IDF intelligence analysis and production, since the topic of intelligence covering of the Territories had not been part of its mandate. The lack of cooperation also had been a function of the Shabak's overweening certainty that as long as terrorist attacks were under control, no essential change could occur in the Palestinian territories. However, it is possible that if all the agencies (both those that had been directly involved and those that had been indirectly involved, such as analysts from non-military spheres) had not been compartmentalized but instead had joined forces, it might have been possible earlier to identify the changes and increased threats presented by the Intifada, a diffused surprise.

Interactions with the Decision Makers

Apparently, the events in the territories had not interested the senior defense ranks or the senior political leadership. They had been left to the care of the Shabak and the COGAT, and to Yitzhak Mordechai, the commander of the Southern Command, and Amram Mitzna, the commander of the Central Command. Their approach had been that if nothing significant happened, there was nothing to discuss. In 1986, the "territories forum" had met every week, in the office of Defense Minister Rabin, but only routine events in the territories were discussed (Haber 2013; Moran 2013). Even when there were significant events, such as terrorist attacks, the issue of the territories was not a top priority for the decision makers. As noted, even when Yitzhak Segev had issued a warning shortly before the outbreak of the Intifada, it was dismissed because it did not seem realistic. The concept that nothing in the territories was going to change, because the Palestinians accepted the status quo and were doing nothing to change it, was also influenced by the expectations of the political leadership, who were of the opinion that there was no need to take action beyond preserving quiet. External factors, such as academics, had had no influence on the defense establishment or on the events in the territories. Such factors had seemed political and therefore were not integrated into the issue, although they would have been able to have presented different viewpoints, especially regarding trends and processes occurring in the territories.

The Israeli government and IDF headquarters had discussed the Intifada only after more than a month had gone by. Shamir had not been receptive and, as far as he was concerned, the events were insignificant and would soon end on their own—and if they did not, the IDF would end them. Thus, the implied message from the decision makers had been the necessity to preserve the status quo. Since the situation in the territories had never been a particular point of interest for the media, and thus not for the public at large, when the time came to assess the real situation, the decision was made to continue the routine and ignore the few indicators that existed. Not only Israeli but global decision makers, as well, had tended to ignore warnings of diffused surprises, such as the First and the Second Intifadas, the fall of the Shah, the collapse of the Soviet Union, and the Arab Spring, because the occurrences had been the culmination of ongoing processes and not the results of specific events. Also, it had been unclear if and how these situations would develop, and there had not been clear signs to indicate their relevance.

QUESTIONS DISCUSSED IN THE TEST CASE OF THE INTIFADA

1. Before the crisis broke out, what had been the assessment regarding the possibility of its occurrence?

   There had been no predictions of a crisis. Based on summaries of deliberations held in the office of the Israeli COGAT in Judea, Samaria, and the Gaza Strip, no alert was sounded before the Intifada broke out. The deliberations had been held to provide responses to events as they occurred on the ground, mainly bureaucratic responses, but no discussions were held about long-term developments. Discussions had focused on the PLO, on the assumption that it would be the source of any threat. Terrorist attacks and riots had become routine. According to security assessments, the Palestinian public had become apathetic and would not carry out any acts that deviated from the profile of its activities over the past twenty years.
2. What signs had indicated a coming crisis?

   Although signs had been present, they had not been recognized for what they were because of blind adherence to concept. Even during the first days of the Intifada, their significance had not been correctly assessed; they had been regarded as a wave of riots, despite their massive attendance, which was different from previous instances. The situation on the ground had not seemed dangerous, because the Palestinians did not carry out terrorist attacks— they rioted and threw stones. According to the concepts of the decision makers, Israel had struggled against organizations: if the PLO had not initiated it, it would not happen, and if something did happen, it was likely to have limited importance and to be short-lived. All the people involved in security honestly had believed that, as long as the PLO did nothing to change the situation, the situation on the ground would remain unchanged.

3. If there had been signs, over a long period of time, indicating a developing threat, why were the developments and their possible significance not correctly assessed?

   Most of the signs had been in the field of macro, but they were not investigated. Monitoring events in the realm of political subversion had been part of the ISA's activity on the ground, but its priority was low, and no one in the intelligence organizations had had responsibility for it. To a certain extent, the advisor for Arab affairs had dealt with political subversion, but because of the COGAT's relatively limited deployment in the territories, and the limited attention it had been given, a genuine picture of the situation was unavailable. Moreover, contacts generally had been with local actors, who had been prepared to talk to representatives of the administration, with the result that the information that was received had been biased. The ISA had focused on preventing terrorist attacks, and the Analysis and Production department was small and had focused on terrorist attacks and riots, not political subversion. A significance revolt in the Balata refugee camp in May 1987 did not receive the attention it deserved and was seen as a pinpoint occurrence. The possibility of a broader development had not been correctly assessed.

4. Nevertheless, were there, among people with clout, assessments of the possibility of a significant crisis? What led to the failure of assessors in the establishment and to the success of alternative assessors?

   The ISA and the COGAT had felt the situation on the ground was calm and that there were no developments or changes on the horizon. Within the ISA, there had been a minority opinion that the Palestinian street was about to explode. The opinion was brought to the attention of senior ISA officials a few months before the outbreak of the Intifada, but it was ignored. One of the people sounding the tocsin was Brigadier General (Ret.) Yitzhak Segev, and his warning was noted twice by Chief of Staff Shomron at meetings with the Ministry of Defense, about a month before the Intifada began, but it was rejected. The opinion had been shared by a few isolated people and did not receive special attention. Amram Mitzna,

Commander of the Central Command, in an interview with the *Jerusalem Post* on October 12, 1987, had correctly read the map regarding the increase in locally initiated attacks, but had added that they would not lead to a popular uprising in the territories. Within the defense establishment, no one had issued a warning. They were held captive by the concept that no change was to be expected. Part of that concept was that if a change did occur, it would be the result of activity from the Palestinian organizations, as usual, initiated by the PLO which, at that time, had not been interested in igniting the territories, especially not with an Intifada. Some of the media correspondents who had covered the territories and had dealt with security, such as Yehuda Litani, Ze'ev Shiff and Uri Nir, had been of the opinion, from the beginning, that this time the situation was different.

5. Had this been an intelligence failure and, if so, what kind?

   The Israeli defense establishment had been held captive by the concept that there was no visible sign of a change, and if there were to be a change, it would come from the organizations, especially the PLO, as it had in the past. The possibility of a popular rebellion had not been considered. The situation in the territories had been considered to be calm. The general assessment was that the PLO had no interest in effecting a change. The PLO had seemed to be focused on international political activity and in directing attacks in the territories. No one in the defense establishment had thought that the situation could or would change. No serious alarms had been raised because intelligence collection had not been directed at looking for them. Even during the first weeks, after the outbreak of the Intifada, the concept was still in force. According to assessment, it was a wave that would pass and there was no need to respond with force. The possibility that a fundamental change was about to occur was not raised for discussion, nor was the question of whether the usual forceful response would be able to return the situation to the status quo ante.

In summation, the intelligence failures of the first Intifada were the following:

One: the decision makers had been surprised by the timing and rapid spread of the events throughout the Palestinian Authority-administered territories.

Two: even during the weeks after the outbreak of the Intifada, the IDF and the Shabak had not understood the true significance of the events, having mistaken them for a wave of riots that would wane on its own within two or three weeks.

Three: the uprising had come from an unexpected direction, from the unorganized Palestinian masses. The PLO initially was not in the picture, although it jumped on the bandwagon, at a later date, as did Hamas. Neither was present at its inception.

Four: both the IDF and the PLO had been surprised by the Intifada. The Israeli Intelligence Community had examined what the PLO knew and had understood that the PLO had known nothing, but were surprised when it joined the Intifada and began leading it.

Five: the assessment of the IDF and the Shabak was that if there had been a rebellion, it would be organized by one of the terrorist organizations, principally the PLO, which was being monitored to prevent terrorist attacks and, to a lesser extent, political subversion. However, the surprise came from a different direction; it was diffused, spontaneous, and unorganized.

Six: the Shabak, which had been the dominant organization dealing with the territories, had been responsible for preventing terrorist attacks and not political subversion. The Commission, which had been headed by Moshe Landau, an Israeli Supreme Court Judge, had issued a report in October 1987 about political subversion that had dealt with the Shabak's methods. According to the report, political subversion had been an important part of the PLO's activities in the territories. It had praised, glorified, and encouraged terrorist attacks or activities that showed solidarity with the organization. Agencies had been established on the public front to draw the masses closer, mainly among the younger generation; students had played an important role. The agencies had taken their orders from the PLO and had been a convenient human foundation for recruiting individuals to conduct subversive activities. In the years leading up to the Intifada, the number of organizations of young people in the territories had increased—young people who had gone from open solidarity to supporting terrorist attacks.

Thus, the importance of preventing political subversion was clear, but the Shabak had given it low priority and had assumed that every activity had been organized and directed by the PLO in Tunisia.

Seven: Military Intelligence and the COGAT had not dealt much with the issue of political subversion. The Shabak, however, had HUMINT sources (i.e., informers) spread throughout the territories. Every month, it had interrogated hundreds of Palestinians, of every age, but most of them were guilty of throwing stones and Molotov cocktails. The Shabak had focused on the wrong key intelligence target and had assumed that if a change in anti-Israeli activities had been being planned, they would have heard of it. However, they did not hear about it because political subversion had not been a key intelligence target (table 4.2).

Table 4.2 Factors Influencing the Intelligence Failure

Number	*Question/Issue*	*Response*
1	Was the event routine?	No
2	Was it familiar from the past?	No
3	Were the threatening factors familiar?	No
4	Was the modus operandi familiar?	No
5	Was there a specific organization directing the events?	No
6	Was the information received unequivocal?	No
7	Was it clear what was intended?	No

Source: Avner Barnea 2020.

The consequences of the intelligence failure were the following:

One: the State of Israel had to deal with the Intifada for six years, until the Oslo Accords were signed in 1993. Apparently, the Intifada had led to the Oslo Accords and to the signing of an Agreement of Principles with the PA (Pundak 2014,17-18).
Two: the Intifada did enormous damage to Israel's image.
Three: the Intifada had reduced Israel's short and long-term deterrent capabilities, which took years to return to their former strength.
Four, the Intifada had severely damaged the reputation of Israeli intelligence for its inability to predict the Intifada and to end it, as ending it took a long time.

The characteristics of Israel's intelligence failure were the following:

One: despite the vast amount of information and Israel's intelligence command of the territories, the wrong key intelligence target had been chosen (common in diffused surprises).
Two: large quantities of information had been collected in the territories by the IDF and the Israel Police Force as well, but the information was partially contradictory and often irrelevant, again because of the wrong choice of intelligence target.
Three: there had been a tendency to adhere to previous assessments, especially because of the calculated determination that the situation was under control and the populace appeared calm. As a result, there had been no need to change strategy. Monitoring the PLO's activities in Tunisia only had served to reinforce the assessment.
Four: there had been an interagency lack of cooperation, even though they had sat together in joint forums of the Shabak and the COGAT. In effect, the COGAT had led the way and the defense establishment had not disagreed with its assessments. Danny Rubinstein, head of military intelligence, had claimed that there had been no cooperation between

the military secretaries of the prime minister, the defense minister, the COGAT and the IDF's Production and Analysis department (Danny Rothschild, formerly head of Research Division, Israel Military Intelligence, interview by author, April 2013). The Shabak and the COGAT had not collaborated. Shmuel Goren, who had been the COGAT at the time, claimed that during the six years that he had held the position, he had never seen a single Shabak report (Goren, interview by author, October 2013). Dr. Levenberg (interview by author, October 2013) who wrote a summary about the Intifada, between 2000 and 2001, for the IDF's Historical Department, called "The IDF against the Intifada," had said that there had been limited sharing of information between the Shabak and the COGAT (Levenberg 2013).

Five: while it is difficult to evaluate the influence of external factors on intelligence assessment, it is possible that Israeli Prime Minister Shamir's position of not to rush to inform him of the real situation in the territories, had influenced both the IDF and the Shabak. For several weeks, the assessments had been, by both Shamir and, to a similar extent, by Rabin, that the uprising was a wave that would pass.

The Explanation of Israel's Intelligence Failure

The main explanation for the fact that there had been no prediction of the Intifada before it broke out, and no understanding of what it was for weeks after, is that it had been a diffused surprise. The main characteristics of a diffused surprise are spontaneous significant events that are carried out by many disparate actors, which develop over a long period of time and are not recognized as threatening; thus, they surprise both intelligence organizations and decision makers. They are not the product of a concentrated or organized effort but rather of spontaneous social and political processes by the Palestinian crowds . In several instances, as in the case of the Intifada, concentrated surprises are instead expected, which lead to identifying false key intelligence targets. Intelligence collection thus brings irrelevant information, which then influences the assessors.

When the information is not interpreted as indicating a diffused surprise, it is misunderstood as not indicating a change; in the case of the Intifada, the analysts had concluded that it was a wave of riots that would soon end as it happened before. The more diffused the intelligence, the greater the danger of an intelligence failure, especially as the assessors tend to see the information through the lens of a concentrated surprise. Diffused surprises can be characterized as unusual events unfamiliar from the past carried out by unfamiliar sources of threats. They can have an unusual modus operandi and not be directed by known agents. The intelligence collected may not clearly indicate a threat or may not be interpreted as indicating a threat.

In addition, the tools used by IDF intelligence and the Shabak had been the routine tools of ordinary intelligence work, especially in monitoring events in the territories. As there had been no apprehension of threat or danger, no special actions were taken and the routine was maintained. The basic assumption of the defense establishment had been that the wave of riots would pass on its own. Moreover, it had not even raised the possibility that there would be a popular uprising in the territories, as the situation on the ground was stable; so, they had claimed, there had been no need for special tools different from those ordinarily used.

MEASURES TAKEN TO PREVENT THE FAILURE

The measures that had been used were those of routine intelligence work, primarily monitoring events in the territories with the Shabak's ordinary tools. As no threat or danger had been detected, no special measures were used. The basic assumption was that nothing would change and the wave of protests would end.

THE IDF AND THE SHABAK COULD HAVE DONE THINGS DIFFERENTLY

One: if there had been a functioning unit in the Shabak responsible for political subversion, and if it had been collecting information over a long period of time, it would have been possible to identify indicators of a potential uprising in the territories.

Two: if such indicators had been identified, an alert could have been given, advising that a threat or at least a change was developing, different from what had been identified so far. If the Shabak had had even partial intelligence-collecting capabilities to identify political subversion, it could have found indicators of a change.

Three: external tools could have been used that might have been able to identify social and political changes.

Four: using open instead of only covert sources would have made it possible to identify the changes in the Arab street.

Five: there could have been greater cooperation within the intelligence community regarding political subversion; had IDF intelligence been made responsible, pluralism would have been created within the defense establishment.

THREE CHANGES THAT RESULTED FROM THE LESSONS LEARNED

First: a Shabak Analysis and Production department was established, responsible for investigating events in the Palestinian Authority-administered territories.
Second: the areas responsible for monitoring political subversion were improved, and a key intelligence target was defined.
Third: cooperation within the intelligence community regarding the territories was improved, including the sharing of information.

Chapter 5

Test Case

The Financial Crisis of 2008

OVERVIEW

On September 15, 2008, the American financial system imploded after the collapse of the Lehman Brothers investment bank, and the crisis became global. An examination of the crisis, using the intelligence discipline, indicates that it had been a diffused strategic surprise, an unpredicted threat to the financial system that had caught the American administration and the world unprepared. It has never been investigated from an intelligence point of view.

The agencies responsible for the financial stability of the United States had had a great deal of information about the developing threat, but the chances of its occurring had been considered low (Wyatt 2010). All prognoses, including those of the Federal Reserve (Fed), had failed to assess the significance of the threat and its ability to turn into a financial crisis, so no resolute measures were taken to prevent it. As a result, the decision makers had received no warning and then had reacted too late, after the crisis had seriously impacted the financial system's stability, first in the United States and then globally (Rose and Spiegel 2010). Research indicates that economists' ability to predict financial crises is not good (Ahir and Loungani 2014).

The Asian financial crisis of 1997 also was a local and global surprise. The International Monetary Fund (IMF) also had been surprised and played a large part in the failure because it had not predicted it, had been unprepared for it, and had intervened too late (Mishkin 1999). For several years, it had been known that Thailand's financial system was shaky, but it had not been assumed that it would influence the entire financial world and slow the economies of many countries for two years, although it mainly hit Asia. The decline of the price of oil affected Russia, leading to a devaluation of the ruble and a financial crisis. The IMF gave Russia a $23 billion loan, enabling it to recover faster than had been expected.

The crisis in Thailand was triggered by the fall of the baht, after the government had decided to end its linkage to the dollar and to allow it to be traded on the free market. As the crisis spread, most of the Southeast Asian countries saw their own currencies and other assets fall. The IMF initiated a program of $40 billion to stabilize the currencies of South Korea, Thailand and Indonesia, the economies most seriously hit. In 1999, Asian economy began to recover.

It is interesting to compare the Asian and American crises, since the situation in Thailand was well known, but the assessment had been that it would be overcome. When the crisis occurred, it had been an enormous surprise for the Thai financial institutions. It rapidly developed to far greater proportions than had been expected and was extremely difficult to overcome (Fox 2014).

The financial crisis of 2008 was a strategic surprise. The American administration had decided not to rescue Lehman Brothers, triggering the collapse of AIG, the largest insurance company in the world, which the administration did decide to rescue, infusing massive amounts of money. The crisis rapidly developed into one of the most devastating in history, the worst since the Great Depression (Fox 2014; Kindleberger 2012). The initial assessment, including that of the Fed, had been that no financial crisis could be expected, and if there were to be a recession, it would be limited in time and extent. There had been strong faith in the free market, America's economy, and its financial institutions, led by Alan Greenspan, who had chaired the Fed from 1987 to 2006. He later admitted that he had been wrong, saying, of the Lehman Brothers collapse, "We missed the timing badly on September 15, 2008" (Belvedere 2013).

After the dot.com crisis, at the end of the 1990s, and the 9/11 terrorist attack, in 2001, Greenspan had decided to lower the interest rate to accelerate the American economy, leading to easy credit which, in turn, had led to the real estate bubble, since the low interest rate on bank deposits and government bonds had made investors look for alternative investment opportunities. Two or three years after the interest rates had been raised in 2005, the real estate sector collapsed, including the subprime market (mortgages given to people who could not pay them off), leading, in turn, to the crisis of 2008 (Morgan 2009).

It lasted for several years. Multi-national companies overcame it more quickly because they could divert their financial activities to less-affected regions (Divoka et al. 2013). While the Fed had not been exclusively responsible for the failure that led to the crisis, its mistakes tipped the scales by not preventing it, as stated by the *Financial Crisis Inquiry Report* (*The Financial Crisis Inquiry Report* 2001 xxiii).

There had been no warning nor assessment about the approaching crisis. The Fed reports, called the Beige Book, of both February and July 2008, had referred to a decline in economic activity and in real estate, but they had not mentioned any sign of a possible crisis. The economic forum that had met in Davos, in January 2008, did not discuss financial stability (Na 2008).

There had been many signs indicating a financial crisis was on the horizon, but the decision makers in the United States and the heads of global finance had ignored them. Principal responsibility for preventing such a surprise belongs to the Fed, whose role has been to preserve financial stability in the United States and macroeconomic stability, by regulating the interest rates and their influence on expenditures, manufacturing, employment, and inflation (Bernanke 2012). For years, the Fed had ignored its historical duty of preventing banks from dealing in speculative credit (Rotemberg 2014). According to Bernanke (Bernanke 2013), for financial stability, the Fed had had to ensure growth and low interest and prevent crises (Bernanke 2013, 3). In retrospect, he talked about the importance of regulation and sufficient liquidity for the financial system (Bernanke 2012; 2013, 3). Bernanke, an expert in the study of the Great Depression, had said that the Fed also should have learned the lessons of the Great Depression, when investors had bought stocks on margin which they could not cover. Then it would have noticed the signs indicating that it had needed to operate quickly, in order to stabilize the financial and macroeconomic system and to ensure a flow of money for financial liquidity for financial institutions (Bernanke 2013, 74). The Fed had been slow to respond. Bernanke had not accepted the assessment that monetary dominance and low interest were the main causes of the real estate bubble, an issue that economists are still debating. The Fed had failed to play its role, according to Nuriel and Roubini, who were among the few who had warned of the crisis, saying that the Fed had done almost nothing to stop the wave of speculations (Roubini and Nuriel 2011).

Before the great crisis of 2008, there had been several smaller ones in the United States. One was the dot.com bubble of 2000 and, before that, the collapse, in 1998, of a hedge fund management company called Long-Term Capital Management, better known as LTCM. The American economy had overcome both crises, thanks to correct policy judgment calls made by Fed Chairman Greenspan. His economic positions had been accepted, without question, by the administration, the economic-financial system, and an enormous majority of economic experts.

Starting in 2003, not only banks but financial companies had marketed stocks that were difficult to understand, and they created temporary credit lines for millions of customers, until prosperity turned into the real estate bubble. Greenspan had objected to the implementation of regulatory measures and had not rushed to act against the rise in real estate prices. According to common wisdom, real estate prices would continue to rise, the market was always right, and the correct thing to do would be to not interfere, or to interfere as little as possible. The refusal to recognize the danger of the situation had been so strong that, in 2007, Bernanke had said that it was reasonable to assume that the influence of the subprime problems on the American economy, in the broader sense, and on the financial markets, would be halted. He had been aware of the problem and had monitored it, but he had not thought that the situation was dangerous and had been surprised by the collapse (Crutsinger 2014). In May 2008, after the collapse of the investment bank, Bear Sterns, Secretary of the Treasury Paulson said he expected an improvement in the economic situation and that the real estate market would recover and motivate the financial markets (Roubini and Miehm 2011, 19). He had been optimistic and had not identified the real situation. According to Greenspan, only five or six people had correctly identified the situation (Fox 2014).

Between 2006 and 2008, five large investment banks had had problems; a few months later, Lehman Brothers collapsed and, after that, Merrill Lynch ran out of money and was bought by the Bank of America. In the spring of 2008, Goldman Sachs and Morgan Stanley acceded to the demands of the Fed and became ordinary banks, thus escaping bankruptcy through a government bailout, like other financial institutions. In December 2007, the Fed began lending the banks money, as did the banks in Europe and the Bank of England, and the general feeling was that the situation had been stabilized. It quickly became obvious that this was not the case. About one thousand banks failed, including large financial institutions, mainly in the United States, and most of them in the first two years of the crisis. The financial collapse had cost the American government about $29 trillion, far more than what had been estimated. Globally, a total of thirty-four banks around the world failed, most of them outside the United States (Jenkins 2013).

THE FINANCIAL CRISIS INQUIRY COMMISSION (FCIC)

The United States had appointed two commissions to investigate the crisis: the FCIC, chaired by Phil Angelides, which issued its conclusions in January 2011 (*Financial Crisis Inquiry Report* 2011), and a bipartisan Senate committee headed by Senators Carl Levin (D-Mich) and Tom Coburn (R-Okla) (the Levin-Coburn Committee), which published its report in April 2011 (United States Senate Investigations Subcommittee Wall Street and the Financial Crisis: Anatomy of a Financial Collapse 2011). Both commissions, acting independently, had reached similar conclusions about the causes of the crisis and had noted the faulty functioning of government and Congressional bodies. Both reports stated that there had been no lack of information about the increase in subprime mortgages and other financial apparatus, which had issued "toxic" loans that could not be redeemed.

Very few observers had noted that the crisis had reflected a genuine danger to America's economy (Stockman 2013). Bernanke, speaking in 2013, admitted that the Fed's actions, before the crisis, had been divided, that the Fed had not been methodical in monitoring the financial system, and that it had not collected information which could have been analyzed. Apparently, even before 2008, the risky procedures of the banks had been known, but they had been ignored.

In 2009, Professor David Biem was invited to audit the Federal Bank, in New York, to determine why it had not predicted the crisis that would end up affecting the large New York banks. According to his reports, which were classified at the time and published later, in 2013, the Fed in New York had known about the dangers facing the investment banks but had done nothing because it had not wanted to confront them (Nicolaci Da Costa 2014). Both the FCIC and the Levin-Coburn commissions noted that, while the crisis had been preceded by a long process of signals of a rising threat to America's financial stability, nothing had been done to stop it (Walton 2012; Rose and Spiegel 2010).

A financial crisis is not generally considered an intelligence failure by intelligence scholars, with the exception of Shulsky and Schmitt (Shulsky and Schmitt, 2002). Others (Courtney et al. 2009; Medina and Fisher 2009; Walton, 2012) had noted that applying intelligence disciplines could have helped prevent the financial crisis of 2008 or could have identified it earlier, but still they had not defined the crisis as an intelligence failure. The criticism that had been issued by the commissions concerned the failure of the assessors to predict the threat, but not the failure to identify the assessed intelligence target—that is, the various organizations, which had included financial institutions, customers, and economic developments, which is characteristic of diffused surprises caused by steps taken by numerous organizations, make it hard to receive an alert in time.

THE MAIN EXPLANATION FOR THE INTELLIGENCE FAILURE—A DIFFUSED SURPRISE

Thc financial crisis of 2008 principally had bccn an intclligcncc failurc of the Fed, which had not predicted nor warned of the threat approaching the financial system. The conception (I prefer to use the term "conception," since it encompasses a wider view taken from national security and intelligence thinking) prevalent at the Fed was "Too big to fail"; that is, the financial institutions in the United States had been so big and strong that they could not be significantly damaged. If there were to be financial problems, they would be minor, under control, and resolved in a short period of time, as they had been, in the past. If a crisis were to occur, it would involve one bank, or a few banks, and the administration would not hesitate to step in and rescue them.

My main explanation of the crisis had been that the agencies that were supposed to sense a threat on the banking system had failed: they had not assessed the threat and therefore had not halted the dangerous practices of the financial institutions, nor had they warned the decision makers. Despite the early warnings, among them from Willian White, the chief economist of the Swiss Bank of International Settlements (BIS), that a crisis was on the horizon, the business system had failed to create an intelligence model that would have led to the entire financial system's having made preparations.

The crisis had been a diffused surprise for the Fed and the American and global financial systems. Since diffused surprise means having to recognize diffused, broad, gradual developments, it is difficult to identify. It grows from within a large, public organization or from within many organizations; it is not directed by a familiar or an unidentified organization; it develops spontaneously; and generally, there is no past precedent. Those responsible for identifying the dangers to the system find it hard to construct a cumulative, integrative picture of the threat and therefore are in error and do not issue a warning.

Before the crisis, Greenspan had been convinced that the financial products, in use at the time, had contributed to the stability of the American economy (Greenspan 2005). The Fed's oversight of the financial institutions had been limited because of the gradual deregulation that had occurred, after 1999, with Greenspan's support and that of the secretary of the Treasury, Robert Rubin (Taylor 1995). In the Fed's assessment, the competition between the financial institutions and the internal oversight of the directors and bodies for handling risks would prevent dangerous measures. The Fed's main difficulty had been in assessing the cumulative effect of the threat, as each financial institution had operated independently, within its own sphere and had not coordinated with the others, in order to maximize its profits. This had made it possible for the danger to mount, since many of the financial institutions had taken great risks.

Rubin, Greenspan, and Charles Prince, the former CEO of Citigroup, testified before the Senate subcommittee that the crisis had been extraordinary because it had no precedent and therefore could not have been predicted. The decision makers, the regulators, and the financial institutions themselves knew what had been happening but had not understood the seriousness of the situation. According to Senator Levin, the crisis had not been a natural phenomenon: it had been man-made, and a future occurrence could only be prevented if the rules were changed (Levin-Coburn Committee 2011, 9). Other causes of the crisis had been the policy failure of the ongoing limitation of the regulatory oversight, changes in the global economy, and the conduct of the decision makers, the banks, and investment houses, caused by corporate greed (Chossudovsky et al. 2010). The boards of directors had failed to assess the threats and the institutions had been unprepared to deal with them (Montgomery, Moore, and Urbany 2005). The role of intelligence, in this case, of the Fed, would have been to examine what had been occurring in the markets and what the competition had been doing, which would have made it easier to assess threats. That had been done by Morgan Chase, which had used advanced prediction tools (Siegel and Davenport 2013) and was thus prepared for the crisis.

DEVELOPMENTS IN FINANCE AND ECONOMY IN THE UNITED STATES AT THE END OF THE 1990S

In 1998, the American LTCM, the largest hedge fund in the world, collapsed. Because of its size, there had been concern that it might start a domino effect. The Fed, in New York State, had convinced a group of investors to buy control of the fund, and thus LTCM continued its operations. The Fed had lowered the interest rate twice in 1998, once in September and once in October, and the markets had rebounded. Greenspan, by lowering the rate twice, had successfully rescued the financial system (Greenspan 2009). At the end of the 1990s, there had been a stock market bubble, and in 2000–2002, after 9/11 and the dot.com crisis, the market had fallen by 40% and it looked as though the United States was headed for a recession (Krugman 2009;158-160). However, Greenspan aggressively cut the interest rate, and in a relatively short time, the economy had recovered and then the real estate bubble began to develop (Herring and Wachter 2002). That meant a sharp, rapid rise in real estate prices: the value of the properties had reached levels disproportionate with the levels of income and other economic market indicators.

THE DEVELOPMENT OF THE REAL ESTATE BUBBLE AND THE INFORMATION ON THE FINANCIAL SYSTEM

Since the Great Depression, it has always been assumed, in the United States, that real estate is an investment with a good return, an opinion reinforced by the media (Wiltz 2005). However, in reality, its yield is less than an investment in the stock market (Shiller 2005; Eaves 2007). According to the U.S. Census Bureau, the number of homeowners had risen by 64.2%, between 1994 and 2004. People had bought houses, assuming that they could sell them for a profit, which would have enabled them to cover their mortgages (Knox 2006). The improvement in the economy, at the turn of the millennium, had been considered a success for Greenspan (Greenspan 2009, 200-201). However, the 9/11 attack had had an immediate and negative effect on the economy, with the result that the Fed lowered the interest rate and undertook a monetary policy that had contributed to the recovery of the economy, through increased consumption and a decrease in unemployment. Greenspan decreased the interest rate until, in 2004, it was only 1% (Greenspan 2009, 481-482).

At the same time, there had been an acceleration in the securitization of mortgages—mortgages were pooled and parts were sold to investors, who bought them with loans that they had received. When the real estate bubble began, securitization had been limited to prime mortgages; that is, money had been lent to people who could pay a substantial amount initially and whose income was sufficient to cover the mortgage payments. The number of borrowers who could not cover their monthly payments had been relatively low, and the risk to purchasers of bonds from mortgage collectors and to financial institutions also had been relatively low. The level of risk changed when securitization began for subprime mortgages, including Collateralized Debt Obligation (CDO), Credit Default Swaps (CDS), and Mortgage Backed Security (MBS), which are types of bonds similar to the bonds that periodically pay interest, but lose their value if the borrower cannot afford the payments.

By the early 2000s, there had been economists, including people like Paul Krugman, Nouriel Roubini and Kenneth Rogoff, who had warned of the developing real estate bubble and that, when it would burst, it would strongly endanger the economy. Their assessments had been unacceptable to many people, including Greenspan and Bernanke, who had claimed that their criticism was unfounded. Economists and financial experts generally had been in accord with Greenspan and of the opinion that the new financial products were not only not dangerous but would contribute to economic growth.

According to the study of Colander et al. (2009), economists had been unaware of the development of a crisis and its consequences, and had not ascribed enough importance to the chances that a financial crisis would occur. They had focused on examining models and had ignored many developments that had been easy to see. Scholars talk about the systematic failure of the economics profession, which had failed to assess the possibility of a significant crisis. In addition, scholars say that no early indicators had been developed to detect changes in the financial markets—changes indicating a worsening of the situation and necessitating that an alert be given to the decision makers. They claim that many economists had not known how to integrate into their models and assessments the significance of the decline in the level of regulation and the influence of the risks that the financial institutions had taken on themselves (Colander et al. 2009, 14).

The decision makers had suffered from the same blindness. In 2008, *The Economist* had noted the great risk to the financial system in the United States and had shown that, in 2000, the profits of the financial institutions had soared, compared with other economic bodies in the United States. It had warned that the situation could not continue over time. At the same time, Greenspan had said that it was improbable that a decline would begin in home prices to significantly damage the financial system. He said there could be a little "froth" in housing prices in certain areas, but not in the national real estate bubble.

Housing prices had become so high that it had become difficult to purchase a new home. A decline began in housing prices in 2005 and, in 2006 and 2007, prices fell more quickly— during the second quarter of 2007, prices fell by 3% and by the end of the year, by 15%. With falling prices, it had become difficult to sell house, and the number of households which could not meet their mortgage payments rose quickly. People with mortgages and banks began to panic. When many people all over the country could no longer meet their mortgage payments, the large financial institutions suffered great losses. The institutions had been leveraged and did not have enough money.

At the beginning of 2007, there was a rise in the number of people who had held low-rated bonds and could not get their money back. The demand for those bonds had ended, as had the availability of subprime loans. There were no buyers for low-rated bonds, and banks were less willing to give loans because they could not be certain the loans would be repaid. Funding for buying houses had become scarce, and the recession in the housing market worsened markedly. Investors had continued to believe that the bonds they held had value, despite an economy that was getting worse. The drop in housing prices had a direct, negative influence on employment, which began to drop by the end of 2007 (Krugman 2009, 155). Prospects of insolvency grew, following the loss of jobs and unexpected medical bills. It had become clear that lenders and investors who had bought stocks backed by mortgages were beginning to lose enormous sums of money on them, and their value quickly plummeted. However, most of the losses were suffered by homeowners who could not pay their mortgages, and they lost both their homes and the money that they had already repaid on the home loan.

When the real estate bubble began to burst, the Fed and the Bush administration had maintained the assessment that if there were to be a recession in the housing market, it would be short and limited in its influence on the financial system. In July 2007, the White House issued a financial assessment, claiming that the president's policy of encouraging growth had helped guard American resilience and had allowed it to be flexible and dynamic (Krugman 2009, 179). In August 2008, after two government mortgage banks had failed and had been bailed out by the government, Secretary of the Treasury Paulson said he hoped that they were on the way to finding a solution for the housing problems, despite the fact that the two mortgage banks had operated under instructions from the administration ("Meet the Press" 2008). He added that the problems in the housing and mortgage markets had been halted to a great degree (Krugman 2009, 179). Both the Fed and the Treasury had been of the opinion that the financial situation was good and improving, that there was no imminent danger.

In July 2008, Citigroup analysts estimated that the bank would lose $5 trillion of its worth because of assets that could not be recovered. The total balance of the five largest investment banks had stood at only $4 trillion (RepoWatch 2008, 7). The risk to the stability of the banking system had been immense.

When things had begun to be disrupted in the United States, and people couldn't meet their mortgages, investors rushed to get their money out of America, which only worsened the situation. Setser (Setser 2009) had noted that it also had been a problem to manage risks inside the financial institutions, and the Fed's oversight of the activity, when administrative agencies had not believed that the real estate bubble was a threat and did supervise closely the financial system.

In March 2008, Bear Stearns, a relatively small investment house, had had financial difficulties that led to its insolvency, and the Treasury Department had convinced JP Morgan Chase to buy Bear Stearns. This marked the outbreak of the financial crisis, and Lehman Brothers fell on September 15, 2008. Because of Lehman Brothers' size, the Treasury Department had decided to let it go bankrupt. The decision had turned out to be destructive for the trust of investors. The prices of assets had continued to drop. Days later, the administration decided to rescue the insurance giant AIG, the largest insurance company in the world, whose collapse was liable to have an immediate global effect worse than Lehman Brothers. The degree to which the depth of the financial crisis had not been properly assessed can be seen from the cost of bailing out financial institutions in the United States, which initially had been estimated, by the Troubled Assets Relief Program (TARP), to be about $700 billion and turned out finally to be about $29 trillion (Wray 2013). Freezing credit had dealt a heavy blow to international trade, and within a few months, the marine transport market had fallen by 90%.

Thus, there had been many signs of a developing threat, but the government system, especially the Fed, had ignored them and had not correctly assessed the complex situation in which threats were developing from many directions—the banks, the mortgage banks and other financial institutions, households, real estate prices, and investors. The Fed had done almost nothing to stop the collapse. The faith that there could be no collapse was what had led to the mistaken assessment of the economic situation, despite the fact that there had been people, especially academics, who had issued warnings. In 2013, Secretary of the Treasury Paulson admitted that he had been mistaken when, after the fall of Lehman Brothers, he had not foreseen a domino effect (Bloomberg Businessweek 2013).

THE CRISIS DEVELOPS TOWARD A PEAK IN 2008—WARNINGS IGNORED

The 2008 crisis has been considered to have been the worst since the Great Depression (Ozkan and Unsal 2012). Bernanke told the Congressional investigation that, as a student of the Great Depression, he had believed that September and October 2008 had been the worst financial crisis in global history, including the Great Depression (*Financial Crisis Inquiry Report* 2011, 354). Historian Neil Ferguson claimed that the responsibility for the Great Depression and the 2008 financial crisis had rested with the Fed which, in both instances, had implemented an incorrect policy that almost collapsed the banking system (Ferguson 2011, 241). According to the U.S. Government Accountability report, the financial crisis of 2007–2009, like previous financial crises, had not been linked to a sharp drop in the GDP, but also to the worst financial crisis since the Great Depression of the 1930s (U.S. Government Accountability Office 2013).

The decision makers in the administration and Congress had not received warnings of an approaching crisis. In 2013, Secretary of the Treasury Paulson (Bloomberg Businessweek 2013) had said that, three days after the fall of Lehman Brothers and the AIG bailout, it had become clear to him, in a meeting with members of the Congress, during which they authorized $700 billion to rescue the market, that they had not known the American economy had been in the middle of a deep financial crisis (Yoaz 2014).

Between 2003 and 2007, there had been concerns over the real estate bubble, but they had never reached the point of concern over the stability of the financial system. The prevalent assumption had been, according to Mary Shapiro, deputy Security Exchange Commission (SEC) commissioner, that the markets and Wall Street would defend the financial system better than the regulators (Wyatt 2010). The Council of Economic Advisers' report for 2007, presented to Congress in February 2008, did not indicate that a crisis could be expected. The annual Lehman Brothers report for 2007, Form 10-K, showed no signs that the bank was in trouble. In July and August 2008, it already had been known that the bank had been having financial difficulties following the losses in the subprime market (Kulikowski 2007; Ganagher 2008). The SEC and the Fed had known that the Lehman Brothers' situation was dangerous, because it had been seriously leveraged due to the financial market's being backed by mortgages, but neither agency did anything because they had been unprepared for a risk to the bank's stability (Valukas 2010). The Treasury Department decision not to bail out Lehman Brothers had surprised the bank's directors, who had thought that an investment bank, as large as Lehman had been, was too big to fail. Robert Fuld, the bank's CEO, had not read the bank's situation properly, had refused to listen to opinions contradictory to his own, and had been convinced that it would be impossible for such a large bank to collapse (Hertz 2013). He had not believed that the bank's situation had been serious and therefore had not instituted any significant measures. Fuld, who had been willing to take risks (Green 2013), had dug his heels in and had reduced the chances of saving the bank (Stein 2013).

According to the *Financial Crisis Inquiry Report* (2011 xvii-xviii), it had been a systematic failure of Congress, the administration, the SEC, and the Fed. Despite the fact that the crisis had been preceded by a long process with many warning signs of an increasing threat to the financial stability of the United States, no assessment had been made of the significance of the threat and its seriousness, and nothing was done to stop it in time. The commission had determined that regulation, which had been greatly weakened in the years before the crisis, had capitulated to political pressures to enable financial institutions to expand their activities. Greenspan had admitted, in retrospect, that there had been many indications in the Fed that had never turned into an alert (Fox 2014). The economists who had dealt with the issue and even had warned of the danger, like Krugman, Steiglitz, Roubini, Rogoff, and others, agreed that the failing actions of the Fed and the entire administration had brought about the financial crisis in the United States.

The Levin-Coburn Committee reported that there had been warnings from employees of financial institutions, credit rating companies and senior economists, such as Krugman (Krugman 2009), Ferguson (Ferguson 2008), and Roubini (Roubini 2006), but they had been in the minority and their opinions had not been taken into account. Both the Fed and the administration had been of the opinion that the Great Depression had been a unique phenomenon and would not be repeated. The various inquiry committees had noted that the crisis had been a complete surprise for the regulation, the government agencies and the influencing institutions. Before the crisis, various agencies and people who had held political and financial office, had minimized the significance of the threat. According to Eckstein and others (Eckstein, Fisher, and Flug 2011), the credit rating companies had failed because of conflicts of interest and because the incentives for high credit had been flawed. The new financial apparatus was complex and had incorrectly assessed the ability to pay off loans.

Senior economists like Krugman, Ferguson, and Roubini (Roubini 2006; Roubini and Miehm 2011), Robert Shiller (Shiller 2005), Kenneth Rogoff (with Carman Reinhart), Dean Baker, and William White had personally warned Greenspan (Blinder 2013). Rogoff and Reinhart had asked themselves if the subprime crisis and the financial crisis, whose inception could already be seen during the middle of 2000, were different from the eighteen previous financial crises from which the country had recovered (Reinhart and Rogoff 2008). They had indicated that the situation in the United States was dangerous and could develop into the first great financial crisis of the twenty-first century. Based on the cases that they had analyzed, a drastic fall in real estate prices was an indicator leading to a financial crisis. Michael Lewis said that there had been many financiers on Wall Street, including himself, who had not accepted the opinion that the market would right itself, and that they had tried to warn the large investment banks but had been rejected (Lewis 2010).

At the end of 2005, a festive retirement ceremony was held for Greenspan. Raghuram Rajan, an award-winning professor of economics from University of Chicago, gave a speech warning of a threat of an approaching financial crisis caused by the financial sector's risks (Rajan 2005). He said that he had wondered if the banks could meet the demands for liquidity, as others also had wondered (Krugman 2009; Lahart 2009). Former Harvard President Summers had said that Rajan's analysis was misleading, calling Rajan a Luddite (one who opposed changes and progress). In 2008, Rajan had proposed limiting the activities of stock traders, but his proposition was rejected (Rajan 2008). In the summer of 2007, Rajan was quoted by two heads of the Fed, Janet Yellen and Gary Stern, when they criticized the disregard of warnings and measures that had led to the crisis. The Fed and the Treasury Department had been more worried about the liquidity of the banking system and the navigation of the control of inflation, to keep it low (Morgenson and Rosner 2011; Zandi 2009), but what should have worried them was the solvency of the financial institutions.

In 1999, Greenspan had said that the most important act of the past decade had been the exceptional development of financial derivatives (Financial Crisis Inquiry Commission 2011, 48). It had been an expression of satisfaction on the one hand, and of not having correctly assessed the danger in the measures employed, on the other. In the five following years, the housing market in the United States had grown by 5% a year, which had never been seen in the past. In 2007, most of the mortgages had been backed by derivatives and bonds with a value of $13 trillion, and the parameters had indicated that the economic situation was excellent (Tett 2009; Morgenson and Rosner 2011). In the 1980s, economist Hyman Minsky had described the theoretical foundation by saying that the financial institutions were fulfilling a growing role in modern economy, but that he was concerned by speculative lending; he said that a speculative explosion could occur, especially in the real estate market (Minsky 1986). According to Minsky, when a collapse has begun after a bust that has been difficult to define, financial institutions face a lack of cash and cannot pay their departments, which leads to insolvency and bankruptcy. According to Minsky, the Fed has to intervene to prevent such a situation.

THE WARNINGS ISSUED BY WILLIAM WHITE

One of the most prominent economists who had issued a warning was William White, head economist for the Swiss BIS. At the beginning of the 2000s, he had warned of a great approaching financial crisis (Balzi and Schiessl 2009). The heads of the central banks in the United States and the rest of the world had preferred to agree with Greenspan and to ignore White. According to White, the financial crisis had surprised the decision makers, and for a long time they had denied the information in their possession (White 2012). The case of William White, which is almost unknown, is characteristic of what had happened in the financial world. The governors of the central banks around the world had aligned themselves with Greenspan and had ignored anyone who had said that the subprime problem would lead to the collapse of the financial markets.

When the OECD met in France, in October 2012, White raised certain issues regarding the ability to evaluate threats and to make preparations for them (White 2012). He had said that Daniel Kahneman was of the same opinion, that the reason for the misleading evaluation had been the false beliefs of the investigators and their belief that financial crisis would not occur. Kahneman had noted that the false beliefs were so strong that, even after the financial crisis broke out, responses had minimized its importance. For example, the head of the Fed had said that only $50 billion had been lost and it would focus, therefore, exclusively on the subprime mortgage market.

CRITICISM VOICED BY ROBERT SHILLER

In 2005, Robert Shiller, Sterling Professor of Economics at Yale University, had published the second edition of his book *Irrational Exuberance*. It dealt with the possible consequences of the real estate bubble. Shiller and Karl

Case had developed the Shiller-Case Home Price Index, which had indicated that the risks of the approaching collapse of the real estate bubble could lead to a deep recession and the bankruptcy of individuals and financial institutions, and possibly even a global recession. In 2005, a year before the prices of homes in the United States had begun to drop, Shiller said that the American housing market had developed a destructive bubble which would end in disaster. Thus, Shiller had reinforced White's assessment (Ibid: 233).

THE FAILURE DUE TO THE LACK OF REGULATION

Laws protecting investors and the regulation of the money market in the United States had failed after years of weak regulation of financial institutions, mainly after the Glass-Steagall Act had been revoked in 1999 (Gorton 2012). Greenspan, who had supported deregulation, said that the markets had become large, unwieldy, and had been changing so fast that it was impossible to oversee or regulate them (Greenspan 2009, 6). The *Financial Crisis Inquiry Report* emphasized the contribution of deregulation to the crisis. It claimed that for more than thirty years, there had been a combination of lack of oversight and trust in the self-regulation of the financial institutions. More recently, this had been led by the former chairman of the Fed, Greenspan and others, but had been supported by consecutive administrations and Congress, and also had been actively pushed by the strong financial industry; as a result, the regulation government had been stripped of any means of defense that could have helped prevent a catastrophe.

According to various economists, including Stiglitz and Krugman, who had won Nobel Prizes in economics, the lack of regulation had been the beginning of the development of the real estate bubble (Krugman 2008; Baram 2008). According to others, the removal of regulation had enabled the banks to compete better and to improve conditions for their clients (Fried 2012). The regulators had not overseen the investment banks the way that they had overseen regular banks; even with regular banks, the regulators had not been strict and had not realized the great danger. The system actually had been working under the radar (Gorton 2009, 42). According to Gorton and Roubini, the investment banks had catalyzed the development of the crisis (Roubini and Miehm 2011, 61).

Greenspan had opposed oversight of the Fed's financial measures for financial institutions that had not been banks that had been dealing extensively with subprime mortgages; he had thought that it would have been sufficient to have had the institutions regulate themselves. He had said that it was fortunate that he had never lost sight of the fact that governmental regulation could undermine the effectiveness of self-regulation in the private market, and by itself government regulation could not effectively protect public interests (Greenspan 1997). According to the *Financial Crisis Inquiry Report* (*Financial Crisis Inquiry Report* 107), it had not accepted Greenspan's testimony that there had been resources for it (Ibid: 18), saying that they had not accepted the opinion that the regulators had lacked the ability to protect the financial system. The report went on to say that the regulators had had a great deal of power but had chosen not to use it.

Economist Joseph Stiglitz (Stiglitz 2010) had noted the blindness of the banks and investment banks, to the point where leverage had been at a 1:40 ratio, in addition to the risky products on the backs of the mortgages that they had given. Unlike Greenspan, Stiglitz had argued that much more could have been done to prevent the crisis. He said that the Fed had not used its authority. In 2012, Bernanke said that the subprime mortgage market and the housing bubble were the match that had lit the crisis, although a high level of leverage, unstable financing and an absence of risk management and oversight had been the Achilles heel (Bernanke 2012). Greenspan only recently admitted that he had been mistaken in his assessment of the danger of the real estate bubble (Fox 2014). About a year before the crisis, on October 17, 2007, *The Economist* had issued an article marking the twentieth anniversary of Black Monday, the day the market had dropped by 23%, saying that it had expected a similar situation, in the near future, because of the great exposure of the banking system to dangers. According to the article, nothing was being done by the regulatory system, especially the Fed, to address the danger (*The Economist* 2007). The article ended by saying that "One day, investors will realize central bankers are not magicians. That might be another Black Monday." Blanchard and others had said that the reason behind the collapse of the financial system had been the absence of willingness to act in time, especially when it had come to a familiar threat to the system (Blanchard et al 2012). They had noted that the solution was the implementation of more effective oversight tools and increasing the power of the regulation in states and the global financial system. In 2013, Bernanke (Bernanke 2013) gave a speech in which he discussed the lessons learned from the 2008 crisis, in the area of oversight of financial institutions. He had called what was currently being done "increased oversight and more intensive oversight," as lessons learned from the past.

According to Bernanke, the body responsible for the lack of regulation in the Fed had been the Office of Financial Stability Policy and Research, which had continually updated the Fed and Federal Open Market Committee (FOMC) and other government agencies. The unit had been established in November 2010 (Lehnert 2013).

In addition to the Fed, the *Financial Crisis Inquiry Report* accused the Treasury Department's Office of the Comptroller of the Currency (OCC) of part of the systematic blindness of regulation in the United States. Employees of the authority admitted to the Commission that they had noticed that in a significant percentage of the mortgages, the risk taken by the bank had been too high, but they had not issued a warning (*Financial Crisis Inquiry Report* 2011, 21, 162).

Among those who had opposed reducing regulation in the 1990s had been economists like Krugman, Stiglitz, Rajan, Eichengreen, Roubini and Simon Jenson from Britain, but most of them, among them people from the Fed, had worked to reduce regulations, having faith in the free market (Greenspan 2009, 335-339). In April 2012, at a conference in Atlanta, Bernanke said (Bernanke 2012) that one of the lessons that had been learned from the crisis of 2008 was that the Fed now placed strict supervision over the banking institutions and non-banking financial institutions, to ensure stability in the banking system.

As an expression of the Fed's faulty oversight Greenspan said that such an event was a flood that happened once in a hundred years (Greenspan 2010). The *Financial Crisis Inquiry Report* noted (*Financial Crisis Inquiry Report* 21) that even after the collapse of Bear Stearns, the Fed had regarded it as "relatively unique."

The two reports of the FCIC had indicated that the regulatory authorities had been aware of the risk but had decided not to change their policies, after an incorrect assessment had been made that the financial system was not at risk.

The Senate Banking, Housing and Urban Affairs Committee, headed by Senator Tim Johnson (D-SD), had dealt with the housing issue. The list of topics for discussion in 2006 shows that of the fifty-five meetings held by the committee that year, only a few had been devoted to the risks of the housing market (US Senate Banking, Housing and Urban Affairs Committee 2006), which indicates a low level of awareness among those who were supposed to have overseen risks and to have issued alerts. Only in March 2007 did committee Chairman Senator Chris Dodd (D-Conn), hold a meeting devoted to dangerous loans, saying after the meeting that the policy had endangered the stability of the homes of millions of Americans, but that he had not related this danger to the nation's overall financial stability (Pointer 2007). At the beginning of 2008, senators such as Charles Schumer (D-NY), had said that the federal administration would have to intervene and help home owners who could not pay their mortgages; however, their opinion had been that the danger was to home owners and not to the financial system (Schumer 2007).

OVERSIGHT OF FINANCIAL STABILITY INSIDE THE FED

Dr. Akiva Offenbacher (Interview by author. Tel Aviv, January and February 2012), who is currently the director of Monetary/Finance Division of the

Research Department at the Bank of Israel, and who had worked at the Fed in the 1980s, recalled that on a visit to the Fed, in 2008, he had been told that, before the financial crisis, a department for monitoring financial security had been working, secretly. He said that the department had been established in 2003, after the financial crisis in the markets in Asia at the end of the 1990s, and that it had belonged to the Division of Research and Statistics. Its job had been to monitor the financial situation of large financial institutions in the United States. Its operations had been in addition to those for the department for monetary financial stability, whose mandate had been to oversee financial transactions. Nothing about the activities of the department to monitor financial stability had been published. It had been compartmentalized within the Fed, since its acts might have been interpreted as an expression of concern about the financial stability of the banking system. According to Offenbacher, a similar unit, called the Financial Oversight Authority, had operated in Britain's Central Bank. Offenbacher claimed that the Fed department of financial stability had continually monitored about fifty of the largest financial institutions in the United States, including the investment banks, and the relevant information had been right in front of its employees. He went on to say that the Fed had held daily briefings, and in his opinion the information had been transmitted to the heads of the Fed. The information had been located on an internal Fed website, which had been accessible to only a few. In Offenbacher's opinion, the unit had had very little influence.

Offenbacher's statements contradicted Bernanke, who had said that the department only had been established in November 2010 (Bernanke 2013). I personally had discussed the issue by phone in 2013 with the Fed's deputy chairman, Kohn, and with Andres Lehnert, from the Fed's Stability department; both, like Bernanke, had said that the unit had been established in 2010.

Lehnert, deputy director of the Fed's Office of Financial Stability and Research, which had been established in 2010, said that the department had operated in cooperation with the unit for bank oversight, and had dealt with worst-case scenarios. Lehnert also said that after 2008, the department had received new tools, including the Marginal Expected Shortfall model, which had been developed by Noble Prize winner Robert Engle, and had been routinely used by them (Greely 2012).

According to Lehnert, the great change in oversight that had come about, after the crisis, was in focusing on what he called "macro-financial oversight." Following the banking reform law, two units were established in the Treasury Department, one in the Office of Financial Research (OFR) and another in the Financial Stability Oversight Council (FSOC), to improve the quality of the financial information received by the decision makers.

Contrary to what Offenbacher had told me, I found no information indicating the existence of the department at the time of the financial crisis or before. In both reports that were issued by the inquiry committees regarding the crisis, there was no mention of a department for financial oversight that had operated in the Fed before the crisis. Whether such a unit had operated before the crisis or not, it does not change the assessment that there had been no lack of information. The Fed's failure had been not only in its evaluations but also in its assessed key intelligence target which, to a great extent, had dealt with economic growth data and less with monitoring financial stability.

THE FAILURE OF THE CREDIT RATING AGENCIES

International credit rating agencies, whose role has been to estimate the danger of various stocks, had failed in assessing the dangers inherent in bonds backed by subprime mortgages and had given most of the agencies inflated credit ratings. The reasons were that they had had no accumulated picture of the large number of people who had taken out risky mortgages, and the products had been very complex, making it difficult to assess the degree of their risk (Keidar-Levi 2013, 112-122).

The rating agencies had operated in areas of conflicting interests when they had received payment for rating the financial institutions. Internal documents of employees of Moody's and of Standard and Poor's were revealed to show that the agencies had been rewarded by the financial institutions, in return for high ratings, and that there had been no genuine assessment of the value of the bonds and of their inherent danger (Taibbi 2013). Yahoo Finance called the revelation, "The last mystery of the financial crisis" (*Financial Crisis Inquiry Report* 2011, 118-121). The Reddit.com Internet site posted correspondence that had been conducted in the years before the crisis, in which Standard and Poor's had written that they had met with the investment banks to coordinate the ratings of the bond, otherwise, there was a risk we would lose the deal" (Chan 2010).

Michel Madelian, Moody's president, had ignored the significant influence of the unrealistic ratings on the outbreak of the crisis. He later wrote that the rating agencies had not predicted the force nor the speed with which the mortgage market would deteriorate (Bergman 2013).

STRUCTURAL FAILURES

According to Donald Kohn, who had been deputy head of the Fed between 2006 and 2010, a dynamic had been created in which the Fed's assessments were reinforced by regional offices; this, then, strengthened Kohn's opinion that they had been going in the right direction (Kohn 2013). He argued that, later on, there had been no constructive differences of opinion within the Fed that could have raised the level of economic deliberations, even with other bureaus within the administration. Agreement among so many bureaus had strengthened the opinion that their path was correct and without danger.

Another structural aspect to the inaccurate assessments was the fact that several government bureaus had been responsible for overseeing financial institutions; it seems that the problem had not been only within the Fed. There had been no wide range of opinions: everyone had been working to decrease regulation. The prevalent opinion had been that the situation was under control, which reinforced the opinion that no change should be expected.

After the crisis, in 2010, regulation was designed in a way that increased the oversight of financial institutions. Various government oversight bodies were established by the Dodd-Frank Wall Street Reform, the Consumer Protection Act, and the establishment of an FDIC unit to oversee financial institutions.

THE CONCEPTION THAT CAUSED THE BLINDNESS

The characteristics of the conception that are presented, below, have never before been described as such. It is my assessment, based on an analysis of information in the context of the financial crisis before and after it had occurred. The conception was strong and had been supported by Fed heads Greenspan and Bernanke and many others. Those who had seen things in a different light had not succeeded in influencing the decision makers. The conception had been based on a low-key concern that a concentrated surprise (but not a diffused surprise) could occur in a specific financial institution, but that the Fed would know how to deal with such an event quickly and successfully, as it had in the past.

The characteristics of the conception are the following:

1. Faith in the strength of a free market: Beginning in 2002, Greenspan had claimed that the financial system was sufficiently strong to face difficulties in complex financial products, as it had shown that it had been able to, in the past. He had added that the central bank, with its unlimited power, could halt dangers before they would become destructive; he said that he had faith that the financial system would not allow such conditions to occur (Greenspan 2002). He and Bernanke had believed that deregulation had been a positive measure by providing an "invisible hand" to operate. When he had spoken about economic flexibility, in 2005, he had said that the economy would grow if the government would not interfere, if it would stand aside and let the markets operate (Greenspan 2005), and he had repeated the statement in

2007 (Allen 2013 130-131). Mary Shapiro, former chairperson of the SEC, had said the same thing, that the markets and Wall Street would protect the financial system better than regulation (Wyatt 2010). The report that was issued by the Council of Economic Advisers for 2007, which had been presented to Congress in 2008, had estimated that the American economy would continue to grow, saying that the chances for continued growth in the coming years looked good. "Subprime," which had been identified with the main causes of the deep financial crisis that had begun about half a year after the report had been presented, was mentioned forty-nine times in connection with developments in the housing market, but not in connection with the risk to the stability of the American economy.

Public statements that had been made by Fed Commissioner Bernanke and others in the administration, among them Secretary of the Treasury Paulson, had given the impression that the situation was under control, that the American economy was growing and in good condition (Paulson 2011). In October 2008, Greenspan told the Congressional Inquiry Commission that for 40 years, deregulation had worked well, and that he had never imagined that the banks would dare to harm the interests of their stockholders (Clark and Treanor 2008). Faith in the free market and the dismissal of the possibility of a financial crisis had been reinforced by indicators showing that the economy in the United States was growing.

2. Faith that housing prices would continue to rise: The second element of the conception was that housing prices would continue to rise and, as long as that was the situation, the economy would continue to grow because the housing market had created a great many jobs, and financial renewal had created large incomes. According to Roubini, in 2005 alone, the bonuses that had been distributed by the five large investment banks had totaled $25 billion; they had totaled $36 billion in 2006, and $37 billion in 2007 (Roubini and Miehm 2011, 68). Apparently, the rise in housing prices had not threatened the banking system; the rating agencies had given very high ratings to stocks of the mortgage payment collectors, which showed how low their risk was. Housing prices had risen more quickly than salaries, according to the FDIC, and had reached 7% per annum, for reasons such as the high demand that had been caused by easy mortgage money, including subprime mortgages. When real estate prices began to decline—a process that had begun to speed up, in 2006—there had still been the belief that the situation was under control. The significance of the change in the trend had been minimized.

3. Belief that the economic influence of the real estate market had been limited: The third element of the conception was that in the event that there would be problems in the mortgage market, the problem would be limited and would be regulated by the free market. The real estate market had comprised only a small part of banking activity and therefore the possible damage would

be limited and under control. The subprime market would not become a problem that would cause serious economic damage. The conclusion had been that the free market would regulate problems if they should arise, and there had been no need for oversight of the financial institutions. Financial problems would be stopped by the real estate market. In the 1990s, Greenspan had already been urged to oversee subprime loans, but he had refused (Roubini and Miehm 2011, 72). One of the most important banking regulation laws had been the Glass-Steagall Act; its revocation indicated the belief that the free market would regulate itself. It had been revoked with support from Greenspan and Rubin and opposition from Paul Walker, the previous head of the Fed. The Gramm-Leach-Bliley Act of 2000 also deregulated mortgage-based bonds, with the result that securitization had developed rapidly, reaching about $50 trillion in 2008 (Rubini and Miehm 2001, 73).

Until 2008, the regulators, mainly the Fed, had not correctly understood the threat. The Fed's deliberations of 2006 and 2007, in the FOMC meeting, had shown that the heads of the Fed had not related to the possibility that difficulties in real estate, which had been known, would have a significant influence on the American economy (Damon 2013). When, in February 2007, it had become clear that Freddie Mac, one of the two federal government mortgage companies, was having financial stability problems, Bernanke told the FOMC that Freddie Mac's wider influence on the economy and financial markets and on the problems in the subprime market were under control. In August 2007, the American Home Mortgage Investment Corporation declared bankruptcy, and the matter was discussed at a FOMC meeting; Bernanke's suggestion, to do nothing, was accepted, and no discussion was held about the significance of the event (Damon 2013).

4. Belief that the crisis in the United States was isolated from the rest of the world: When there had been concern regarding the influence of the subprime market and the bonds had endangered the financial system in 2006 and 2007, a conception had been developed, according to which, even if a financial crisis would occur in the United States, its influence would be limited to the United States alone and would not reach the rest of the world. That idea was first raised by the economists of the investment bank, Goldman Sachs, and became the consensus (Roubini and Miehm 2011, 109). According to this conception, successful economies, such as those of Brazil, Russia, India and China had recovered from crises because they had been based on local demand, and therefore if the subprime loans collapsed, such countries would be affected less, if at all. Even in Europe, it had been the prevailing conception, and after the collapse of Lehman Brothers, the German Treasury minister, Steinbruck, had said that the financial crisis was first and foremost an American crisis (DW Staff 2008). He added that the other G-7 Treasury ministers had agreed with him. Their approach has been hard to understand,

in view of the leverage relations between liquid capital and credit in European banks, which had been dangerous (Barr 2008). A few days later, part of the European banking system collapsed, and Germany had been forced to stream huge amounts of money to rescue the giant Hypo Real Estate Bank. At that point, the German Treasury minister admitted that Germany was looking into the abyss. Other European banks rapidly had to be rescued, among them the Dexia Group, Fortis, and ABN Amro and ING in Holland. The Irish banking system collapsed, and Britain nationalized part of its banking system. The crisis also struck Brazil, Russia, India and China. What had begun as a crisis in one country rapidly turned into a global crisis, because of the interconnections between the American banking system and the financial institutions in the rest of the world.

THE COLLAPSE OF THE CONCEPTION

Greenspan, testifying before the House Oversight Committee on October 24, 2008 (The House Oversight Committee 2011), admitted that he had erred by not halting the deregulation process of the financial system, which had weakened it. He said that the crisis had reached unimaginable proportions, adding that for 40 years, deregulation had worked well and he had not imagined that the banks would dare to harm the interests of their stockholders (Clark and Treanor 2008). After the crisis had begun, he had found a fault in the way the economic system had worked (Fox 2014). Secretary of the Treasury Paulson had said, on the same occasion, that he should have seen the subprime crisis coming much sooner.

The Fed's well-rooted method was called the "mopping up approach," meaning that it was best to wait until a problem popped up and then to either minimize it or remove it (Binder 2008). The approach had worked in the past, during the dot.com crisis of 2001 to 2002, and it had been mistakenly believed that it would work again, before the financial crisis of 2008. That is, the Fed had operated by using what had been the solution for the previous crisis, which now was unsuitable. The Fed had decided not to burst the bubble, because it had not correctly assessed its significance. The Fed had had enough time to raise the low interest rate and thereby attempt to stave off the crisis. It was unclear why the involved parties had not taken careful, preventive measures that could have prevented the crisis (Arieli 2011). The main assumption had been that housing prices would continue to rise, so that investments in real estate would be safe (Posner 2009). Group thinking had been prevalent in the banks, and bankers had not changed their methods and had not wanted to hear bad news, even after it had begun to trickle in (Tett 2009, 137).

Fed documents about the FOMC meetings (FOMC: Transcripts and Other Historical Materials 2006), which had been attended by senior Fed officials and were held every six weeks, indicate that the committee had not related to the difficulties in the real estate market (Appelbaum 2012). The committee generally had agreed that the situation was under control, that the American banking system had been in no danger, and that the American economy certainly had not been in any danger, even though there had been several signs indicating problems in the housing and mortgage market. The FOMC material clearly showed that there had been no lack of information, but the focus largely had been on America's good economic situation and much less on financial threats. For example, in the same year, there had been a significant increase in losses from people who had been unable to meet their mortgage payments (Roubini and Miehm 2011). The problem had been in the lack of understanding of the situation: it was the result of the certainty that the committee members had maintained, because they had been working with familiar economic models that had predicted that no crisis could be expected. There were people in the FOMC who had claimed that the decline of the real estate market would be good for the economy (Appelbaum 2012). Professor Janet Yellen, the president of the Fed in San Francisco, had said, at a meeting held in March 2006, that the problems in housing would not have broad consequences, because the housing market was a small part of the economy and the downturn would right itself. Kevin Warsh, from the Fed, had said, at a meeting in September 2006, that the financial markets were more profitable than they had been in the past (Applebaum 2012). At the beginning of 2006, when Greenspan had retired, the opinion of the committee, as expressed by Geithner and Yellen, was that it was fitting for Greenspan to leave his position at a time when the economy was so good.

Transcripts of FOMC meetings show that the members had been aware that real estate prices had ceased to rise. The Fed had assumed that there was no reason to worry about the situation and the negative influence on the financial sector (Goldfarb 2012). One of the members, Susan Bies, had warned that the housing market could have an influence on the banks, but Bernanke had told her that, at that point, while a recession was evident in the housing market, the situation was far from being a genuine decline (Goldfarb 2012). At an FOMC meeting, in June 2006, the Fed's economist reported that no broad decline had been expected in the quality of mortgage credit (Goldfarb 2012). In August 2006, when the slowdown in the housing market had accelerated, Geithner said that the Fed's most important challenge had to be the threat of inflation (Goldfarb 2012). The meeting at the end of 2006 had been optimistic, and Geithner had said that the economy's weakness had been caused by the decline in construction and did not require a reassessment of the risks (Goldfarb 2012). That is, the measures that had been taken by the Fed were influencing the market in the right direction and the housing market was cooling off. Contradictory assessments had appeared in the BIS report, and it is reasonable to assume that they had been brought to the attention of the heads of the Fed, but no deliberations were held. The committee members and the heads of the Fed had supported Greenspan and Bernanke's assessments.

While the Fed had been holding optimistic meetings, dangerous events were occurring in the financial markets. A large mortgage company, called Merit Financial Services, had collapsed in 2006. By the end of 2006, mortgage brokerage institutions had failed, and at the beginning of 2007, the number of failed non-bank loan companies had reached about 50 (Roubini and Miehm 2001). On April 22, 2007, New Century Financial, which had been the second largest subprime loan company in the United States, failed: in 2007, it had had 7,000 employees, and in 2006, its profits had been $417 billion (Missal 2011). In 2007, Bernanke appeared before Congress and had said that there were problems in the subprime market, but "it was a disease and not the beginning of an epidemic" (Roubini and Miehm 2011, 87). In October 2007, Kevin Warsh, one of the Fed's heads said that the economic indicators had showed that it was possible that the economic situation was stabilizing, and the conditions of the banks were improving, after they had sold a substantial part of their risky stocks. He added that there was a significant decline in people taking out mortgages and fewer new bonds were being issued (Warsh 2007). In the summer of 2007, the CEO of Citibank had talked about the risks of the real estate market, saying that there was no need to worry, because "they would dance as long as the music played, and the music was still playing" (Posner 2009). At the same time, Secretary of the Treasury Paulson had said that the problem of the mortgages seemed to be under control (Financial Crisis Inquiry Commission 2011, 234).

Bernanke also had said that the extension of subprime mortgages apparently had had only marginal significance and that most of the mortgage market had been continuing to behave well. Market forces, he said, had been balancing the situation (Bernanke 2007). He had believed that the markets would correct themselves (Territory 2009, 251). In 2007, when the banks had begun to fail, and there were serious economic problems in the United States, Greenspan had not changed his mind, saying that the collapse had not been caused by blindly relying on an unbridled, unregulated market, but rather by people who, once every ten years, lost their sanity and rationality and were swept away, initially by euphoria and later by depression (Greenspan 2009, 461-483). He had said that every so often, there was a surprising discontinuity, whose roots were psychological, because a phenomenon that had occurred inside people's minds could not be cured by government intervention, oversight, or regulation. In 2007, Greenspan had written that he was becoming more convinced that governments and central banks could not substantially change the course of the inflation bubble (Greenspan 2009, 461-483). He claimed that various bubbles would burst without causing long-term damage. He had relied on what had seemed to him to have been a measured, slight decline in the prices of real estate and the various stocks that had backed assets. Greenspan had concluded his book, at the end of 2007, with a calming prophesy, saying that economic bubbles—the phenomenon that had fashioned and had shocked our lives, to such a great extent, in recent years—would not be a worry in the foreseeable future (Greenspan 2009, 483).

In October 2008, Greenspan had shared his astonishment with the Congressional Committee for Oversight and Reform and had said that he was amazed, because the free market system, with government involvement, seemed to him to have worked well for decades, and now a fault had been found with it. He was, he had said, shocked (Greenspan 2009, 4). He claimed that the crisis had been far more than what could have been imagined. People who had assumed that lending institutions would guard the assets of their stockholders—Greenspan, himself, included—were in a state of shock (Tett 2009).

HOW HAD THE AMERICAN INTELLIGENCE COMMUNITY REGARDED THE FINANCIAL CRISIS?

The report of the U.S. Worldwide Threat Assessment, originally called the Annual Threat Assessment, which had been issued in February 2008, had not mentioned the financial crisis. Various external threats had been examined, especially threats to American security, but not the financial stability of the United States.

The report for 2009, issued in February 2009, was different. The report not only began with the financial crisis, but the global ramifications of the crisis made up a significant part. In September 2008, there had been no awareness of a possible crisis, even among those who had been responsible for assessing the risks facing the United States, and even though there had been signs indicating its approach in 2007 and before. The report for 2009, issued just a few months after the crisis had begun, said that it was apparently the most serious global crisis to have been seen in many decades. In the report for 2010, the section on the economy was substantial, but did not appear at the beginning of the report.

Three months after the financial crisis had begun, the American National Intelligence Council issued a comprehensive report that had tried to predict what the world would be like in 2025, called *Global Trends 2025: A Transformed World*, signed by the council's chairman, Thomas Finger. The report had been prepared when there had been clear signs of a financial crisis;

hundreds of experts from leading think tanks and universities in the United States had helped with its preparation. One section related to projected global economic development (Ibid., 6-17); the financial crisis was only briefly mentioned (Ibid., 10). Apparently, the section had been inserted after the crisis had broken out, in September 2008, since the other items in the section did not relate to it. The authors of the report had not predicted the developing crisis.

COULD THINGS HAVE BEEN DONE DIFFERENTLY?

The decision-making process at the JP Morgan Chase bank was such that, in October 2006, CEO Jamie Dimon had instructed William King, one of the bank's senior officials, to immediately sell risky bonds, based on the use of a prediction tool, which had shown that it would be possible to act differently and go against the trend (Tully 2008). The move had been credited to a staff of fifteen senior bank officials who had worked with Dimon for many years and who had held open deliberations and assessments of the situation, which had been passed on to the bank's CEO. Morgan Chase had used predictive analytics tools to examine its strength in the mortgage field (Siegel 2013; Siegel and Davenport 2013). The picture that had been received was of a possible risk to the bank's stability in various scenarios. That was the background for Dimon's decision to reduce the bank's exposure to toxic bonds.

The Wells Fargo Bank (Brady 2012) and Bill Gross, the CEO of Pimco, then the world's largest investment fund, had operated in a similar way to JP Morgan Chase. In 2005, Gross had sent his employees into the field and had received a clear recommendation that the real estate bubble was about to explode (Ablan 2007). His main competitors—Citigroup, UBS and Merrill Lynch—had ignored the warning signs and had continued issuing more bonds of the same type (Tully 2008). They had been busy with their own affairs and had not noticed what had been going on around them (Courtney, Horn, and Kar 2009). If other large banks had acted the way that Morgan Chase had, it would have influenced the financial system to stop the issuing. At Lehman Brothers, the messages that CEO Fuld had received from his subordinates were those that he had wanted to hear, and if anyone had thought differently, they were afraid to tell the senior figures (Stein 2013). There had been small banks, most of them local, which had seen the signs of impending danger and had decided not to enter the subprime area, among them the Hudson City Saving Bank, the New Jersey Community Bank, and the Hingham Bank (Gilad 2011).

Shulsky and Schmitt had seen a similarity between financial and political crises and were of the opinion that they were strategic surprises (Shulsky and Schmitt 2002). Both had suggested using intelligence tools to prevent crises. Courtney, Horn, and Kar had suggested that the use of competitive intelligence tools could have prevented the financial crisis (Courtney, Horn, and Kar 2009). In the case that the events did not occur, with the exception of Morgan Chase (which correctly assessed the situation and decided to act differently from the way its competitors acted). Experts have recommended using the same tools that intelligence uses, such as war games and scenario planning, to assess developments. In their opinion, the key is to get into the minds of competitors and to understand their thought processes, in order to learn the correct action to take.

Fuld and Chodnowsky, experts in competitive intelligence who had analyzed the intelligence failure of the leading companies in the United States, between 2007 and 2009, had claimed that the reason for the failure was that economists had not focused on the critical issues and for that reason they had been surprised (Fuld and Chodnowsky 2010). As far as they were concerned, it would have been preferable for the economists to have cooperated with intelligence experts who had been capable of identifying signs indicating significant changes, and not been fixed on the contextual conceptions of professionals developing similar understandings. They had thought that giving the correct weight to alerts had depended on the degree of involvement of the senior leadership in the process. There is an intelligence problem when conviction about existing assessments is strong and no doubts are raised, so there is no motive to examine the possibility of detecting discontinuity, or of identifying, in time, when a change will occur and what its importance will be. Fuld and Chodnowsky's opinion was supported by the terrible mistake by economists in predicting financial crises over the years (Ahir and Loungani 2014).

Certain banks in the United States had used competitive intelligence tools, especially early warning and risk management tools, to identify the threat of a financial crisis, in time. One of these banks had been mentioned, in an article, by Sawka, without mentioning of its name, for reasons of commercial security (Sawka 2010). After the crisis had broken out and Lehman Brothers had collapsed, an effort was made to identify threats and opportunities. One of the tools was scenario analysis, which had not been used before the crisis; this had been one of the lessons learned. After the crisis, the Fed had undergone a process of learning the lessons of the event (Greeley 2012). The Fed examined thirty-one economic models which could effectively help identify crises. That had not been done before the crisis, because no one had believed that such a disaster could occur.

Regarding the use of intelligence tools, Medina and Fisher had dealt with the crisis, from an intelligence viewpoint, and had asked the question whether or not it might have been possible to prevent it (Medina and Fisher 2009). Medina had held a senior position in the CIA. Medina and Fisher had suggested that economists operate according to the intelligence discipline that gives the best chance of early identification. Walton, who also had held a senior position in the CIA, agreed that intelligence conceptions could have provided an early warning, and had related to the influence of cognitive bias on financial oversight factor in the United States. However, the conclusion that Medina and Fisher had reached was that intelligence officers with intelligence conceptions regarding the use of alerts would have foreseen the crisis better than the economists (Walton 2010). Medina and Fisher had noted six lessons to be learned from the intelligence failure in the 2008 crisis:

> One: It would have been possible to have correctly assessed the threat, even in a situation which had lacked information.
> Two: Incorrect sources had been relied on and there had been a lack of willingness to accept information from additional sources, especially open-source material.
> Three: It would have been possible to have found concrete information which would have indicated the critical nature of the situation, but no search had been initiated to understand which direction the crisis had been taking, before it began.
> Four: It would have been possible to have issued a warning in time, but the actions taken had been incorrect. There had been no teamwork. Economists wrote articles on their own, as had been customary, in academic circles.
> Five: It would have been possible not only to rely more on open-source material but also to have operated according to scenarios and assessments, and then the critical nature of the situation would have become apparent.
> Six: It should have been realized that the world was far more complex than what economists had thought, and then they would have better understood the significance of the processes and events.

CONCLUSION—REASONS BEHIND THE INTELLIGENCE FAILURE

Intelligence Collection Capabilities

The Fed had had no lack of information. The bank's procedures for giving subprime mortgages and creating mortgage-backed bonds as investment were known. The financial institutions had had a great deal of information about what had been happening, and a picture of the situation of every bank had been known to the Fed and bank CEOs. Events in bank competitors had been known, even if banks were not following systematic oversight using competitive intelligence tools, since the information had been made public in economic publications and in reports that had been issued by financial institutions. The fierce competition for credit, even high-risk credit, was an open secret. And despite the fact that there had been no lack of information, there had, in fact, been a lack of information about events on the ground with borrowers (households) and on the way that the worsening of the economic situation, especially in real estate, had influenced their ability to repay their mortgages. The banking system, including the Fed, had not dealt with collecting open-source information, but had focused, if they had focused at all, on business results. No examination had been made of events in the mortgage agencies and on people who had taken out mortgages. One of the lessons of the financial crisis that since then, has been applied, is that the banking branch, in the United States today, uses information systems that measure the ability of clients to repay mortgage loans, on the basis of information on clients appearing on the social networks to offer them alternative credit firms that allow other mortgage options.

Thus, there had been a lack of information about the situation of the borrowers, especially those who had taken out subprime mortgages, most of whom did not have a realistic ability to repay them. One of the mid-level managers at Lehman Brothers had visited an area where many mortgages had been taken out and was shocked when he learned who the borrowers were. He had known that their financial situation would not permit them to repay their loans (Lewis 2010). He did not report the information to the senior bank management. No effort had been made to contact the borrowers or to examine their positions, to assess the chances that they would repay their loans. When it came to collecting information, the Fed had continued acting routinely to oversee the condition of the banks, while the SEC had decided to stop reviewing the financial institutions, because there had not seemed to be any reason to.

Thus, there had been no lack of information about the banks' situation, but not enough information about the situation of the borrowers. There had been no focus on the assessed target: the borrowers, the households, and other factors that influenced the stability of the financial system, and therefore the information received had been irrelevant to the developing threat. In addition, the Fed had examined other parameters, which showed economic growth, and thus cancelled the warning signals. There had been no awareness of the possible consequences of the lack of warning signals, especially for the stability of the financial system.

Noisy Information Environment

The information environment of financial institutions had been characterized by noise. On one side, there had been official factors stressing that the situation was under control, that the financial system was stable and that the American economy was very good and getting better. That opinion had been led by Fed Chair Greenspan and, after him, his heir, Bernanke. Most economists had supported the view. There had been a handful of economists at the turn of the century who had claimed that America's financial policy was incorrect and would lead to a crisis, among them William White, who had headed the BIS. The voices of those who had seen things differently were silenced by the majority. The voice of Congress had gone unheard and, if it had been heard, it had favored the policies led by Greenspan and Bernanke. The vast quantity of information had contained contradictions, especially between short-term and long-term information. While it had been seen that the situation of the banking system and the American economy were improving, there also had been signs indicating that a change was taking place, especially the decrease in real estate prices and in mortgage-repayment capabilities, after the Fed had raised the interest rate, in 2005. People who had thought differently had said that it made no economic sense that the trends would continue over time, that a recession could be expected and that preparations had to be made. There had been signs indicating that the financial system was entering a tailspin, because it had been taking risks that were too great. Others had said that the free market was strong enough to balance the situation and that things would remain under control.

The conclusion is that most of the information about financial stability had indicated that the situation had been good and that no problems could be expected. There had been contradictory opinions that were not examined seriously. The Fed had focused its attention on specific financial institutions, but it mainly related to information that had reinforced its assessments, which had prevented it from relating to other information. The general opinion had been that the possibility of a concentrated surprise, of the sort familiar from the past, was low, and that if it would occur, it would have a short-term influence on isolated, financial institutions, and no more than that.

Human Failures

Given the development of the events, it can be seen that a solid conception had been formulated, which had led to decisions made by the heads of the government systems and financial institutions. The conception had had four components: (1) faith in the strength of the free market; (2) a belief that real estate prices would continue to rise; (3) an assessment that the economic influence of real estate was limited and, therefore, even if the market would fall, its influence would not lead to an economic crisis; and (4) a belief that if a crisis would occur, it would be limited to the United States.

The heads of the financial system, led by the Fed, had concluded that the markets and Wall Street bankers would protect the financial system better than the regulators. Regulation was removed from events and instead, the heads of the financial institutions and the Fed's ongoing oversight were relied upon. The real estate bubble and the threat that it had created would be regulated by the free market. Like every conception, dominant factors had been its supporters, and it had been difficult to disagree with them. Those who had believed in the conception had received support from (allegedly) independent sources, such as rating agencies, which not only had ignored the signs indicating that the situation was unstable, but had found creative explanations that minimized the importance of the signs. For example, signs included the collapse of a mortgage bank, or an investment bank that was about to collapse and the aid it received to solve the problem; minimizing the signs, would claim, for example, that they had only pinpoint importance. There had been no tendency to examine the broader picture. There had been occasional threat of collapse as happened during the Great Depression, but it did not have a central place in the conception, because it never seemed like the same thing could happen again. Great improvement had been made in regulation, in competition between financial bodies, and in the banking system, which was large and stable. In such a situation, it would have been impossible to raise the need for examining the feasibility of a crisis, by using scenarios. The Fed had used a limited number of scenarios, but only for a stress test of a specific bank. There had been no scenario for the simultaneous collapse of several banks. There also had been no scenario concerning what would happen if the fall of real estate prices worsened and led to a significant decline of mortgage-repayment capabilities and the resulting ramifications for the financial-economic system, in general. It had been assumed that there might be problems, but that they would be minor, and if one financial institution folded, a quick, good solution would be found, as had happened in the 1990s and at the turn of the century. Assessors had had a strong tendency to adhere to previous assessments, concluding that what had happened in the past would also happen in the future.

The conclusion is that the prevailing conception, which had been supported by the heads of the Fed and by most of those influencing the financial system, had damaged the ability to correctly assess the situation and the threats that had been piling up. It had been difficult for the various assessors to internalize the change in the situation and therefore they had reacted too late. The financial system had not changed its assessments until the crisis began, even though there had been many signs indicating its approach. The knowledge and experience of the assessors had not included thinking in terms of diffused surprise, since they had not been not aware of its special characteristics.

Organizational Difficulties and Inadequate Cooperation

Since the Fed had been responsible for the stability of the financial system, it was possible to have expected that it would have an ongoing assessment of the situation. However, not only had there been no collaboration between other bodies in the government, which had dealt with various parts of the financial system, but the Fed had been regarded as the leader; the other governmental bodies fell into step behind it without question. Even inside the Fed, collaboration had been weak and there had been a maximum amount of compartmentalization. Further, collaboration between federal banks and with the Fed in Washington was not as good as it could have been. Until the crisis had broken out, the Fed had broadcasted a sense of satisfaction and control of the situation. The strong leadership of Greenspan and Bernanke had not been questioned, even when a reservation was raised. The financial system, that is, the large financial institutions, had not seen a need to collaborate with the Fed, regarding what had occurred, lest the Fed try to stop or limit their activities, especially since their profits had been enormous. It had been convenient for everyone for the situation to continue, with almost no oversight. The Fed had operated as the leading body, generating policy and especially allowing the financial institutions to continue as they had in the past; it had backed them up and had not demanded that they be careful or watchful. Greenspan had admitted, in his testimony before Congress, that he had made a mistake and had been completely surprised, when it had become evident that the basic premises, according to which he had operated were not relevant, and that the financial institutions had gone along a different path which, he claimed, he had known nothing about. He had added that his basic principles about human behavior—that people operate rationally, had collapsed; he had said that this had hocked him and had made him change the way that he looked at the world (Luscombe 2013; Fox 2014).

Thus, it can be concluded that there had been a lack of information sharing between the Fed and the other agencies in the government, the Congress and the financial institutions, which had damaged their ability to understand events prior to the crisis. The lack of collaboration had been the result of the heads of the Fed's overconfidence, and the fact that no agency had had a full picture of what was happening, especially about the threats to the financial system. It is possible that in cases of diffused surprises, which are rarer and depend on processes and not events, additional collaboration, such as with experts in business and social fields, can make an important contribution.

Interaction with Decision Makers

There had been people in the Fed who had thought differently from the heads and who had expressed their opinions. According to the publications, in the Fed there had been a few people who had raised an alert. The financial institutions and the rating agencies had had a few people who had expressed different opinions, and the information had been made public knowledge and also had been reported by investigatory commissions. However, those were lone and, generally speaking, not influential voices in the lower echelons. The political system apparently had not interested itself in financial stability, and Congress had received continually optimistic reports and therefore chose not to intervene. There had been no gap between the viewpoint of the Fed and of most of the economists and financial institutions on the one hand, and of the overseers of the financial system, such as Congress, on the other. Since there had been no sense of danger, no one had thought it necessary to take any action. The broad agreement had not led to a gap between the conception of those who dealt with the issue on a daily basis, such as the Fed and the banks, and those whose role it had been to ensure that the system was working correctly. Apparently, there had been no governmental influence on the assessment of the health of the financial market. However, there had been support from the Treasury Department for steps taken by Congress, among them the significant reduction of regulation in 1999, through a change in the law; this can be seen as one of the causes of the financial crisis.

Thus, the government and Congress relied on the Fed and did not demonstrate any active interest in events until the crisis began. The administration did not have continuous contact with the Fed for updates and it did not seem that a crisis was on the horizon. The decision makers had a tendency to ignore the warning signs of a diffused surprise when the signs were not unequivocal, since it was an ongoing process and not a specific event and it was unclear if and how it would develop.

QUESTIONS EXAMINED IN THE TEST CASE

1. What had been the assessments, before the crisis, regarding such a possibility?

   Before the crisis, it had been assessed that there would be no significant crisis in the financial system, and if there would be a crisis, it would be local, and affect one bank, or isolated banks, and the authorities would know how to deal with it rapidly, as they had successfully done in the past.
2. What had been the indicators of the approaching crisis?

   There had been many indications that a crisis was approaching, and they had been brought to the Fed's attention. There had been information about the worsening of the mortgage market and of the bond market backed by mortgages, which potentially could have influenced the stability of the financial system, but the overriding assessment had been that the free market and competition would know how to regulate the situation.

3. Had there been long-term indicators of a developing crisis and, if so, why hadn't preparations been made to deal with it?

   Before the crisis, the ruling conception had been that the financial system was under the oversight of the authorities, especially the Fed, and therefore it would not be likely that a significant crisis would occur. All the relevant agencies had accepted the assessment of the Fed chairmen, Greenspan and Bernanke, and had not questioned them. Indicators that had shown an ongoing improvement in the overall financial situation had lessened the weight of other indicators and of warnings from actors outside the Fed, mainly from academics, that financial stability had been in danger.

4. Had there been any serious assessments about the possibility of a significant crisis? What had led to the failure of establishment assessments and the success of alternative assessments?

   There had been alternative assessments of the situation, mainly from academic economists, some of them among the most senior in the United States, and also from abroad, but they had been in the minority and were ignored. Everyone had more-or-less the same information, but the argument had been over the significance of the information. The critics had argued that it would be unreasonable for the real estate bubble to continue without a crisis, while the prevailing opinion had been that, while there was in fact a real estate bubble, it would end without causing shock waves, and the economy would continue, because of the strength of the free market.

5. Had there been an intelligence failure, and if so, what had characterized it?

   The intelligence failure resulted from a lack of assessment that a crisis was impending and an inability to recognize the indication when it would occur. Therefore, the decision makers in the administration and the Fed had not been warned that the situation was taking a turn for the worse. Even when the crisis did break out, midway through September 2008, its depth, scope, and direction—where it was leading the financial system—had not been correctly assessed. Thus, it had turned rapidly from an internal American financial crisis to a global economic crisis. The administrative system had been surprised and had been caught unprepared. The timing and rapid spread of the crisis had surprised the decision makers: initially, they had not understood the full significance of its impact, because they had not expected that it would affect the economy as strongly as it had, and that so many factors had influenced it.

6. How had the failure affected the country?

   As a result of the intelligence failure, no preparations had been made and the crisis had not been prevented. It could have prevented it and/or better preparations for it could have been made. The economic price was steep, and the damage suffered by many Americans was enormous. As it developed, it also caused immense economic damage to other countries, which took years to overcome.

7. What had caused the intelligence failure?

   One explanation for the intelligence failure has been the mental fixation of senior figures in the American financial system, both among overseers and policy makers on the one hand, and senior officials in the large financial institutions, on the other. Another explanation has been the focus put on the key intelligence topic—on intelligence targets which had been incorrect for the situation, which is characteristic of diffused surprises. The relevant targets were the problematic nature of the housing and real estate markets. A third explanation has been the particularly strong tendency of assessors to adhere to previous assessments. There had been no way of shaking their faith in the free market and the rational, seemingly cautious activity of the markets and financial institutions. For several years before the crisis, there had been a developing conception that had relied on the faith that the markets behaved rationally and that real estate prices were not divorced from the economic reality; therefore, there had been no reason for regulatory intervention. Anyone who had tried to contradict that view—and they had been few and far between—had adopted the conceptions of developmental psychology, based on the understanding that people do not behave rationally. Such individuals had been criticized or ignored. The regulators had done very little to limit the real estate bubble, subprime loans, and mortgage securitization. The lack of inter- and intra-organizational cooperation also had contributed to a rise in the risk of a surprise.

8. What kind of intelligence failure had this been?

   This intelligence failure had been based on a crisis that was a diffused surprise. The crisis had developed over time and had been caused by many uncoordinated factors, mainly financial institutions and other bodies that had dealt with marketing mortgages, and from the worsening situation of homeowners, especially those who had taken out subprime loans. The general assumption had been that even if a specific financial institution had been in a dangerous situation, it could be rescued, but the accumulated influence of the worsening situation of many bodies at the same time, without coordination or direction, had not been predicted by overseers and therefore they had been prepared for a crisis. Such an event had never occurred: the Great Depression had seemed far away and irrelevant to the way that the financial system had operated at the time of the crisis.

9. Which factors had influenced the intelligence failure (table 5.1)?

   In this test case, the causes that influenced the intelligence failure have been presented. In our assessment, the most influential factor was the Fed, which had been responsible for the issue, and which had failed. The Inquiry Committee also pointed a finger at the Fed and had said it was the main factor responsible for the failure.

   Apparently, in cases of diffused surprise, it is more difficult to identify a developing threat. The intelligence system (in this case the regulatory system, mainly the Fed) has not been focused in the right direction, in its collection efforts, and has not assessed all possible developments.

10. Which tools had been used to prevent the failure?

    Routine tools had been used, primarily the ongoing oversight of the financial system. However, following the legislation that had been enacted years before the crisis had broken out, the scope of the oversight had declined and had become limited, and therefore its effectiveness had been low. This was made clear after the issue had been investigated by two investigation committees. In addition, there had been economic surveys written by economists, but they had not correctly interpreted the essence of the developing danger to the financial system, because such processes had not occurred in the past. The possibility of a domino effect in the financial system had never been discussed, not one that would develop after the collapse of a large financial institution; further, the economic consequences for the United States had never been taken into consideration.

11. Which tools could have been used to prevent the intelligence failure?

    Two investigation committees had raised various suggestions, especially increasing the oversight of the financial institutions, extending the use of scenarios, inter-agency information sharing and increasing inter-agency cooperation. The committees had not related to the lack of open-source information and its potential influence on the assessment of

Table 5.1 Factors Influencing the Intelligence Failure

Number	*Issue*	*Response*
1	Was the event routine?	No
2	Was the event known from the past?	Yes
3	Were the threatening factors known?	Yes
4	Was the type of action known?	No
5	Was the crisis directed?	No
6	Was the information received clear?	No
7	Was it clear what was intended?	Yes

Source: Avner Barnea 2020.

the ability of people who were purchasing homes to repay their loans. If the financial system had used intelligence tools, especially tools of indicative signs to raise the alert that the situation was changing for the worse, there might have been a greater chance of preventing the failure. Other possible tools that could have led to a better understanding of the situation were the collection of open-source information, especially on occurrences in real estate regarding mortgages, sharing information within the Fed and between the various agencies that deal with finance and the economy, which could have helped in understanding the nature of the threat. Although there had been no lack of information about the banks, there had been room for improvement, but because of the lack of regulation, which had begun in 2000, it became difficult to collect information about bank occurrences. However, that was not significant and not what had prevented an alert. The Fed had had enough information about the developing risks, but it had not correctly assessed the full significance and great danger that had been posed to the financial stability of the United States.

12. Which intelligence lessons have been applied?

An intelligence unit was established in the Fed to monitor what occurs in financial institutions. Changes were made in legislation to increase the Fed's oversight of what occurs in those institutions and the strength of managing dangers in the financial system. While no national intelligence or competitive intelligence tools were introduced, tools were developed for receiving alerts from various indicator when the financial situation worsened, tools which had not existed before the crisis. Insofar as is known, lessons were learned, especially in the greater use of possible scenarios, in sharing information, and in monitoring the situations of the banks—not just for individual banks. Since the administration restored regulation and strengthened the oversight of the financial institutions, there is naturally more information about what goes on in such institutions. Improved indicators were also developed, which are expected to raise alerts regarding a worsening in the situation of an individual financial institution, using intelligence early warning indicators.

Nonetheless, the Fed apparently has not internalized the conception of organized intelligence to prevent the next failure. While indicators have been developed, it is unclear to what degree they are appropriate for receiving alerts, and it is also unclear if open-source collection has been developed for dynamic key intelligence topic activity, or if the variety of information sources has been expanded. One of the lessons of the crisis was that economic models do not necessarily provide an appropriate response, and in that respect, improvement has been made in the use of additional tools.

Chapter 6

Test Case

The September 11, 2001, Terrorist Attack on the United States

OVERVIEW

On September 11, 2001, a total of nineteen al-Qaeda terrorist operatives used hijacked planes to attack the World Trade Center, in New York City, and the Pentagon, in Washington D.C. Fifteen of the terrorists were Saudi Arabian, two were from the UAE, one was Egyptian, and one was Lebanese. They had been carefully chosen and indoctrinated and were highly motivated. Two of the planes crashed into the World Trade Center (the Twin Towers), the third plane crashed into the Pentagon, and the fourth, which was supposed to have crashed into the Capitol or the White House, crashed in Pennsylvania. American Airlines flight 111, to Los Angeles, which had taken off from Logan International Airport, in Boston, crashed into the North Tower at 8:46 a.m. United Airlines flight 175, to Los Angeles, which had taken off from the same airport, crashed into the South Tower, at 9:03 a.m. American Airlines flight 77, to Los Angeles, which had taken off from Washington, D.C., crashed into the Pentagon at 9:37 a.m. United Airlines flight 93 from New Jersey to San Francisco at 10:02 a.m. was supposed to hit the Capitol or White House crashed in Pennsylvania.

The terrorist attack had been a strategic, concentrated surprise. It was the first time that a terrorist attack had been carried out on American soil, by an Islamic terrorist organization whose headquarters were located outside the United States. Osama bin Laden had been behind it, and the Pakistani, Khalid Sheikh Mohammed, had apparently commanded the September 11th attack (*9/11 Commission Report* 2004); Sheikh Mohammed had financed the Twin Towers attack in February 1993.

The al-Qaeda attack on the United States, known universally as "9/11," had been a strategic concentrated surprise attack, planned beyond America's borders. It had consisted of four simultaneous suicide bombing attacks, which had been perpetrated by terrorists, who had hijacked commercial flights. The attack had been an American intelligence failure, mainly of the FBI and CIA, and many had regarded it as a second Pearl Harbor, including one of the intelligence committees that had investigated the events leading to the attack. 9/11 had been carried out by a well-known, designated, enemy organization and had been the result of an inaccurate assessment of the threat.

Despite al-Qaeda's attempts to hide its intentions, American intelligence had significant information indicating a coming attack—not inconclusive information, as had been claimed by some (Roberto et al. 2006). There had been enough time to warn of an attack and either prevent it or decrease its potential damage. Some people have regarded it as a fundamental surprise, not situational, since its influence on the security of the United States and on the global fight against Islamic terrorism had been extensive and unprecedented. It had made the United States go to war with Iraq and Afghanistan and against global Islamic terrorism in general (Lanir 2006).

The 9/11 attacks had led to the appointment of two investigatory commissions. One was the Congressional Joint Inquiry (2002), which had been headed by Senators Bob Graham and Richard Shelby, and the other was the National Commission on Terrorist Attacks Upon the United States (also known as the 9/11 Commission), headed by Thomas Kean and Lee Hamilton, which had issued the *9/11 Commission Report* (2004).

According to the *9/11 Commission Report*, there had been many indicators that had been ignored; this had made the attack a shock but not a surprise. The commission had elaborated on the information known to American intelligence, and it is reasonable to assume there had been much information that had not been revealed for reasons of security. But the clear conclusion was that intelligence had had information about the coming attack but had failed to warn of it. The same was said by Richard Clarke, White House advisor for the war on terrorism (Clarke 2004) and Tim Walton, a senior CIA official (Walton 2010).

After the publication of reports by the two commissions, an internal CIA examination was held by the internal affairs agency. This examination indicated findings that criticized the functioning of the intelligence agencies, which had not shared information with each other nor with law enforcement; some of the findings apparently had not been known to the investigatory commission (Giraldi 2005). Regarding this, Richard Clarke, who had been national coordinator for Security, Infrastructure Protection, and Counterterrorism for the United States, had said (interview by author, Tel Aviv, June 2013) that it had been a conscious decision made by senior CIA officials, not to share information with the FBI about terrorists who had been known to his organization. Thus, the names of the terrorists, which had been known to the CIA, had not been transmitted to the FBI and perhaps had kept the attack from being prevented.

The 9/11 Commission issued a long list of recommendations for reorganizing the intelligence and internal security operations of the United States, after it had reached the conclusion that beyond not understanding the threat and its importance because of a lack of *imagination*, there also had been organizational problems that had kept the attack from being prevented. The combination of analytic and organizational/structural problems explains the intelligence failure in preventing 9/11, which has been the opinion accepted by many analysts (Malfatto 2007). Former senior National Security Agency (NSA) official Thomas Drake claimed that the NSA had very important preventive alert intelligence about a coming attack which had not been correctly assessed (Nakashima 2010) and which had not been shared within the intelligence community.

Beginning in May 2001, the CIA repeatedly had transmitted alerts about a possible attack on the United States, as reported by Eichenwald, in *500 Days: Secrets and Lies in the Terror Wars* (Eichenwald 2012), and in an article entitled "The Deafness Before the Storm" (Eichenwald 2012); this was according to the President's Daily Brief (PDB), the daily intelligence report for the American president. Among the president's team, no one seriously had related to the terrorist threat of al-Qaeda; in addition, there had been those who had claimed that the CIA had been wrong in its assessment of the threat of bin Laden to the United States and had given it less importance, because the focus of attention had been on Saddam Hussein's intentions and capabilities. An intelligence report from August 6, 2001 (Ibid) contradicted the claims of the Bush administration that no concrete alert had been received. According to the report, at the briefing it had been specifically mentioned that al-Qaeda intended to attack the United States, but the president had not responded and his team had ignored the intelligence information.

Most intelligence experts and those who formally had investigated the issues agree that the lack of warning had been an intelligence failure (Marrin 2011). According to a different report, more responsible for the failure had been the decision makers, to whose attention the raw information had been brought, and less responsible had been the analysts who issued the strategic alert (Pillar 2006). CIA Director Tenet had not considered it an intelligence failure, which he explained by saying that an intelligence failure is defined as a "lack of focus and attention to a threat," and in his opinion that had not been the case (Congressional Joint Inquiry 2002). Others add that the absence of warning was the failure of those who had determined policy and who had not devoted enough attention to the prevention of terrorism (Baer 2002; Clarke 2004, 2013; Steele, 2003).

IT COULD HAVE BEEN PREVENTED!

American intelligence had not been the only organization that had been guilty of blindness, in the face of approaching threats. Others had assumed that what had been was what would be. Despite the warnings and assessment that a civil aerial attack against the United States was liable to occur, many people in positions of authority had chosen to ignore the warnings and had failed to make preparations. The Federal Aviation Authority (FAA) had received intelligence reports and had done nothing to improve plane security on the ground and in the air, especially because of pressure from the airplane companies, which had been concerned lest improved security would be very expensive and would damage the quality of service (Bazerman and Watkins 2001; Pasternak 2001; Robinson and Johnson 2001). The civilian aeronautical authorities in the United States had known that the security systems had not been prepared for a terrorist attack on the United States (Ibid, 5-10), but the tendency to preserve the status quo had been very strong. Before there had been alerts of terrorist threats to the United States from al-Qaeda, the White House Committee on Aviation and Security (1997) had indicated faults in aerial security, but nothing had been done.

The commission also had determined that the CIA's analysts had not written an assessment that took an attack on the United States into consideration (*9/11 Commission Report* 2004, 347). Information had existed about intentions to carry out attacks inside the United States, but it had not been taken seriously.

The FBI's assessment, before the 9/11 attack, had been that bin Laden had needed pilots to fly planes that would be purchased in the United States, and that the FBI had information that two al-Qaeda operatives had acquired flight training in Afghanistan, with the intention of carrying out terrorist attacks. One of these operatives came to the United States, had learned how to become a pilot and had flown one of the planes in the attack (Hill 2002, 14). Nevertheless, this information had not been part of the intelligence report that had presented the threat and the possible avenues that had been open to al-Qaeda.

According to Clarke, a warning about an al-Qaeda threat had been transmitted by the CIA, during the interim between the end of the Clinton administration and the beginning of the Bush, but the new administration had not assessed the information properly (Clarke 2004). In August 2001, the President's Daily Briefing had included a warning about an approaching attack (*9/11 Commission Report* 2004, 261-262), which the president did not respond to. That was made especially clear, in the Cabinet meeting that was held on September 4, 2001, which Bush did not attend. The Cabinet had to decide on policy regarding al-Qaeda in Afghanistan, but had made no decision, even though, during deliberations, al-Qaeda's plans for an immediate attack on the United States had been mentioned (Clarke 2004; Coll, 2004). According to the commission, the new administration had begun formulating a strategy to destroy al-Qaeda, but there had been no policy in place for the immediate future.

Between March and September 2001, the intelligence community had identified signs of an upcoming terrorist attack against the United States, inside the country (Hill 2002, 20). Tenet had called the information a "stream of alerts" (9/11 *Commission Report Final Report*, Executive Summary 2004, 6), and it was unclear why no action had been taken.

The Commission Report noted that despite the information about intentions to attack inside the United States, the eventual assessment had been that an attack would be carried out on American targets abroad (Ibid, 22). The commission noted that the information had not been integrated into preparations for preventing al-Qaeda's expected attack (*9/11 Commission Report* 2004, 358-360).

Even after the al-Qaeda attacks on the American embassies, in Dar es-Salaam (Tanzania) and Nairobi (Kenya), in 1998, the American intelligence community had not placed bin Laden at the top of its priority list, despite instructions from Tenet. His role as CIA director had not given him authority over other organizations in the American intelligence community, and his instructions had not been followed as they should have been (*9/11 Commission Report* 2004, 357; Hill 2002).

One of the most significant criticisms issued by the commission was the claim of the "lack of imagination" of the administration's intelligence analysts, whose intelligence-operational importance had been explained for several pages (*9/11 Commission Report*, 2004, 339-348). They had not considered the use of planes as weapons, even though there had been information about it (Ibid, 346). That was the reason, according to the commission, that the attack had not been prevented.

Thus, it can be seen that the alerts provided by the intelligence community, regarding the heightening of Islamic terrorist threats, had been known to the administration, but preventing terrorism had been a low priority, in both the Clinton and Bush administrations, as was noted by the *Commission Report* (Ibid, 10).

The commission had determined that, despite al-Qaeda's having been an intelligence target for many years, no organized National Intelligence Estimate had been carried out before the 9/11 attack, and the most recent assessment had been written in 1997 (Ibid, 12).

Apparently, American intelligence had been in possession of sufficient intelligence to have prevented a mistake in predicting bin Laden's intention and also could have prevented the attack itself. The focus on the assessed intelligence target, al-Qaeda and its concentrated activities, had been correct; the concentrated surprise had been the result of mistakes made in the "intelligence cycle," as had occurred in other strategic concentrated surprises.

THE ATTACK ON THE WORLD TRADE CENTER, 1993

It is impossible to understand the events leading up to 9/11 without understanding the attack on the World Trade Center in 1993, especially the lessons that had not been learned by the intelligence community. On February 26, 1993, a booby-trapped vehicle was driving into the underground parking lot of World Trade Center Building B-2 and exploded in the afternoon. Six people were killed and about a thousand were wounded, most of them not seriously. The *New York Times* and the *New York Daily News* had received claims of responsibility from an Islamic organization and a notice of its intention to destroy the Twin Towers. A small number of suspects were arrested, but Ramzi Yusef, the main person who had been suspected of having orchestrated the attack, escaped to Pakistan. All those who had been arrested and the suspects who had disappeared had belonged to a mosque in Jersey City, whose imam was a blind Egyptian sheikh named Omar Abdul Rahman. He had been known to the CIA because he had recruited Muslims to fight against the Soviets in Afghanistan. He had been tried in Egypt for his involvement in the assassination of Sadat but was found not guilty. Once released, he had managed to obtain a visa for the United States and entered in 1990. In retrospect, it turned out that the CIA had not informed the consul that the sheikh was known as a radical Islamic (Weiner 2009, 370). It later became known that, before the 1993 attack, some of the suspects had been known to the police and FBI after news had been received of their radical Islamic activities (Copeland 2006).

In 1992, the group head by Omar Abduk Rahman had planned an attack to release Sayid Nosair, who had assassinated Meir Kahane. They had contacted two Muslim brothers, Ahmad and Yousef Ajaj, who had trained in terrorist camps in Afghanistan and had specialized in manufacturing bombs. The Ajaj brothers had prepared the bomb that had been placed in the vehicle that was driven to the World Trade Center's parking lot. The FBI had known of their intentions to carry out the attack, but had not succeeded in preventing it (Lance 2003).

The 1993 terrorist attack on the Twin Towers had been the first Islamic attack ever attempted on American soil. Investigators had found a note on the computer of one of the suspects: it stated that the bomb had not been properly prepared and that only slight damage had been caused, but the World Trade Center would continue to be a target for a future attack (Childers and

DePippo 1998). Following the attack, there had been analysts who had said that this might have been a turning point in American-Middle East relations, because the United States had become a target for Islamic terrorism. However, the American administration had regarded the event as a criminal rather than as a terrorist attack. In a speech given by President Clinton, the day after the attack, he had described it as an explosion, not a bomb, and had said, in a short statement, that the perpetrators would be caught. The investigation had been left in the hands of the FBI, which had not had experience in preventing Islamic terrorism; the CIA did not participate in the investigation (Miniter 2003). The event was investigated as a criminal event, and the focus was on finding evidence that would make it possible to bring the perpetrators to trial. No attention had been paid to the intelligence aspects of preventing terrorism, such as exposing additional suspects in the second circle of involvement or examining consequences, to prepare for preventing a similar attack, in the future. The importance of Ramzi Yousef, who had been in the United States in 1992 and had left for Afghanistan on the eve of the attack, and who had been an al-Qaeda operative, had been ignored, and his connection to the attack had not been investigated. In 1995, Yousef was arrested in Islamabad, Pakistan, and was deported to the United States, where he was tried and sentenced to life imprisonment. In 1998, al-Qaeda attacked the American embassies in Tanzania and Nairobi and, in 1996, the Khobar Towers in Khobar, Saudi Arabia where, among those who had been killed were nineteen American Air Force soldiers. The attack in 1993 had been the first time that it became evident that there had been a connection between al-Qaeda and anti-American terrorist activity. However, it is important to note that the attack had been a local initiative, in which Ramzi Yousef himself had been involved; while he had been in contact with al-Qaeda, the organization had not been behind it.

The 1993 attack had been carried out with the involvement of Egyptian citizens who had been active members of the Muslim Brotherhood. The CIA had had very little information about the organization, which was both radical and Sunni. The CIA's Richard Baer, who had been active in the Middle East (Baer 2004, 98-99), said that the CIA's file, from 1985, had contained a few newspaper articles about the Muslim Brotherhood, some reports from American agencies, and other reports that Baer had called "analytical pieces." Sayid Qutb, one of al-Qaeda's founders, was Egyptian and a prominent Muslim Brotherhood activist in Egypt.

The 1993 attack had been a concentrated surprise; it had been an intelligence failure, because it had not been prevented, even though the FBI had had early information about radical Islamic activity that had focused on the mosque, in New Jersey. The attack had not changed the preventive intelligence concept, relating to the war on terrorism in the United States. The FBI, whose function was defined as "law enforcement" (Hudson 2014), had not understood that it should have provided intelligence cover of local terrorist networks, within the Muslim population, and should have examined their intentions and ties to terrorists and other extremists, beyond the borders of the United States. American newspapers had reported the event as part of a larger plan to turn the United States into a target for global terrorism (Farrall 1993). However, this had not been the concept maintained by the FBI.

Following the Khobar attack, in 1996, and the attacks on the American embassies, in 1998, there had been no American intelligence assessment of the possibility that terrorism would leak into the United States, even though information had been received from random open sources. No methodical open intelligence collection had been carried out, regarding bin Laden's threats to attack the United States (Copeland 2006). Clarke reported that after the 1993 attack, the FBI had decided on significantly increasing its counter-terrorism activities and had allotted resources to that end, but nothing was done (Clarke, interview by author, 2013). Instead, the FBI had continued focusing on its "regular" issues, with only a few dozen agents dealing with counterterrorism. There had been almost no awareness of the subject, and therefore an Islamic center was not established within the agency. The only FBI offices that had understood something about it were in New York and Washington; the other offices had not dealt with it at all. According to Clarke, at the end of 2000, a meeting was held for the heads of the FBI offices in the United States, attended by the agency's deputy director, to brief them on al-Qaeda and its intentions. The meeting did not lead to the change that had been hoped for. The FBI, which is not an intelligence agency, had not internalized the change in threats to the United States and the way in which these new threats should have influenced its methods (Jeffries-Jones 2009).

THE REASONS FOR THE INTELLIGENCE FAILURE IN 1993

Intelligence Collection Capabilities

The 1993 attack on the World Trade Center had been the work of radical Muslims inside the United States. The Islamic operatives had been in contact with other operatives in the country, some of whom had trained in Afghanistan, apparently in al-Qaeda camps, and had specialized in making bombs. Although the FBI had had early information about the network, its exact intentions had not been known, partly because the FBI had not used an aggressive intelligence system to obtain additional information to discover the operatives' intentions. The FBI in New Jersey had had leads that could have focused the agency in its intelligence collection. However, it had acted out of a lack of understanding of counterterrorism, especially on how to prevent Islamic terrorism. The FBI had had several informers inside the Muslim community, in New Jersey, but their contribution was small since they had not been briefed on the key intelligence topics and methods for collecting information, and therefore had given no warning of the attack (Reeve 1999). Even after the attack and the exposure and arrest of some of the operatives who had been involved, the FBI still did not focus its intelligence activity on radical Islamic operatives in the United States. An FBI agent had told journalist Peter Lance (Lance 2003, 113) that there had been FBI supervisors in the New York office who had been so sure of themselves, that they had said that no one would ever dare to attack the United States; as a result, they believed that Muslims did not pose a risk, going on to say that the Muslims were uneducated Bedouin, while the United States was large and smart, and they weren't. Richard Clarke argued (interview by author, 2013) that the FBI's professional knowledge about preventing terrorist attacks had been negligible and the resources allotted to it had been insufficient; thus, the agency's chances for success had been low.

The conclusion to be drawn is that despite the FBI's lack of professionalism, with regard to counterterrorism, there had been no lack of information. The agency had had early information about the specific Islamic cell, but its professional capability in the field had not been good enough, and therefore it had not prevented the attack.

Noisy Intelligence Environment

After the First Gulf War (1991), there had been strong anti-American feeling, and in the West, the intelligence organizations suffered from an anti-Arab bias. Jervis (Jervis 1985) discussed the bias among the decision makers as they had dealt with the threat. President Clinton, responding to the terror attack of 1993, had referred to "isolated" operatives and had ignored the possibility that it had been carried out under the direction of a terrorist organization, operating against and from outside the United States. Clinton, at that time, had focused on the country's economic situation, which had influenced how terrorist threats had been assessed. The threat environment in 1993 had been complex. Saddam Hussein had been in power, after losing the Gulf War, and American troops were in Somalia. As early as 1991 and 1992, the FBI had had information about attacks planned by the cell to which Sayid Nosair had belonged (Copeland 2006, 51). In January 1993, Secretary of Defense Dick Cheney said that there were terrorist threats against the United States; the information had been passed along to Clinton's incoming administration and had been noted by the new Secretary of State, Warren Christopher, in one of his first speeches (Farrall 1993). The FBI's investigation into the Islamic cell in New Jersey had focused on obtaining information about the activities of some of the cell members, who had been of Egyptian origin and had opposed Egyptian president Mubarak. About six weeks before the attack, the Justice Department had ordered the investigation to be closed, because apparently there had been no legal basis for it (Dwyer 1994, 170).

It can therefore be concluded that in the absence of an orderly assessment of an Islamic terrorist threat, and in the absence of studies carried out from the perspective of national security, general information remained that could have predicted the First Gulf War, but not the change in the way Islamic elements had related to the United States. The 1993 attack had been regarded as an isolated incident and had not been examined as the product of a more profound change in the way radical Islam had related to the United States. It is unclear why the investigation had ended—an investigation of an organization, whose intentions had been to carry out an attack, whose intentions had been known—unless there had been an assessment that it had been an isolated event. There had been no such assessment.

HUMAN FAILURES

The FBI's incorrect assessment, regarding preventive intelligence, in general, and preventing terrorism, in particular, had resulted in the fact that in 1991, the agency transferred 350 agents from intelligence to other positions, and in 1992, it transferred another 1,200 (McQueen 1993). Even after 1993, the FBI had continued giving preventive intelligence low priority and had focused on the war on drugs. At the same time, the number of agents in the CIA and the State Department also had declined. The problem had been not only the low priority that had been given to preventing terrorism, but the lack of a focus for collecting information on terrorist organizations that had threatened the United States. There had been signs that Ramzi Yousef, who had orchestrated the attack, had been in contact with bin Laden both before the attack and after he had escaped to Afghanistan (Reeve 1999, 246-248). Some of the human failure had been linked to the skills of the FBI agents who had dealt with the Islamic cell. The Islamic issue had been unknown to them. For example, some of them had previously dealt with Soviet espionage (Lance 2003). The FBI had not had the skills to deal with such new, complex matters, and it had no agents with the appropriate training (Riebling 1994). In 1991 and 1992, FBI analysts had indicated that the United States might be attacked by Iraqis, in the wake of the First Gulf War, but a bin Laden terrorist attack had not been considered (Marlin Tepper 1991). In January 1993, Sheikh Omar Abdel Rahman issued a fatwa against American interests around the globe, and it had been a declaration of intent. There had been more information about terrorist intentions against the United States, arising from individuals within the United States, but they had not been assessed as strategic alerts and had not been discussed at a high level. Following an assessment that there had been no threat, the FBI had not used covert means, such as wire taps and surveillance, to collect information (Mylroie 2002).

The conclusion is that the assessors had not fully considered the Islamic issue and the assessments had not been based on a systematic study, but rather on intuition and general knowledge. There had been no one who had presented a systematic assessment that said that the issue demanded attention. The result was that the terrorist threat of the Islamic cell in New Jersey had not been correctly assessed.

Organizational Difficulties and Faulty Collaboration

Beyond the fact that preventive intelligence and the prevention of Islamic terrorism had been given a low priority, the FBI had not operated like an intelligence agency. The agency heads had never considered intelligence as their main activity, and others had not regarded the FBI as an important member of the Intelligence Community intercom (Zegart 2009). FBI-CIA collaboration had had a very low profile. Information had not been methodically transferred from one agency to another, regarding terrorist threats to the United States. The CIA had not given the FBI information about terrorists operating outside the United States or about their ties to people inside the country. The FBI had not given the CIA information about the ties between suspects inside the United States with terrorists or terrorist organizations outside the country. There had been information that one of the terrorists, Abdul Rahum Yassin, who had left the United States immediately after the attack, had gone to Iraq, where he was in contact with the local authorities (Mylroie 2000). Yassin had not been the only subject for whom there had been information but no collaboration between the FBI and CIA; there had been others, as well. For example, before the attack had occurred, one of the terrorists had been in frequent telephone contact with someone in Iraq. The lack of collaboration had damaged the construction of a preventive intelligence picture. There had been assessments that Saddam Hussein had been behind the attack to avenge the First Gulf War, but that never had been deeply examined (Mylroie 2000) and apparently had not been the case. The Immigration and Naturalization Service (INS) had allowed the suspects to enter the United States, because it had not had access to the FBI and CIA databases. Thus, Ramzi Yusef, who had planned the attack, and Sheikh Omar from Egypt, who had been known as having ties to Islamic terrorism and had been the spiritual leader of the terrorist cell that carried out the attack, had been able to enter the country. The entrance visa given, with the approval based on authority from the CIA and the State Department, had not been brought to the knowledge of the FBI. When it was brought to their attention, the FBI had claimed that the ability to monitor Yusef in the United States had been compromised (Riebling 1994). The attack had not led to collaboration or information-sharing within the America intelligence community. Instead, it had been considered to be an isolated event with little significance.

The conclusion is that the lack of cooperation and information-sharing within the intelligence community had caused significant damage and perhaps had kept the 1993 attack from being prevented. Lessons had not been learned and no deliberations had been held for improving the situation in the future.

Interactions with the Decision Makers

At the beginning of the Clinton administration, the issue of counterterrorism, both within the United States and beyond its borders, had not been given high priority. Clinton's policy had not been substantially different from that of his predecessor, Bush Sr. The general feeling inside the intelligence community had been that the issue was not particularly important for the decision makers. The FBI, which had been responsible for preventing terrorism inside the United States, had access to the president or senior decision makers to make them aware of issues, yet it had continued to operate the way it had before the attack. The director of the FBI, Louis Freeh, who had held the position until 2001 (replaced a few days before 9/11, by Robert Mueller), had not brought his concerns to the decision makers.

Thus, the FBI, subordinate to the Department of Justice, had not had close interactions regarding counterterrorism with other agencies and had operated alone. It had not attempted to bring its point of view to the attention of the decision makers. This had damaged the FBI's effectiveness but was not a major factor in the failure to prevent the attack.

THE 9/11 ATTACK

Overview

The report of the commission that had investigated the attack had had details about the attackers, including their connections with al-Qaeda and the involvement, of some, in terrorism, before the attack. Most of the information has been based on what had been known to the American intelligence community before the attack had occurred.

In January 2000, the NSA found a link between al-Qaeda operatives and persons suspected of terrorist activity, and the CIA identified three of them.

They were Salem al-Hamzi, Nawaff al-Hamzi, and Khalid al-Midhar. It later became apparent that they had participated in the 9/11 attack, but the CIA had lost trace of them. About a week later, they entered the United States, without having been identified, and began learning how to fly, at a flight school, in Florida. The same was true for Mohammed Atta and others who had been known to the CIA, which had cooperated with German intelligence, after the suspects had lived in Hamburg, for a number of years. Atta and others had learned to fly at flight schools in Florida and New Jersey, and others at a flight school in Minnesota. Richard Clarke accused the CIA of having withheld the information from the FBI, which perhaps had kept it from preventing the 9/11 attack (McGovern 2011).

The terrorists had arrived in the United States between January and April 2000 and had not been arrested upon arrival, or later. Some of them had been known to the CIA and possibly also to the NSA (*9/11 Commission Report* 2004, 157-158). While the FBI had received information about them, from the flight school in Florida which had made them suspect, the information had not been formulated into an assessment about the danger they had presented, because of lack interagency cooperation and the FBI's low level of intelligence awareness. The terrorists had learned how to fly in the United States, had rented planes for aerial reconnaissance in the regions they had wanted to attack, and had collected intelligence about the civilian aerial security (Framer 2009).

The 9/11 commission noted that preparations for the attack cost half a million dollars (*9/11 Commission Report* 2004, 169). The terrorists had opened bank accounts, using fictitious names, and regularly had received bank transfers from abroad (Farmer 2009, 45; 64). They had been very circumspect in their actions, had not approached mosques, and had behaved like ordinary young men. They had not phoned al-Qaeda operatives, in Afghanistan or elsewhere. They had not been permitted to ask after their families. The compartmentalization between them had been strong (Farmer 2009, 59). Some of them, especially Atta, who had been known to the CIA and apparently had been the senior terrorist, had exited and had entered the United States and had even flown to the Far East and Afghanistan (Posner 2004). They could have been monitored by following their flights to and from the United States, but that had not been done because they had not been treated as suspects. Most of them had had Saudi Arabian passports and therefore had not roused suspicions, and they had had no problem in extending their tourist visas. They had lived successfully in the United States for a long period of time, having remained under the radar of the FBI and other American intelligence agencies. That had made it possible for them to plan and carry out the attack, without pressure, and to choose the right time for it. They had been very self-confident, to the point where some of them had been in contact with one another, despite the fact that it had been contrary to their rules of compartmentalization.

While the 9/11 attack had been regarded as a surprise, the American intelligence community had had enough information for it not to have been a surprise. It had come as a shock to the decision makers. The commission had called it "a shock, not a surprise" (*9/11 Commission Report*. Final Report, Executive Summary 2004, 2). The administration, the intelligence agencies, and the general public had been shocked, but when it came to intelligence, the attack had been an intelligence failure. Bin Laden's plans to attack the United States had been known for years, but the preparations made by American intelligence and the decision makers had been incorrect, during both the Clinton and Bush eras (Bossie 2004). The FBI had received information in 1995, from Philippine intelligence, including the names of some of the terrorists who later participated in the 9/11 attack (*9/11 Commission Report* 2004, 345). In 1999, the Library of Congress prepared a report for the National Intelligence Council, which had predicted various threats, including an aerial suicide bombing attack on government buildings, but the report had never been used (Solomon 2002).

INTELLIGENCE PREPAREDNESS AND PREPARATIONS FOR PREVENTING TERRORIST ATTACKS

Between the fall of the Soviet bloc, in 1991 and 2001, the American intelligence community had been preparing intensively for the new situation. Six Congressional committees, three national commissions, and three think-tank committees had been dealing with it (Best 2004; Zegart 2009, 8- 9). The main subject that all had dealt with was the need for essential changes in the intelligence community, in order to make it functional in a situation that no longer focused on the Soviet Union and its satellites.

After the fall of the Soviet bloc, the change in the intelligence effort and the setting of America's new priorities had been slow and weak, because of inherent conservatism and the lack of internalizing of the new threats. The Congress, especially its intelligence committees (the House and Senate), had tried to influence the American intelligence community regarding new directions for action, but their ability to influence them had been limited (McCubbins 1985). It is difficult to make changes when many organizations work within the same framework, such as the intelligence community (Simon 2000). Analysts have believed that America's preparedness to deal with terrorist threats had not been good. There had been a general failure throughout the entire intelligence cycle, so that it has been impossible to point at specific areas, where the failure had been greater (Betts 2007, 105). Goodman has argued that it had been inconceivable that the United States would have had to have faced a surprise along the lines of Pearl Harbor, when it had had thirteen intelligence agencies, with a budget of more than $30 trillion, to have provided warning of intentions of an enemy attack (Goodman 2003).

Both intelligence and the president's security advisor must have given counterterrorism low priority; otherwise, it is difficult to understand why the National Security Council (NSC) had discussed terrorism prevention, for the first time, three months after the start of the Bush administration (Clarke 2004, 197-201). The intelligence community, which usually had worked according to Cold War models, had not implemented changes, nor had the administration (Zegart 2009, 35). Apparently, counterterrorism had been given high priority by the administration, a few years before 9/11. In 1995, Clinton issued a Presidential Decision Directive (Presidential Decision Directive, 35) that had defined intelligence's priorities. Counterterrorism had had a high priority in the US intelligence and its budget was doubled (Congressional Joint Inquiry, 46-48). According to both investigation commissions, the fact that there had been more intelligence had not led to increased effectiveness in preventing terrorism, because of structural problems within the American intelligence community and perhaps also because the terrorist threat had not been internalized. A discrepancy had been created between the instructions given and the intelligence situation in practice.

The CIA's image had been badly damaged in 1997, when the House Intelligence Committee, headed by Porter Goss, formerly a CIA official, issued its report, which criticized the organization's capabilities in every field, saying it had lacked the depth, breadth, and expertise necessary for following political, military, and economic developments around the globe. At the same time, Russ Travers, a senior Defense Intelligence Agency (DIA) officer, wrote an article for the organization's internal organ, in which he alerted his readers to the fact that the United States' intelligence capabilities had diminished. He had warned that the year was 2001 and fact-gathering had been collapsing under the load of available information and could no longer distinguish between important data and background noise. The quality of the organization's analyses was becoming, he said, more and more suspect. The data was available, but the agency had not understood their full significance. Travers said that, from the perspective of 2001, the intelligence failure had been inevitable (Traver 1997). In 1998, the CIA had had the opportunity to eliminate bin Laden, in Afghanistan, but it had been decided, at the highest level—apparently by the president himself—not to act, because it had been unclear to what extent the intelligence was reliable. According to Gary Schroen, who had been head of the CIA branch, in Pakistan, the United States apparently had missed a rare opportunity, and he testified to that, before the Commission (*9/11 Commission Report* 2004, 112).

After the attacks on the American embassies in Nairobi and Dar es-Salaam (1998)— which had been identified as having been carried out by al-Qaeda—Tenet, as head of the DCI, had instructed the intelligence community to give priority to counterterrorism. However, his instructions were not followed, and funds enabling their implementation had not been budgeted (*9/11 Commission Report* 2004, 341, 357; Hill 2002, 9-10). The attacks had been carried out one after the other and showed al-Qaeda's ability to execute simultaneous, coordinated attacks, which is what had happened later, in 9/11. As opposed to 9/11, in which there had been good, early intelligence, the attacks on the two embassies had been complete surprises and without warning, which shows the quality of the intelligence coverage of al-Qaeda.

Bin Laden had been well-known to the CIA because he had operated for it, in Afghanistan, against the Soviets in the 1980s. Once the Soviet Union left Afghanistan in 1989, bin Laden had turned his efforts to terrorist activities in various countries—like many who had fought against the Soviets—and bin Laden had made use of the experience he had gained in Afghanistan (Reeve 1999). When the Cold War ended, a wave of global jihad began, and the United States and its allies have been its main targets (Ibid, 4). Following that, asymmetrical clashes began with the participation of non-state players, who had threatened the countries (Treverton 2011). The new global terrorism had exploited the information revolution, gathering and transmitting information and communicating across borders; the information revolution had been the catalyst for political, secular, and religious outbreaks around the world (Neumann 2009, 2-5). Neumann had argued that al-Qaeda was a terrorist organization, based on the social network and its lack of a formal hierarchy, which had made monitoring it difficult (Neumann 2009, 153).

In 1991, bin Laden returned to Saudi Arabia; following the First Gulf War, he had begun preaching against the United States. After he was expelled from Saudi Arabia, he settled in Sudan. The CIA station in Sudan had monitored him, after it had been assessed that he and his followers had been liable to attack American targets abroad. Bin Laden later moved from Sudan to Afghanistan (Weinter 2009, 382-383). From Afghanistan, he had financed the training of young Muslims who had wanted to join the global jihad, and he had provided financial support for Islamic terrorist activities in various countries (Sageman 2008).

Another aspect of the lack of preparation for a possible terrorist attack in the United States was demonstrated by the FAA's conduct. As with the FAA, the lack of preparation had resulted from the lack of a belief that such an attack could take place. The FAA which, among other things, has been responsible for air travel security, had held a meeting in 1999 with agents from the NSA, including Richard Clarke, during which NSA agents had presented terrorist threats. However, the FAA had been unconvinced that there had been a significant threat and therefore had not allotted resources to strengthen security aboard planes (Pillar 2004). The FAA did not change its position, even though, before the attack, it had received significant information about possible aerial threats (Lichtblau 2005). The FAA's intelligence unit had had a scenario for an attempted plane hijack and suicide bombing attack, but the possibility had been rejected and no preparations had been made (*9/11 Commission Report* 2004, 344-345).

At the end of 1999, the CIA began to formulate a new strategy to apprehend bin Laden. The agency had joined Afghan fighter Ahmed Shah Masoud, who had worked for the CIA and had wanted to get rid of the Taliban and its allies and had wanted to attack bin Laden. However, the action had not been put forward because of CIA hesitation. In February 1999, the CIA had had an opportunity to assassinate bin Laden, which had not been authorized. President Clinton had been regularly briefed on the CIA plan to arrest bin Laden, but the feeling among CIA officers had been that the agency was not acting with determination, and that its problem had not been lack of resources, as Richard Clarke had claimed and had testified to, before the commission. The Congressional Intelligence Committees, which had been required, from time to time, to deal with the war on terrorism, had not given terrorism first place, in their reports, at the turn of the century, to the FBI (*9/11 Commission Report* 2004, 102-107). According to the commission report, one of the reasons had been the lack of experience and knowledge of the members of the Committees, when it had come to complex intelligence and classified information.

At a Congressional hearing for Robert Mueller, the new FBI director, on September 4, 2001, a week before the 9/11 attack, Mueller had been asked ninety-four questions. Only three had dealt with preparations for a terrorist attack, a sign of the low importance the subject had received when "hot" warnings had been given by both covert and open-source intelligence (Zegart 2005, 145). Before the 9/11 attack, approximately 80% of the intelligence community budget had been devoted to the Department of Defense. After the 9/11 attack, the intelligence community budget changed and 50% of it had been allotted to internal security (*9/11 Commission Report* 2004, 93, 391). Additionally, there also had been difficulties dealing with terrorism in the United States because of the sensitivity of the issue of civil rights, but that had not been the reason for the FBI's difficulties, and the commission had not indicated it as a problem that had influenced the agency's functioning (Naftali 2005). Following the Church Committee report of 1975, the FBI had had the authority to improve the monitoring of suspected terrorists inside the United States, but had not used it (Johnson 2008).

The FBI had lacked knowledge of terrorism, had had no expertise in counterterrorism and had given little importance to the issue. The agency had focused on bringing criminals to trial; it had not perceived of itself as being intelligence-driven and thus had not involved itself, much, in counterterrorist intelligence (Jeffreys-Jones 2007). After the attack, Louis Freeh, who had been the FBI director until a week before 9/11, had explained the problematic nature of the FBI's approach to counterterrorism. He said that they had dealt with terrorist threats to the United States as though they had been a matter a law enforcement, like dealing with organized crime or white-collar crime. Al-Qaeda had not been in the Sicilian mafia, he had said (Freeh 2005). It had taken the intelligence failure of 9/11 to understand that. The attack on the World Trade Center in 1993 and the information that had been presented by the commission indicate that the covert activity methods of the Islamic operatives in New Jersey and their contacts with al-Qaeda had not been sophisticated: they had made mistakes that could have led to the prevention of the 1993 attack. The commission gave a long list of examples that, had there been sufficient alertness, especially within the FBI, it would have been relatively easy to have identified the operatives who had planned the 9/11 attack before they had carried it out.

On October 12, 2000, the United States Navy destroyer USS Cole, which had been anchored in the Yemeni port of Aden, was attacked. The missiles that had fired at the Cole killed seventeen crew members. It very quickly became clear to American intelligence that al-Qaeda operatives had been behind the attack. After George Bush had won the 2000 election and before he was sworn in, CIA Director Tenet briefed him about bin Laden, but the issue had not yet achieved a high priority in the administration or the intelligence community (Clarke, interview by author, 2013). The FBI had not made an assessment of the terrorist threat to the continental United States; the most recent National Intelligence Estimate (NIE), dealing with al-Qaeda, had been made in 1997 (*9/11 Commission Report* 2004, 77).

At the end of 2000, Tenet said his organization had not sufficiently assessed bin Laden's strategic intentions. The commission had come to the conclusion that since the CIA had not issued a new NIE after 1997, and as no high-level administration deliberations had been held, the way that the United States had understood the threat had been limited (Ibid, 348). Clarke had criticized the new administration for its low awareness of terrorist threats, but his warnings went unheeded (Ibid, 348). As there had been information about al-Qaeda's intention to attack within the United States, the question, in retrospect, was whether the information had been mistakenly regarded as "noise," or whether there had been enough information so that a warning could have been issued. The fact that there had been no orderly assessment had been less significant, because intelligence agents could be expected to act according to the intelligence that they possessed, especially when it came to terrorism. The commission had asked how much information had to be collected in order to formulate an assessment and whether intelligence had been expected to do more than it could have done, especially if such an event never had happened before (Posner 2004). The commission had not accepted Clarke's position, saying that "It is crucial to find a way of routinizing, even bureaucratizing, the exercise of imagination" (*9/11 Commission Report* 2004, 344). As to using tools that would have improved assessment and preparation, including the use of scenarios, the commission had noted that possible scenarios for aerial terrorism had been considered, but that nothing had been done concerning them.

The suggestion to use scenarios had been made, not only for a possible attack and preparations for one, but had been given, very broadly, in a commission report that dealt with the lack of the FAA's security preparations (Ibid, 345). With the help of scenarios, it could have been possible to reach insights that might have led to a change in the approach to flight security.

A significant assessment of terrorist threats had been carried out by NSA, through the Counterterrorism Security Group, and by Richard Clarke, who had issued an alert at the time, but they were not enough to prevent the attack (Ibid, 348).

Clarke had been so frustrated by the lack of attention that the new Bush administration had paid to terrorist threats that he resigned from his post in June 2001, active October 1, 2001. The commission had noted the attention that had been paid to China and North Korea, and the situation that had prevailed under Clinton did not change under Bush (Ibid, 343). Posner had said that understanding the commitments and capabilities of the enemy was most important for preventing surprise attacks (Posner 2005, 77). Accordingly, there had been mistakes made, in the assessments of bin Laden and al-Qaeda, as the administration had believed that counterterrorism in the United States had been efficient (Ibid, 174). Diamond had had a similar opinion, which related to the mental difficulties that members of the intelligence community had, in changing their thinking and moving their efforts, from the Soviets to counterterrorism (Diamond 2008, 14).

It is possible that the lack of preventive intelligence activity, within the United States, on the eve of 9/11, had been the result of the conclusions of the Church (1975) and Pike (1975) Committees, which had focused on improving internal security and had limited the intelligence activity within the country. After 1975, there had been almost no internal security activity (*Church Committee Reports* 1975). There also had been a problem with the concept of counterterrorism activity, since preventive intelligence in the United States, which had been carried out by the FBI, had been influenced too much by legal considerations that sometimes conflicted with the needs of intelligence work and its efficiency. The commission (*9/11 Commission Report* 2004, 72-73) also related to that and criticized the fact that too much attention had been given to the legal aspects of counterterrorism (Strasser 2004). The problems of interagency cooperation, which the commission discussed at length, were critical because the CIA had not reported to the FBI about the entrance, into the United States, of people who had been suspected of terrorist activity. On the other hand, the problems of the lack of internal FBI cooperation had to be solved by the FBI, itself. The lack of coordination and mutual intelligence transmission had been prominent when information had begun arriving, about suspects who had learned to fly at various flight schools inside the country—as this information had not been synthesized into any picture of a threat. For example, investigations had been carried out, separately, in Arizona and Minnesota, but the information which had been received by these states, from various offices in the United States, had not been made into a comprehensive picture at FBI headquarters in Washington (Farmer 2009, 77-79).

In 2000, the FBI began a program for improving its counterterrorism intelligence capabilities, which had been distributed to all fifty-six regional offices. However, no substantial change was made before 9/11, for several reasons, including the fact that the agency's rewards program had continued giving priority to trying suspects and not to bringing intelligence about terrorist suspects. In 2001, only sixty-five agents had dealt with counterterrorism (Zegart 2005, 5; 19). On September 11, 2001, only twenty FBI agents dealt with preventing al-Qaeda terrorist activity (Thompson 2004). Thus, there had been a gap between the instructions issued and the actual practice, which had not changed, even though there had been information about suspects currently in the United States, information that had not passed between the FBI and the CIA.

Terrorist threats had not been an issue in the presidential campaign of 2000, and Congress and the media also had paid no attention to them (*9/11 Commission Report* 2004, 341). A few months after the Bush administration took office, in May 2001, Condoleezza Rice, the director of the NSA, had asked Richard Clarke to prepare presidential guidelines for anti-al-Qaeda activities, including a range of offensive activities, but nothing happened before 9/11 (Ibid, 202-205). Clarke had been dissatisfied with the actions taken against al-Qaeda, as he had been dissatisfied with the actions during the Clinton administration (Ibid, 192-197) and saw that there would be no change. Despairing of the lack of activity against terrorist organizations, Clarke had said that he had proposed to change his role and deal with defensive activities, especially in the realm of cyber security after (Ibid, Clarke 2004). The commission (*9/11 Commission Report* 2004, 213) had understood his frustration at not having managed, over a period of years, to convince the administration of the importance of changing its focus toward al-Qaeda and of creating better cooperation between the CIA and FBI (Ibid, 210). Clarke had been in a position to compare the Clinton administration, which had had a belligerent stance toward al-Qaeda, with the Bush administration, and he often had criticized Bush, which was evident in his testimony before the commission. Clarke clashed with Louis Freeh, the FBI director, after Clarke had claimed that the FBI had not fulfilled its role in preventing terrorism.

On September 4, a week before the attack, Clarke wrote to Rice to complain that the actions he had proposed had not been implemented. He had warned that a catastrophe was coming (Ibid, 213). What he had said had not been accepted, and the director of the FBI disputed his views, claiming Clarke had been inventing facts, including conversations allegedly held with high-ranking decision makers in the American administration (Freeh 2005, 297-300). At the same time, activities that had been planned by the Department of Defense had been conducted, but they had been aggressive, in that they had been meant to attack al-Qaeda in Afghanistan and not to prevent an attack in the United States (Ibid 205-209). No attention had been paid to making preparations for a terrorist attack inside the country. There had been great disappointment because, after the attack on the USS Cole, in October 2000, there had been no American response. The Clinton administration, which was about to come to an end, had been busy with the Israel-Palestinian Authority negotiations (*9/11 Commission Report* 2004, 192-195). The new Bush administration had wanted retaliation to be part of an overall strategy. Clarke expressed his deep disappointment at the lack of action, when testifying before the commission (Ibid, 192-197). However, the chance that retaliation would have changed al-Qaeda's plan to attack the United States apparently was very small.

Teams in the NSA, CIA, FBI, the State Department, and the Department of Defense that had been dealing with the war on terrorism remained, in place, after the Bush administration took power, which ensured continuity. However, Condoleezza Rice, who had been national security advisor, had not permitted Clarke to report to her personally, and that complicated the system even more, when it came to making decisions (Ibid, 198-200). The activity against al-Qaeda had focused on Afghanistan, although there had been information about its intent to attack the United States (Ibid, 204-205).

The commission did not absolve Congress of responsibility for the intelligence failure that had led to 9/11. It said sternly that Congress had not recognized the structural weakness of the intelligence community, adding that Congress, and the administration as well, had reacted only to international terrorism as a threat to America's national security. In addition, according to the commission, bin Laden's threats had not been brought forward by Congress. The commission noted that fourteen different Congressional testimonies related to dealing with terrorist threats and that only a minor effort had been made to create an integrated action. It added that the issue of terrorism had been of second or third priority in the Congressional committees that had dealt with national security (Ibid 102-107). It did not hesitate to accuse the Congress of having ignored the issue, after not having made sure, between 1993 and 2001, that its recommendations had been implemented (Ibid 119). The commission concluded by saying that the United States needed a strong, stable intelligence community that would support America's vision and leadership. The commission summed up the faults that had led to the 9/11 attack: "imagination, policy, capabilities, and management" (*9/11 Commission Report* 2004, 339).

Regarding imagination, the commission had concluded that intelligence had known of an al-Qaeda threat, but had not tried to understand it or comprehend its nature. No use had been made of various tools, for example, scenarios, to better understand the threat (*9/11 Commission Report* 2004, Executive Summary, 10).

Regarding Policy, it had concluded that the policy of the administration leadership had been to minimize the importance of a terrorist threat, and therefore no requests had been made for updated assessments on al-Qaeda (Ibid, 11).

Regarding capabilities, it had concluded that the administration had not used its capabilities to the fullest, to prevent the attack. For example, the Department of Defense and the DIA had not been involved at all (Ibid, 11, 14, 23, 25).

Regarding management, the commission had concluded that the intelligence community's lack of sharing of information and a lack of intelligence cycle activities had created the lack of preparedness for terrorist attacks. The administration also had not been involved in allotting additional resources and determining priorities (Ibid, 12).

REASONS FOR THE INTELLIGENCE FAILURE

Collection Capabilities

Two investigatory committees determined that there had been no lack of intelligence and that the United States had been in possession of precise information, even for the date of an attack on American soil. Richard Clarke had said that, as part of his position as advisor for the war on terrorism, the White House had been briefed daily with intelligence about al-Qaeda's intentions (Clarke, interview by author, 2013). About 90% of the information had been from the NSA and about 10% from the CIA. Clarke added that, according to the information received, the NSA had had excellent coverage of bin Laden's communications system and had been aware of his plans. Nevertheless, an emergency situation had not been declared and no preparations had been made for an attack. The commission determined that the administration and intelligence community had thought that an attack would be carried out inside the country, but they had not known where or when (*9/11 Commission Report* 2004, 254-263). In addition, there had been insufficient open-source intelligence (OSINT) regarding al-Qaeda in the CIA and FBI, and additional information could have contributed to understanding bin Laden's intention. There had not been enough to influence the assessment of the overall picture. The FBI had not collected OSINT on al-Qaeda nor on his connections, inside the United States, because its agents had been unaware of the importance of OSINT and of gathering information from Islamic websites (Paz 2013). The possible contribution of OSINT can be seen by the following: at the end of the 1990s, the United States Army was handed an OSINT project for terrorism called "Able Danger." Its analysts discovered the name of Muhammad Atta, a prominent al-Qaeda operative who, according to the information collected, had been in the United States at the time (in retrospect, it was discovered that he had headed the 9/11 attack). Their findings had been presented to the Army and the NSA, but nothing had been done with them. For an unaccountable reason, the commission did not relate to the issue (McCarthy 2005; Rosen 2005). If the information had been processed by the intelligence community, the attack might possibly have been prevented. The commission had not gone into details about OSINT but had noted the need to improve its use, as the commission on the Roles and Capabilities of the US Intelligence Community (Aspin-Brown Commission) had done in 1996, whose conclusions also had not been implemented (Aspin-Brown Commission 1996, 88). The commission had presented a suggestion for establishing an OSINT center inside the CIA and had said that it was of great importance (*9/11 Commission Report* 2004, 413). According to the commission of inquiry that had been appointed to deal with weapons of mass destruction (WMD), in Iraq (WMD Commission 2005), the conclusions of the 9/11 Commission, regarding using OSINT had not been implemented (Gibson 2014). The instructions that had been given by the director of national intelligence, in 2006, regarding OSINT, had met with difficulties, when it came to implementing them (George and Bruce 2008).

Since the threat had come from within the United States, there had been no human sources of intelligence (HUMINT) that could have contributed to preventing the attack, according to the FBI. An analysis of the information in the hands of the FBI had indicated that no effort had been made to recruit HUMINT sources, who would have reported on the suspects in the flight schools. The FBI had not believed that a terrorist attack would be carried out from inside the country and had given low priority to methodological intelligence actions. The commission was very critical of the FBI, saying it had had a risk-averse culture. In other words, the FBI's intelligence operations had not been carried out correctly; in fact, it had transferred analysts, who had dealt with intelligence, to the problem of drugs (*9/11 Commission Report* 2004, 76-77).

It can be assumed that if there had been better cooperation within the intelligence community, and if the CIA had transmitted to the FBI the information it had had about some of the suspects, such as Mohammed Atta, it would have been possible to focus prevention efforts and to have improved intelligence quality. The main reason that the FBI had not tried to recruit sources that would have assisted in surveilling the suspects was that its orientation was limited and had not been familiar with Islamic matters. In its attempts toward preventing possible al-Qaeda activity inside the United States, the FBI's activity had been marginal and had not been focused on identifying possible suspects. The commission determined that the intelligence community had had important information about al-Qaeda's intentions to operate within the United States, and there had been no awareness of other tools that the FBI could have used. An example of the FBI's poor professionalism had been its arrest of Ahmed Ressam, an al-Qaeda operative, who had been accused of an attempt to attack Los Angeles' international airport at the end of December 1999. Ressam was sentenced to twenty-two years in prison and he cooperated with his interrogators, giving them valuable information about al-Qaeda's intentions to carry out an attack inside the United States (O'Malley 2006). He told the FBI that he knew, because of what he had heard during training in Afghanistan, that al-Qaeda had been planning to use planes to attack the United States. That information had not been given to the CIA which, at the time, had collected information that two al-Qaeda operatives were currently in California. It can be assumed that if the CIA and FBI information had intersected, the chances that an assessment of a threat from al-Qaeda inside the United States would have been more likely. In July 2001, an FBI agent in Arizona noted that Islamic suspects had been learning how to fly at flight schools in the state. He had recommended that action be taken against them, but he never heard back from FBI headquarters, in Washington (Thompson 2004, 23; Congressional Joint Inquiry 2002, 20-21), and the event had been filed as "routine" (Farmer 209, 56). If the information from Ressam had been joined to the information that the CIA already had had, it is reasonable to assume that the matter would have been given a higher priority.

At the time, counterintelligence activity in the FBI had been marginal, and until the 9/11 attack, the agency had made no changes, such as in an increase in resources and manpower, following the lessons that had been learned from the attack on the World Trade Center, in 1993 (*9/11 Commission Report* 2004, 76-77). The commission stated that the administration's ability to collect information inside the United States and to share it with the intelligence and law enforcement agencies had not been priorities, before the 9/11 attack (*9/11 Commission Report* 2004, 238).

The 9/11 Commission had focused its criticism on the CIA and the NSA, particularly on the lack of cooperation between them and with other intelligence agencies. CIA collection officers, who had been dealing with al-Qaeda, had not agreed to being directed by the CIA's investigation branch, toward key intelligence topics, claiming that people who sat in offices had not understood the problems of fieldwork. Clarke (interview by author, 2013) argued that the FBI needed to investigate the possibility that, in that situation, it could have prevented the attack. The commission criticized the CIA, as well, for not having focused sufficiently on specific terrorists and for having spent too much time covering territories, instead of personally monitoring terrorists and searching for them (*9/11 Commission Report* 2004, 268). The criticism had been directed not only at the lack of information-sharing, which the commission had referred to as, "the wall"—to them, the most serious problem—but at the 'professionalism"of the activity of the CIA and FBI (*9/11 Commission Report* 2004, 78-80).

Parker and Stern (Parker and Stern 2002, 601-603) had identified three main reasons for the intelligence failure, and none of them had involved a lack of information. The reasons that they had identified were psychological, organizational, and political. In discussing the psychological aspect of assessing a threat, they had related to over-confidence, underestimation of the enemy, and wishful thinking that nothing would happen (Parker and Stern 2002). In discussing the organizational aspect, they had claimed that the organizations accompanying intelligence activities, at the administrative level, had not correctly examined the intelligence and the threats and had not instructed intelligence as to the proper orders of priorities. In discussing the political reasons, they had argued that there had been a failure of the political leadership, to interest themselves or to give instructions on matters of importance.

In the years before 2001, the CIA, FBI, and NSA had amassed a great deal of information about the terrorists who later would participate in the 9/11 attack, and also about bin Laden and al-Qaeda. The problem was that, not only did the matter not have a sufficiently high priority, but there had been no information sharing, which could have made it possible for the intelligence organizations to have focused attention on the right target and thus have improved the quality of the intelligence. There also had been a language problem for translating open-source information and other material. The CIA had not translated this information, at all, or not in time; however, this had not strongly influenced the chances of preventing the attack. The commission had not related to information-collecting as a critical problem, but noted that it was necessary to improve HUMINT and to recruit and train speakers of foreign languages. Dahl argued that collection had not been exhaustive and was insufficiently focused, and therefore it had become difficult to issue a warning (Dahl 2013). The commission had not related to the fact that in prevention less research is necessary, but rather action should be taken based on information which can be used for a warning.

In addition to the information that American intelligence had possessed, regarding al-Qaeda's intentions to operate against the United States, inside the country, there had been specific information from an al-Qaeda operative named Khan, who had defected and had turned himself in, to the FBI, about a year before the 9/11 attack. He said that he had come to the United States to hijack a plane, and he revealed a detailed plan for the way that the attack would be carried out. He had been interrogated by the FBI, for three weeks, and the interrogators were of the opinion that he had been telling the truth, but it was decided to fly him back to London and to forget about him (Myers 2004). At a certain point, a few days before the date of the attack, the FBI had been very close to identifying some of the terrorists. An examination had revealed that two of them, Hazmi and Mihdhar, who had participated in the attack on the USS Cole, were currently in the United States. The Border Patrol had been instructed to report if they entered or left the country. On August 25, 2001, two weeks before the attack, the FBI had decided not to open an investigation into Mihdhar. It was unclear why. The commission noted that Hamzi apparently had been the number two commander of the 9/11 attack, and that Mohammed Atta was apparently number one (*9/11 Commission Report* 2004, 242). Both Hamzi and Mihdhar had been known to the CIA and should have been on the watch list for at least a year, before the attack, but their names had been added to it only a week before, at the request of a CIA agent, who had been stationed in the FBI office (CIA, OIG Report 2007,13). By that time, they already had been in the United States and had been prepared to carry out the attack.

The FBI had had information that in Minnesota, Zakarias Moussaoui had learned to fly a Boeing 747. His flight instructor had said that he had been more interested in takeoffs and flying than he had been in learning how to land. On August 17, 2001, he was detained, after a problem had been identified with his visa (O'Malley 2006). Apparently, he had visited Afghanistan and Pakistan and he had $32,000 in his bank account that he had not been able to explain. French intelligence had informed the FBI that Moussaoui had been known as an Islamic terrorist operative who had operated in Chechnya. He was interrogated but he told his interrogators nothing. The FBI could have increased the investigation to have included an examination of his computer, but they did not receive legal authorization and therefore the agency had not made a particular effort to examine it, apparently unconvinced of its suspiciousness.

The investigation was not concluded, although Moussaoui had been identified as an al-Qaeda operative. An FBI agent named Colleen Rowley had thought differently and at a certain point had said that, in her opinion, Moussaoui had been part of a plan to crash a hijacked plane into the Twin Towers in New York (Ibid). Before the attack, Rowley had warned that the investigation of Moussaoui had not been concluded and that he had to be interrogated about others who had been learning how to fly, but she was rebuffed by her superiors. After 9/11, she wrote a critical report (Rowley 2002), which she sent to FBI Director Mueller, elaborating on the FBI's failure to prevent the attack and had testified to that fact before the commission (*9/11 Commission Report* 2004, 540).

These instances had been America's intelligence opportunities to have prevented the attack, but they had received no organizational attention and no preventive steps had been taken, with the exception of the other opportunities noted above. The day before the attack, the NSA recorded transmissions from al-Qaeda operatives who had said, "The match is about to begin," and "Tomorrow is zero hour," but the transmissions were only deciphered the day after the attack, September 12 (Friedman 2005). More than thirty encrypted transmissions, with warnings about a terrorist attack inside the United States, had been recorded in the months before 9/11, but no alert had been given. They had been considered routine because no attack had followed them. It is not clear why they had not raised an alarm (Betts 2007, 107). The commission noted nine reports, from 1998, which had dealt with bin Laden's intention to attack inside the United States (*9/11 Commission Report* 2004, 324). The last was from August, stating that "bin Laden determined to strike in the US."

There had been problems with intelligence collection that had been noted by the commission (*9/11 Commission Report* 2004, 138) and by other sources (Congressional Joint Enquiry 202, 64; Wright 2006), but they had no decisive influence on the intelligence picture. The Congressional Community had determined, as its Number One Finding, that even though there had been clear, pinpointed intelligence, the American intelligence community would not have reported information relevant to the 9/11 attack, at the time, as it had not seen the accumulated importance of the intelligence (Congressional Joint Inquiry 2002, xi).

It is clear, from the above discussion, which has presented the conclusions reached by two inquiry commissions and several researchers, that there had been no lack of information about an upcoming al-Qaeda attack. Issues in intelligence collection and the lack of intelligence had not been the main reasons for the intelligence failure. The intelligence collection system had operated properly and had provided information, from which a warning could have been prepared, about an al-Qaeda threat of an attack in the United States. The intelligence target had been identified and had been known to the intelligence community.

Noisy Work Environment

There had been a great deal of information, some of which had indicated an attack inside the United States and some indicating attacks on American installations around the globe. There also had been conflicting information that attacks would not be carried out, because of internal al-Qaeda objections. On the other hand, there had been information that bin Laden had decided to attack. The information environment had indicated al-Qaeda's intention, based on intelligence from American intelligence collection agencies. Apparently al-Qaeda had not tried to hide its intentions to continue operating against the United States: the information had arrived from the mass media, and in most instances, from the publication of information initiated by al-Qaeda.

According to the open-source information, in 1996 and 1998, bin Laden had issued two fatwas justifying an al-Qaeda declaration of war against the United States, accusing it of killing a million Muslims around the globe, including 400,000 children (Freeman 2012). Clarke noted that he had received valuable information daily, in most instances from the NSA and also from the CIA, adding that his analysts and those of the CIA had correctly interpreted bin Laden's intentions. Thus, the failure had been that the fact had not been assimilated that an attack was going to be carried out against the United States. There had been no assessment of where it would occur, whether inside the United States or against its interests abroad. This was in spite of the fact that bin Laden had threatened that he would attack the United States. Intelligence had not been taken into consideration—information that had come from the FBI, after the investigation of al-Qaeda operatives Ahmed Ressam and Niaz Khan, along with information about flying lessons in the United States. On September 4, the week before the attack, Clarke wrote to Rice, complaining that the measures that he had recommended had not been implemented. He warned that a catastrophe was approaching (Clarke 2004, 213). His warning was not accepted and no action was taken.

Gary Schroen, who had headed the CIA office in Pakistan, claimed, both in testimony to the commission and in an interview he had given, at the end of 1999, that the CIA had begun to formulate a strategy with one aim in view: to apprehend bin Laden (*9/11 Commission Report* 2004, 112-114; Schroen 2006). Thus, less emphasis had been placed on monitoring possible threats that bin Laden had made, against and inside the United States. In 1997, DIA agent Travers had warned that the collection of facts was collapsing under the weight of accessible information, and it was no longer possible to distinguish between important facts and background noise. The quality of the analyses, he said, had become increasingly suspect, and the data were there, but they could not fully appreciate their importance, an intelligence failure had been unavoidable (Travers 1997).

Part of the noisy information environment had been caused by the very large number of targets and items of interest that the intelligence community had had to deal with, especially the NSA. The Congressional Joint Inquiry had noted about 1,500 targets and 200,000 items of interest, not necessarily ordered in terms of priority. According to the commission, there had been no one list that included the information about the terrorists who should have been focused on (Congressional Joint Inquiry 2002, 497). The FBI had used almost no SIGINT in dealing with local targets. The weight of intelligence analysis bodies, in directing items of interest in relation to al-Qaeda, had been low. Responsibility had been more in the hands of the units inside the CIA, which had dealt with operational coverage of al-Qaeda. Integrating information from the CIA, NSA, and FBI had been carried out, personally, by Richard Clarke, of the NSA (Clarke 2013). The assessment bodies had found it difficult to help in focusing the effort on counterterrorism. Clarke testified that the White House (meaning the NSA) had never instructed the intelligence community, regarding items of interest, and had left the intelligence community to decide for itself (*9/11 Commission Report* 2004, 455-457, 470-471). The commission noted that there had been serious faults in all parts of the intelligence cycle and, as a result, no alert had been given (*9/11 Commission Report* 2004, 343-344).

It can be concluded that an important cause of the intelligence failure had been the difficulty in assessing intelligence, due to the large quantity of information, which at least partially contradicted itself, regarding the question of where al-Qaeda would attack. However, the intelligence possessed by the American intelligence community could have enabled it to assess that bin Laden would attack inside the United States, after he had carried out successful attacks on American targets abroad.

Human Failures

The commission determined that the American intelligence community had failed to read the signs indicating the coming attack (*9/11 Commission Report* 2004, 343-344). As a result, the correct preparations had not been made for receiving the intelligence that had arrived from outside the United States (which had been the responsibility of the CIA) and there had not been cooperation in preventing an attack inside the country (which had been the responsibility of the FBI) (Ibid, 258, 263). In addition, when it came to the need of issuing a warning about an attack that would occur in a short time, there had been a problem with the way the threat had been perceived and the way its significance had been assimilated. The essence of intelligence agencies' activities should have been to provide a warning, but this never happened. That was evident in the testimony to the commission of CIA Director Tenet, who had said that they had assumed that intelligence would continue functioning and would warn of an attack, as it had done in the previous instance (Ibid, 428).

One of the important findings of the two inquiry commissions had been the lack of imagination on the part of intelligence analysts, which had caused them to fail in their assessment of the threat. That had been a serious criticism of the human factor in American intelligence. Clarke said that about a week before the attack, the United States had not decided whether al-Qaeda was a serious threat (Clarke 2004, 213). According to the commission, al-Qaeda had not been assessed as a significant threat demanding broad offensive activity against it, and the focus had been mainly on the use of drones to kill bin Laden. The order to kill bin Laden was waiting for Bush's signature, when the 9/11 attack took place (*9/11 Commission Report*.Final Report, Executive Summary 2004, 6).

The commission had noted examples of plans for hijacking planes and flying them to strategic targets, which had taken place, around the world, before 9/11, and it had wondered why the matter had not been discussed, as one of al-Qaeda's methods, especially in view of the information that had been received. The commission regarded it as a human failure, primarily of the analysts (*9/11 Commission Report* 2004, 128-130). The commission also had criticized the intelligence analysts' inability to "connect the dots," as a human failure, as they had been responsible for creating a picture of the threat and presenting it to the decision makers (Ibid, 408). Jones and Silberzahn claimed that one of the problems of American intelligence had been the CIA's perception of bin Laden, manifested by their scorning of him, because of his external appearance, and the fact that he had lived in caves. That contributed to the analysts' underestimating of his capabilities, which had been an important factor in the surprise caused by the attack (Jones and Silberzahn 2013, 201-202). They noted that the way that "the Other" is perceived significantly influences how he and his ability to implement his intentions to attack are evaluated; therefore, to a great extent, the surprise had been the result of the inability to understand information, and not only the information existing about the Other. The intelligence failure is regarded not only as a problem of intelligence work, but also of the general difficulty in analyzing information and in creating a clear picture in complex situations, skills that are also relevant to the field of business (Lundberg 2002).

The FBI had given the issue of studying al-Qaeda low priority, and only two analysts had dealt with it. At a time when the CIA had focused on monitoring al-Qaeda's activity and threats, the FBI should have identified the covert activity inside the United States, as it had had information about it. There had been neither coordination nor integration of the threats beyond the United States' borders (*9/11 Commission Report* 2004, 258-263). If that had been done, it would have been possible to have identified the al-Qaeda operatives who had been in the United States, preparing for a terrorist attack.

Why had the possibility of hijacking planes not been analyzed, especially after warnings had been received? The report on the CIA noted that if the intelligence community had been capable of analyzing the entire range of available information before the 9/11 attack, it could have assessed the developing threat, as early as the spring and summer of 2001 (CIA, OIG Report 2007).

The Comptroller of the CIA noted that there had been no strategic analysis performed by the relevant CIA unit, the DCI Counter Terrorist Center (CTC), before July 2001. The analysis in question had been of the possible methods of al-Qaeda, which the commission had already related to, and the commission determined that the CTC had not done its job (*9/11 Commission Report* 2004, 347). According to the findings, no strategic assessment of al-Qaeda had been carried out, there had been no update of information about bin Laden, no examination of the terrorists' ability to use hijacked planes and no assessment of the United States, as a target for terrorist activity (Ibid, 17018). Thompson noted that of the FBI's 27,000 agents, only 153 had dealt with analyzing terrorism (Thompson 2004, 107). In 1998, *Time* magazine published an article, saying that sources within the intelligence community had indicated both Washington and New York as possible targets for al-Qaeda. In addition, the article stated that Ramzi Yousef, who had planned the attack on the World Trade Center in 1993, said that if he had the means, he would attack it again (Waller 1998).

It is unclear to what extent the speeches given by bin Laden, between 1996 and 1998, had been studied, especially in view of the attacks on the embassies in Kenya and Tanzania. In 1995, Ramzi Yousef and his uncle, Khalid Sheikh Muhammad, had planned to hijack and then blow up twelve planes flying from Asia to the United States. The funding for the operation had come from Muhammad Jamal Khalifa, who was related to bin Laden (Congressional Joint Inquiry 2002, 128).The attack was prevented when Abdul Hakim Mourad was apprehended in the Philippines and confessed that one of the planes was supposed to have crashed into CIA headquarters in the United States (*9/11 Commission Report* 2004, 345). Before the G8 conference, in July 2001, a warning had been issued that bin Laden had planned to attack it from the air (Carroll 2001). A few years previously, a report had been prepared for the intelligence community, stating that a suicide bombing attack, using planes, had been planned for targets, such as CIA headquarters, the Pentagon, and the White House, but apparently it had been ignored (Hudson 1999). The commission noted that despite the information, no assessment had been made of how the terrorists could have carried out a suicide bombing attack from planes (*9/11 Commission Report* 2004, 347).

The commission gave a list of six possible ways the attack could have been prevented, between January and August 2001, based on information that already had been in the hands of the CIA and FBI (*9/11 Commission Report* 2004, 266-276). The commission claimed the dots had not been connected, because no one had been responsible for connecting them. There had been pieces of information, some of them important, but no overall assessment had been made to provide a warning. Given the conditions under which the intelligence organizations had worked, each one operating independently and with no cooperation from the others, the chances of establishing a good threat assessment had been low.

The commission noted that no effort had been made to issue warning signs before the attack (*9/11 Commission Report* 2004, 346-348). Efforts that could have been taken included financing, communications, monitoring targets for attacks, increasing manpower (to identify terrorists and their facilitators), technology (explosives), cover stories to hide the terrorists' identities, and operational security. The commission had been very critical that such warning signs had not been formulated, despite the great amount of available information (Ibid, 348).

The conclusion is that the analysts dealing with counterterrorism had not formulated an assessment of the strength of al-Qaeda's threat, especially for an attack inside the United States. The tendency had been to adhere to existing assessments and to ignore new material, so that good information about an attack inside the country had not been considered. Intelligence agencies had not understood that, to formulate a warning, counterterrorism would have needed more operational analysis, in conjunction with a fundamental analysis of the organizations, their important figures, their motives, intentions, and capabilities.

Organizational Difficulties and Faulty Cooperation

The CIA and FBI had had a long history of faulty cooperation (Goodman 2003), and the situation had not essentially changed before 9/11. It had been the result of activities concerning the Soviet Union and its satellites, especially the lack of capabilities of the rival agency, which had led to strict compartmentalization. The CIA had had no respect for the FBI, following the era of anti-Soviet espionage, and thus did not share information with it (*9/11 Commission Report* 2004, 268). Before 9/11, the FBI had been excluded from the CIA's distribution list of the daily security briefing, which had been presented to the president and which had contained threats about terrorist attacks targeting the United States. The FBI had had an outdated computer system and entering data had been problematic, as was using the information already in the system, making it difficult for the FBI to function (FBI 2004). In 2003, an advanced computer system replaced the old one (*9/11 Commission Report* 2004, 76-77), but it was still not up to the demands placed on it (Eggen and Witte 2006). The FBI had suffered from over-focusing on criminal activities at the expense of counterterrorist intelligence and had not learned the lessons of the attack on the World Trade Center in 1993 (Lichtblau and Piller 2002). Agents dealing with criminal activities were promoted more quickly than those dealing with intelligence, and therefore there had been no incentive to specialize in counterterrorist intelligence (Cumming and Masse 2004). The problems in the relations and cooperation between the FBI and the CIA had been well-known for many years, and most of the recommendations for repairing the situation had not been implemented. Congress had shown no interest in the issue, which did not bring either Senators or Representatives political advantage because they were not in the public eye (Zegart 2005). Beyond this, there had been a difference in culture between the two organizations. The CIA had had a culture of well-developed intelligence analysis, while the FBI had based its activity on law enforcement and bringing criminals to trial. The FBI had been influenced considerably by legal limitations and the recommendations of Congressional committees, especially those of Church and Pike. For example, the limitations that had been imposed on HUMINT had disrupted the development of mutual trust and cooperation between the two agencies.

There also had been a problem of lack of sharing with other administrative bodies, such as local police departments and organizations, like the FAA. Both the commission and the Congressional Joint Inquiry were very critical of that fact (Congressional Joint Inquiry 200d, xvii).

In the late 1990s, there were CIA liaison officers in the FBI and vice versa, but full cooperation and information-sharing had not developed (Clarke, interview by author, 2013). Relations between the agencies had been characterized by a high degree of mutual suspicion, but the CIA had been especially suspicious of the FBI. Several times, it had been Clarke who, when he had received information from one agency, personally had made sure to update the other. In addition, the 9/11 Commission had not been aware that the CIA had made the decision to not give information that it had had, about activities that had been conducted, outside of the United States, by some of the suspects. That only became known after a report by CIA internal affairs, in 2007. According to Clarke (interview by author, 2013), the decision not to share the information about known suspects with the FBI had been made by senior CIA personnel and was not a random mistake. The commission had noted instances in which there had been no sharing of information about terrorists who had been living in the United States before the attack (*9/11 Commission*

Report 2004, 139, 182). Implicit in this observation is that if information had been shared, the attack could have been prevented. At least three of the plane hijackers had been known to the American intelligence community as al-Qaeda operatives, and therefore they could have been refused entry into the country, if their names had been placed on the State Department's list of people who were to be denied entry. In this way, they could have been arrested inside the country. The cooperation between the CIA and NSA also had been faulty, especially in identifying suspects about whom information should be collected.

The commission had dedicated a great amount of space, in the report, to the lack of sharing of information, and said it was the worst fault of the events leading up to the 9/11 attack (*9/11 Commission Report* 2004; Garicano and Posner 2005; Zegart 2005, 3), and the Congressional Joint Committee Inquiry had made a similar comment (2002, 77). Civilian airport security had not been assessed because it was not known to be in danger. The situation changed after 9/11. The Department of Homeland Security was established, one of whose rocket-launchers was to coordinate the intelligence effort regarding terrorism (Graphia 2010). According to the analysis of the terrorist attack on the Boston Marathon, in 2012, the sharing of information was still incomplete (Werner 2013).

Faulty information-sharing also had been the result of the definition of areas of responsibility between external (CIA) and internal (FBI) intelligence. There had been no solution for instances in which the two areas were combined, such as for terrorists from abroad entering the United States (Treverton 2005). Senator Bob Graham, who had headed the Congressional committee, told Bob Schieffer, from CBS, that the lack of information-sharing had been one of the most significant problems in the event. He said that they had found that one of the main causes for the failure of the intelligence community had been that its analysts had not spoken to one another (CBS 2002). Richard Logger, who had sat on one of the committees, said that the culture of the intelligence agencies had been one of "firewalls," that is, compartmentalization (Congressional Joint Inquiry 2002, 307). Ben Gilad, who writes about blind spots in business, regards compartmentalization as one of the main reasons behind organizational blindness. He gives the compartmentalization before 9/11 as an example of what an organization should not do (Gilad 2004, 253).

There had been problems at every stage of the intelligence cycle, but regarding the issue of distribution and sharing of information, the problems had been particularly difficult: after 1997, the NIE had not prepared an updated report on al-Qaeda, despite intelligence reports which had been routinely distributed. According to Zegart, there had been at least twelve opportunities to prevent the 9/11 attack, but various problems interfered, including an incorrect assessment of the force of the attack, the lack of operational information, the lack of an overall assessment, and problems of cooperation with other agencies (Zegart 2007). Tenet, as DCI and CIA director, claimed in their testimony, that there had been a financial problem and that they had not succeeded in acquiring a greater budget for counterterrorism (*9/11 Commission Report* 2004, 90-91).

The commission had criticized the lack of cooperation within the American intelligence community (Ibid, 353) and had determined that there was a need for a complete overhaul of information-sharing. Its recommendation was that the "need-to-know" approach had to be changed to "need-to-share" (*9/11 Commission Report*. Final Report, Executive Summary 2004, 24); this was a revolution in the intelligence approach, which had always been based on almost obsessive compartmentalization.

In 2004, Congress passed the Intelligence Reform and Terrorism Prevention Act as part of the reform of American intelligence, which included improvement in cooperation (IRTPA 2004). The law also broadened the possibilities of counterterrorism intelligence inside the United States. Since the National Security Act of 1947, it had been difficult to carry out intelligence activities inside the United States; and now, it has been permissible to act inside the country, to prevent terrorism, with no relation to the geographic location of the source of the threat.

According to Clarke, one of the reasons that the attack had not been prevented had been the FBI's organizational difficulty, as it had not allotted sufficient manpower, despite instructions received after the attack on the World Trade Center in 1993 (Clarke, interview by author, 2013). After 9/11, an organizational change was effected in the FBI and counterterrorism units were established, and the matter was given a high priority. In Clarke's opinion, this should have been done before 9/11. The commission also noted the legal problems preventing cooperation, inside the United States, between intelligence and law enforcement, but their influence on the effectiveness of the effort to prevent the attack had not been significant (*9/11 Commission Report* 2004, 79-80, 328).

The commission also related to the FAA's lack of preparations, saying that one of the problems had been that important information had been kept from the FAA (*9/11 Commission Report* 2004, 82-85), information that might have enabled it to prevent the attack (Ibid). Since the FAA had received no updated information, it had assumed that hijacking a plane was out of the question, and therefore had not developed indicators to predicting such an occurrence (*9/11 Commission Report* 2004, 344-346). Clarke's attempts to change the FAA's position, even at a time close to the attack, had had no effect, and no relevant scenarios had been carried out to examine preparedness (Ibid).

In the year before 9/11, the CIA and FBI had argued about Operation Foxden, which had been planned as a way to monitor telephone communications between al-Qaeda, in Afghanistan, and operatives in the United States (Cobain 2012). Only on September 8, 2001, three days before the attack, was a plan agreed on. According to Clarke, earlier cooperation would not have prevented the attack, since the relevant information had already been transmitted, and its main points were from NSA sources, not CIA.

Clearly, intelligence's contribution had not been exploited to the full, because of exaggerated compartmentalization and a lack of internal and interorganizational cooperation, which had made it difficult to formulate a full intelligence picture. Without an intelligence picture, it would have been difficult to have issued a warning to prevent the attack. That had been, perhaps, the worst failure which had kept the 9/11 attack from being prevented.

Interaction with the Decision Makers

The commission determined that the decision makers in the administration and in Congress had not internalized the fact that al-Qaeda had been, at that time, the significant threat to the United States (*9/11 Commission Report*. Final Report Executive [Summary 2005, 15]). They had paid little attention to the issue of terrorism, despite the information they had received on a regular basis. According to the commission, the intelligence community had not done its utmost to raise the awareness of Congress and the decision makers to the developing threat. The Congressional Commission was less critical of the Congress and the administration and far more critical of the intelligence organizations. While the commission also was critical of the lack of effort and attention that the Clinton administration had paid to preventing the attack, it largely criticized the Bush administration, which took over from Clinton, in January 2001. The commission determined that the decision makers and heads of intelligence had understood the threat but had done nothing to "institutionalize imagination," that is, to think together about what might happen and to develop tools to prepare for such an eventuality (*9/11 Commission Report* 2004, 339-360). There had been no cooperation between the heads of intelligence and the heads of the administration, in dealing with the threat, and no attempt had been made to prepare for what a terrorist attack against the United States would look like. The commission also determined that in the administration's assessment, there had been no threat from al-Qaeda. The administration also had not asked for assistance from the intelligence community, and had not insisted that the heads of the administration reveal what was bothering them regarding this threat or what they demanded of the intelligence community. After the attacks on the American embassies in Kenya and Tanzania, the heads of the Clinton administration had not demanded a strategic examination of the threat emanating from bin Laden. The heads of intelligence and of the administration had not worked in cooperation, and despite the fact that the heads of the administration had been briefed, on an ongoing basis, there had been almost no communal conceptualization or instruction for action (Gertz 2002). There had been no orderly conceptualization of a preferred way to act to thwart al-Qaeda. No use had been made of other administrative capabilities, such as the Department of Defense. The Department of Defense had been passive in operations against al-Qaeda because it had not been included.

Clarke noted that one of the greatest obstacles in preparing to prevent the attack had been that the new administration, including the new national security advisor, Condoleezza Rice, had not taken al-Qaeda threats seriously, had been passive, and had not made plans nor demands for dealing with the issue (Clarke, interview by author, 2013). In 2012, *The New York Times* revealed information about the briefing that President Bush had received on August 6, 2001, regarding a threat from bin Laden, and implicit in the report was that Bush had not given the information the serious consideration that it had deserved (Eichenwald 2001). The briefing was entitled, "Bin Laden Determined to Strike in the U.S." Eichenwald's claim has been verified by another source (Lichtblau and Sanger 2004). It was referred to only generally, by the commission, but it indicated a lack of cooperation between the new Bush administration and the intelligence community. According to Clarke, the relations between Bush and the CIA had been characterized by a mutual lack of trust (Clarke, interview by author, 2013). The new administration had claimed, to the commission, that it had not been aware of a bin Laden threat to the United States. The White House had been required by the commission to allow the publication of the report (partially and without details), which was done in April 2004, after pressure from the commission. Nevertheless, witnesses for the administration had minimized the importance of the CIA briefing and claimed that it was mainly a historical report which did not require any action from the administration or the president. The administration did not agree to make public other briefings the president had received on the matter. Eichenwald claimed that he had seen sections of the briefings and that they contained a clear picture of a threat. He said that, in May 2001, the president had received a report stating that "a group presently in the United States" had been planning a terrorist attack in the United States. In June 2001, the daily briefing that the president had received referred to an "imminent" attack, with the evaluation that its timing was not yet known.. Eichenwald stated that in conversations he had held with members of the Bush administration, that he was told that officials who had worked in the Pentagon mentioned that the CIA was being fooled by bin Laden. In response, the CIA prepared an assessment which was transmitted to the administration, stating that the bin Laden threat was genuine. According to the president's June 29, 2001, briefing, "The U.S. is not the target of a disinformation campaign by Usama bin Laden"; that is, bin Laden had planned to carry out in practice what he had said in public.

Eichenwald said that similar statements were repeated in later briefings, and the July 1, 2001, briefing stated that "the operation has been delayed, but will occur soon." On July 10, 2001, the CIA received information that al-Qaeda had been planning a large attack against the United States inside the country (Goldberg 2007; Weiner 2009). Tenet did not report the information directly to Bush and did not inform the entire administration, but rather reported it directly to Rice. That would indicate that a warning had not penetrated the consciousness of the heads of the intelligence community nor the White House. Eichenwald reported that, when Bush was briefed on an upcoming attack, on July 24, he had asked for more information about bin Laden and al-Qaeda and had then been given a detailed briefing on August 6, 2001.

Eichenwald added that after the 9/11 attack, members of the administration said that the president had not received specific information about when or where the attack would occur. The heads of the administration had given the attack a low profile and had not given instructions for any action. However, a suspect was caught at the airport in Orlando and deported to Saudi Arabia, and Moussaoui, who had been suspected of being in contact with bin Laden, was arrested in Minnesota, after learning how to fly, and his interrogation served to reinforce the suspicions against him. However, the dots had never been connected to al-Qaeda's intention to carry out an attack in the United States, and no scenario had been formulated about an attack using planes. The commission determined that the oversight of the Congressional committees of the intelligence community had been dysfunctional but, nevertheless, the proposals for change in the oversight were only partial (*9/11 Commission Report* 2004, 420 9/11). The same was noted by the Congressional Joint Inquiry (2002). The commissions related to the fact that Congress had not required the NSC to present a comprehensive strategy for the war on terrorism. It also had not required that the CIA prepare an updated report on al-Qaeda, to follow the 1997 report. In addition, the FBI had not been required to report on how it had been dealing with the problem of terrorism. No examination had been made of how decisions of previous commissions had been implemented, including the issue of information-sharing. The two commissions accused various government agencies, besides the intelligence community, and demanded stricter oversight of the intelligence community, but did not suggest how that would be done. Until at least 2005, there was no significant change in the relations between Congress and the administration, on the one hand, and the intelligence community on the other (Kean and Hamilton 2005).

Therefore, it can be concluded that the administration and Congress had not taken responsibility for the intelligence failure that had prevented the 9/11 attack from being carried out. The administration had had very little involvement in intelligence activities and had made do with general reports. In the case of the attack on the World Trade Center in 1993, the administration had tried to minimize its importance and perhaps had given the impression that it gave little importance to preventing terrorism that had targeted the United States itself. That changed, although not dramatically, after the attacks on the American embassies in 1998 and the attack on the USS Cole in 2000. It is possible that the relatively low priority that the Bush administration had given to counterterrorism had been influenced by how the intelligence community had related to terrorist threats and its preparations for thwarting them.

QUESTIONS DEALT WITH IN THIS TEST CASE

1. What were the intelligence assessments that had been made before the crisis?

   Despite the fact that the American intelligence agencies had had good information about al-Qaeda's intention to attack inside the United States, after it had attacked American installations and civilians abroad, no assessment had been made that an attack inside the United States would occur in the near future, and therefore no preparations had been made to prevent one. The focus had been on trying to hit bin Laden and his close associates, not on preventing a terrorist attack inside the United States.
2. What had been the signs indicating a coming crisis?

   American intelligence had had good information about bin Laden's intentions and clear signs, from both covert and open sources, that he had been planning an attack inside the United States. However, there had not been an organized assessment about his capabilities and the methods he might use. In the days before September 11, 2001, it had been assessed that an attack was close at hand, based on communications intelligence about an increase in the transmissions to and from bin Laden's headquarters. The attack should not have been a surprise.
3. Why had signs indicating the development of a threat, which had been visible over a long period of time, been assessed incorrectly?

   The commission had determined that there had been a great deal of information and signs that could have prevented the attack. The ruling assessment in the intelligence agencies had been that bin Laden would not attack inside the United States. It had been based on an analysis of his past activity and on the assessment that he had not had the operational capabilities to carry out such an attack. In addition, he had been on the run, after an attempt had been made to assassinate him. The American intelligence community had made no methodical assessment of the threat posed by bin Laden and al-Qaeda because of the lack of cooperation within the American intelligence community. Further, no use had been made of advanced tools, such as scenarios. The collection of OSINT had not been at a high level and had been based mainly on information that bin Laden himself had inserted into the global media. The new American administration had given a low priority to preventing terrorism and, therefore, Richard Clarke, senior advisor for the war on terrorism, resigned.

In any case, had there been other assessments, from people whose opinions carried weight, about the possibility of a serious crisis? What had led to the failure of the institutionalized assessments and the success of the alternative assessments?

Clarke had been one of the only people in the intelligence community who had not accepted the prevalent, institutionalized assessment. A few months before the attack, he had demanded an assessment from the FAA, claiming that terrorists would hijack a plane and use it for an attack. His opinion had been rejected. The commission had noted that warnings from CIA's Michael Scheuer also had been rejected; Scheuer had resigned before 2001. Since there had not been cooperation within the intelligence community and dealing with bin Laden's threats had been left exclusively to the CIA, there had been no way for other organizations to present different positions. The intelligence community had not even been exposed to intelligence about bin Laden's intentions. The FBI, which was supposed to have had a position on preventing terrorism inside the United States, had proceeded in an unprofessional manner and had not contributed to the prevention of the attack.

4. Had there been an intelligence failure and, if so, what was it?

Using the information that had been possessed by the American intelligence community, it would have been possible to have prevented the attack. With the exception of Richard Clarke and Michael Scheuer, the ruling concept in the intelligence community and the NSA had been that there would not be an al-Qaeda attack carried out inside the United States. The main intelligence failure had been that the terrorist operatives had not been identified, early on, when they had been learning how to fly in American flight schools. Had they been identified inside the United States, they would have been arrested or deported, and the attack would have been prevented. Counterterrorism had been in the hands of the FBI, which had claimed, in its testimony before the commission, that the CIA had blocked it from receiving information about a significant number of terrorists who had been in the country, which had therefore prevented them from thwarting the attack. However, the FBI had received information about the suspects from the flight schools, but it had not taken action. The intelligence failure had been the CIA's, which had not shared its information about the suspects with the FBI, and also the FBI's, which had not investigated its suspicions.

5. What was the significance of the failure?

   The intelligence failure had failed to prevent the September 11, 2001 attack, in which a total of 2,973 Americans were killed. The eventual result of the intelligence failure was that America went to war in Iraq and Afghanistan and remained there for years. American intelligence took global measures to catch and kill those who had planned the 9/11 attack and to prevent other terrorist attacks on American soil. The war on Islamic terrorism, in general, and on bin Laden, in particular, had become a key intelligence topic for American intelligence. In 2011, Osama bin Laden was killed in Pakistan.

6. How can the intelligence failure be explained?

   The intelligence failure had been a concentrated surprise that had led to the 9/11 attack on the United States. Even though bin Laden and al-Qaeda had been important targets for American intelligence, an incorrect assessment had been made of bin Laden's capabilities and intentions, regarding an attack inside the United States. This had been the main reason for the intelligence failure and why the attack had not been prevented.

7. How was the 9/11 attack different to previous types of surprises?

   The 9/11 attack was a concentrated surprise. While it was similar to other strategic surprises, in this instance it had been made by a terrorist organization that had been an intelligence target. In "ordinary" strategic surprises, the target usually had been the known military forces and/or decision makers of an enemy country.

   In the case of a concentrated surprise from a known enemy, it is theoretically easier, apparently, to identify the developing concentrated threat, since intelligence focuses its efforts on collecting evidence from the correct direction of the threats; if mistakes are made, they are usually in analyzing intentions and capabilities.

8. Factors Influencing the Intelligence Failure (table 6.1)?
9. Which tools had been used to try to prevent failure?

   American intelligence mainly had used covert collection, SIGINT, to discover al-Qaeda's intentions. The American security system had not used defensive tools, such as security and safety systems, inside the United States; no orderly warning had been received about an attack inside the country, even though intelligence had had information that could have been sufficient. The American legations around the globe had

Table 6.1 Factors that had Influenced the Surprise

Number	*Issue*	*Response*
1	Was the event routine?	No
2	Was it familiar from the past?	No
3	Had the threat been known?	Yes
4	Had the modus operandi been familiar?	No
5	Had there been a hand directing the surprise?	Yes
6	Had the information received been clear?	Yes
7	Had it been clear what had been intended?	Yes

Source: Avner Barnea 2020.

been on alert, because of previous attacks, but inside the United States, nothing had been done. The intelligence community had not acted to gain a better understanding of bin Laden's intentions, it had not exploited the intelligence that it had had, to the fullest, and it had not brought its information to the other agencies, which could have helped improve its analysis of the enemy's intentions.

10. Which tools could have been used to prevent the intelligence failure?

    Better use could have been made of intelligence by analyzing possible scenarios and measures that al-Qaeda might have employed. In this way, it could have been decided how to prevent an attack or how to reduce the chances that an attack would succeed. If other experts in the CIA beyond the small group dealing with al-Qaeda intelligence had been approached, then other assessments could have been reached, as to the likelihood of an attack. It is possible that sharing information among the various agencies within the intelligence community could have resulted in formulating a different picture, regarding the threat, and then efforts could have been made to prevent the attack. Using sophisticated information for link analysis could have led to identifying the terrorists, who already were inside the country and learning how to fly; this, in turn, could have led to identifying even more terrorists inside the United States, and to their arrest or deportation. It also could have been possible to improve intelligence work, especially that of the FBI, whose awareness of terrorism and level of professional knowledge about the issue had been low.

LESSONS IN THE FIELD OF INTELLIGENCE THAT WILL BE IMPLEMENTED IN THE FUTURE

The commission noted that the main factor for the failure had been the lack of imagination of the American intelligence community, which could have been related to the lack of using scenario analysis. The second most important failure had been the lack of cooperation within the intelligence community, which had been the result of an exaggerated culture of compartmentalization, as well as the beliefs of the people dealing with the issue. The commission had recommended that essential changes be made in cooperation, saying that "The system of 'need to know' should be replaced by a system of 'need to share'."

The direction instruction of the Intelligence Reform and Terrorism Prevention Act of 2004 (IRTPA), signed by the president in 2004, in the wake of the commission, had been to improve the work of the intelligence agencies, in conjunction with other relevant authorities, to prevent terrorism in the United States. The commission had recommended a change in the definition of the role and authority of the head of the intelligence community, the DNI. It also had been decided to upgrade the FBI's capabilities to prevent terrorism.

Chapter 7

Test Case: IBM

How Did One of the Largest Global Corporations Almost Collapse?

OVERVIEW

In 1992–1993, IBM, then one of the largest global corporations, had suffered enormous losses that had threatened its very existence. Beginning in the late 1980s, IBM had rapidly lost customers when new, fast-moving competitors had entered the market. The organic computer market then changed quickly. Instead of large towers, smaller computers with high levels of performance entered the market and provided solutions for a wide variety of organizations, both large and small, which made it difficult for IBM to compete. According to Gerstner, the CEO who saved IBM, the company had been dying (Gerstner 2014).

Despite the obvious changes that had occurred in the computer world, at the end of the 1980s, IBM's management had been surprised by the company's terrible condition. IBM had ruled the computer market for decades and suddenly it was seeing fundamental changes whose consequences its leadership had not envisioned. Although IBM had conducted competitive intelligence, it had received no warning about the changes in the market and their significance.

In 1990, IBM had been the second most profitable company in the world. Between 1991 and 1993, it had lost about $14 billion, its stock had fallen by 70%, its market value had fallen from $105 billion to about $32 billion, and it was on the brink of declaring bankruptcy. The company's board of directors decided to appoint a new CEO, Louis Gerstner, who had not come from the world of computers but had had experience in rescuing large companies. Within a few years, Gerstner had changed IBM's business strategy and had restored the company's success. *Time* Magazine wrote that IBM was a notable example of a company that had faced difficulties after it had become a prisoner of its basic assumptions: information had been filtered before it had reached management and it had been solving problems of the past and not the present, as it had been misreading the competitive environment and its influences (Teece 2007, 132).

IBM had been surprised to find itself in a relatively inferior position vis-à-vis its competitors, mainly Microsoft and Intel. This had been a concentrated surprise because it had been the result of known competition and technological developments, but the company had not prepared itself for the threat, as has happened in many strategic surprises. However, IBM's business knowledge and experience, its correct (although tardy) identification of the key intelligence topics, such as competitors, customers, and technology, and its openness to solutions from the business world had aided it in recovering from its terminal state.

Within a few years, IBM had gone from a company on the brink of bankruptcy to one that was profitable and growing. So impressed was Howard Friedman, who had written about the difficult economic situation in the United States and the difficulties of dealing with global competition, that he noted that the situation in the United States had been similar to that of IBM, at the beginning of the 1990s (Friedman 2012).

Friedman went on to observe that once a new CEO arrived on the scene, IBM began studying its competitors and using correct competitive intelligence to correctly analyze the strengths and weaknesses of its competitors to identify the needs of its customers and those situations in which IBM had had an advantage—namely, for large and mid-sized companies that were in need of high-quality computer services. IBM rapidly changed its strategy after the losses it had suffered and became, again, one of the most profitable companies in the United States. Within a few years, it returned to lead the field of computer services (Friedman 2012, 5, 6).

IBM CEO Gerstner told *The New York Times* that what had happened was not an act of God. Very simply, other people had poached IBM's customers (Lohr 1994). IBM had been surprised by the increasingly fierce competition and had not known how to combat it, especially in view of the fact that it had had no previous experience in conducting business activities in a complex, competitive environment. Calof (2014) had regarded the issue as an intelligence failure, not only in failing to understand the competition but in not understanding IBM's customers, and he had noted that the two were interconnected.

MILESTONES IN IBM'S DEVELOPMENT

IBM's roots go back to the early twentieth century, when Thomas Watson, Sr., combined a number of small companies to create International Business

Machines (IBM). The company had been a pioneer in computing and had begun by developing calculators for the business world, after having won a contract for providing an information system for American national security, in the 1930s.

IBM's great leap forward came in the middle of the 1950s, when digital computers were being developed (Simmons 1988). In 1964, Watson initiated a new line of mainframe computers called the System/360, which had enjoyed immense popularity, until the middle of the 1980s. IBM had had no significant competition. In retrospect, the System/360 revolution had been similar to Microsoft's Windows revolution or the development and market penetration of the personal computer (PC). IBM had led the market for thirty years with no significant competitor. Like Microsoft in the 1980s and 1990s, it had provided technological improvements, which had given the market new capabilities and had changed the way society behaved. Like Microsoft several years later, IBM had controlled the market, and its earnings had been among the highest in the world and its brand one of the most powerful.

IBM System/360 computers, which had been introduced in the mid-1960s, not only had improved the performance of computers, but also their reliability and, in addition, the price dropped. The future seemed to be based on smart processors, and customers could upgrade their computers with relative ease, as well as the software that had been developed to operate them. The links to peripheral equipment, such as printers, tape drives, and punch-card readers, which had been compatible with the new computers that were being developed, were later made to be compatible with computers manufactured by other companies. Computer standardization had become established. That gave IBM, with its large market share and good reputation, a significant advantage over its competitors. Competitors had found it difficult to challenge IBM's improved technological capabilities and the strength of its sales.

Despite the fact that IBM had manufactured thousands of hardware and software products and sold services as well, basically the company had had one product, mainframes for organizations. They had been joined by a variety of other companies, all supporting the preservation of IMB's edge in the computer market.

IBM's growth had been impressive. Between 1956 and the middle of the 1980s, the company had grown at an average of 14% annually. Its yearly gross profit had been about 60%, and it had had 35% of the market. It had had competitors, but no other company had come close to IBM's marketing capability, its ability to develop new products, and its subsequent financial results.

Thus, IBM had developed and had expanded and in a business environment with little competition. It had led the information field with regard to technology, and its customers had become dependent on it. It had seemed that it would continue in the same way for many years. However, the company leadership slowly had begun to lose its focus on the external environment, since what had occurred in the competitive environment had not influenced IBM. A business culture had been created that had resulted from long years of controlling the market, and a system of technological excellence had been constructed around it. Its employees had enjoyed many benefits and results had improved every year. All of this had changed in the middle of the 1980s, with the increase in competitive companies, such as Fujitsu, which had begun attacking IBM's core markets by lowering prices and by introducing differentiation. A new situation had been created, with completely different rules of engagement and competition. IBM had had great difficulty in adapting to the new situation and had begun losing customers.

In the 1980s, and especially after John Akers had been appointed CEO, IBM almost never looked for other opportunities because its business model had been extremely successful and no need had been seen to change it (Gilad 2004, 231). Under Akers, IBM had failed to identify, in time, some of the changes that had been taking place at the end of the 1980s and the beginning of the 1990s and which had begun influencing the company's business results. There had been the rise of small computers, the entrance of PCs into the market, the entrance of Unix, which had been an open code program, the influence of an antitrust suit filed against IBM, and the rapid rise of Microsoft (operating systems) and Intel (processors), which had led to the swift development of competition, since they had sold their solutions to anyone who had wanted to buy.

With almost exclusive market control, IBM had been operating inefficiently; this had become apparent only when competition had developed, beginning in the 1980s, but particularly in 1989 and 1990 (Kahaner 1996, 98). Its main problem had been that customers, especially customers of minicomputers, had moved to the competition. IBM's main competitors had been Digital Equipment Corporation, Data General, Prime Computers, Computervision, Honeywell, HP, and Texas Instruments. IBM had had leading serious computers in the field of mainframes. However, minicomputers ruined mainframes' previous advantage and they gradually replaced mainframe computers.

In 1990, IBM's earnings and profits had begun to severely decline and investors had begun losing faith in the company, to the point that it was uncertain if IBM would be able to continue its operations. In 1990, IBM had been the second most profitable company in the world, with annual earnings of $69 billion, $6 billion of which had been profit. It had sometimes been called the largest company in the universe, and its future had looked promising. However, within the company, people had been aware that an organizational-structural change was necessary. CEO Akers had said that in April 1992, employees had not known how deep the company's financial trouble was. In 1991, for the first time in its history, IBM had lost $2.9 billion and it continued to lose money for the next two years. The public began calling it a dinosaur, and critics had claimed that it was arrogant, had ignored its customers, and its internal wars had damaged its capabilities.

The new situation in which the company had found itself had made management decide to split IBM into smaller companies to be able to better cope with the competition. The dilemma had been whether to split into seven or eight subsidiaries. No final decision had been made; this had been left to the new CEO (Nissanson 2013).

Management had decided to replace Akers, and in April 2013, Louis Gerstner became the new CEO. He had caused a business and organizational revolution by implementing a model he had used in the past (Gerstner 1973), and within a few years he had restored IBM to its previous status of world leader.

THE DIFFICULTIES ABOUT TO DEVELOP FOR IBM

One of the first signs that something had changed or was about to change was when the Department of Justice filed an antitrust suit against IBM, on January 31, 1969, the last day of the Johnson administration. The case against the company had been based on its having had become a monopoly in the market for the provision of computers to organizations, which violated Article Two of the Sherman Antitrust Act. The suit was dropped thirteen years later, in 1982, but until then IBM had been forced to operate under the threat of a federal liquidation order (Levy and Weizer 1985).

IBM's competitive advantage, which had lasted for many years, had influenced the way it had related to the competitive environment. Terms such as "market segment," "competitor/s," "competition," "to lead," and "to win" had been absent from the company's written materials and had not been mentioned in internal discussion (Gerstner 2002). They had not been part of the perception of either management or labor. However, in reality, the directors had fought one another in attempts to enlarge the company's market segment, and they had never had to look either to the right or to the left to identify what the competition was doing or what its intentions were. While IBM sales personnel had had good intelligence about the competition's products, it usually did not reach the company, as they usually kept it to themselves and had thought it was sufficient to have a technological advantage and a dominant position in the market to preserve its competitive edge. From the beginning, Gerstner had understood that this was insufficient (Utterback 2007).

One of the essential changes Gerstner had made, regarding competitive intelligence, was to convince the board of directors that instead of intelligence on products, which in any event was in the hands of the sales personnel, strategic competitive intelligence had to be collected and analyzed regarding trends in the markets where IBM operated. Gerstner also convinced the board that it was necessary to learn about the market by comparing IBM with its competitors and to decide how to deal with its most prominent market competitors. It had been a fundamental change in IBM's perception of competition (Gerstner 2004, 217-218; Gilad 2004, 115).

Contrary to general opinion, the threat to IBM had not come from PCs, a field in which IBM had been a pioneer, but rather from the development of Unix, an open operating system that had been led by companies such as HP and Sun. Unix had offered its customers an attractive economic alternative to IBM's mainframe products and prices. Within a short time, IBM had been "attacked" by developments in programming and peripherals from Sun, HP, Digital, SGI and others.

According to Gilad, for several years beginning at the end of the 1980s, IBM had operated with industry dissonance, meaning that its strategies had not been appropriate for its environment—but IBM had not understood that (Gilad 2004, 7). The basic assumptions of the directors had been inconsistent with the new situation: for example, some of IBM's products were no longer relevant, because competitors had provided alternative products, and some competitors had been aggressive and had captured market sectors. Thus, IBM had to compete with strong manufacturers of PCs and computers for small organizations. These were serious competitors and they had reduced IBM's earnings, but IBM failed to respond competitively, but rather had continued along its accustomed path.

When IBM finally had formulated its response to increasing competition, it made an important strategic mistake. Instead of improving cooperation among its various units, management had decided to divide the company into independent units, making each compete in its field. It had even been decided to formulate a plan to sell some of the smaller companies. The plan had been led by former CEO Akers, who had said that the company did not have to look to the future but rather had to solve problems as they arose; he claimed that the last thing that IBM had needed was vision. Akers had focused on performance, decisions, and simplifying systems for quick decisions, in order to prevent blockage (Charan and Colvin 1999). In fact, IBM's management did divide the company, but Gerstner canceled the plan during his first couple of days in office.

Only after Unix had expanded the activities of its operating system, causing an increase in competition and weakening IBM did PCs begin to influence IBM's business performance. IBM's failure in the PC field had been that it had not envisioned that personal computers would become part of the business and organization landscape and would also be used by individuals;

as a result, IBM had given PCs low priority. IBM had failed by not having assessed that PCs would threaten its core business and reduce its business market sector, despite the fact that IBM had been the first to develop PCs in the middle of the 1970s (Reimer 2009). IBM also had given control of the production of components it had developed to outside companies. For example, it had transferred its operating system to Microsoft and the development and manufacture of its processor to Intel. The result had been that Microsoft and Intel had grown rapidly and had helped the development of competition, while selling their products to IBM's competitors, as well. IBM had not expected this and had had no response. Microsoft and Intel's business activity had changed the computer market, making it very competitive. IBM had found itself in fierce competition with companies that previously had been either insignificant or had not existed, after the vendor of the operating system and processor—the computer's core—had provided the same solutions as IBM to its competitors.

The first PC that had sold in large quantities was the Commodore PET, in 1977. Later, the Apple II also was launched. At that point, IBM had not sensed any threat, because PCs had been meant for the home. At the beginning of the 1980s, a change occurred, and Commodore came out with a new computer and sold 17 million units. The Japanese company, NEC, also had produced a PC, which sold a similar number of units, as did Radio Shack. In 1983, IBM issued its XT PC, which had been better than anything else on the market, at the time, but it was late in appearing and was more expensive than competing models. At the same time, IBM compatible computers were being manufactured and sold at lower prices. However, IBM had not pushed the sale of its PC, lest it would damage earnings received from its mainframes, and also because it had not understood the potential of the PC market. Its focus had continued to be on mainframes. Meanwhile, IBM compatibles, based on Microsoft's operating system and on Intel processors, had been selling for lower prices. They were of the same quality as IBM PCs and they steadily improved. Apple began expanding with its Macintosh computers, which were very different from IBM compatibles. In the 1980s, sales of PCs had continued to climb and PCs began to be incorporated in business environments; new companies entered the rapidly growing market (Allen 2001).

IBM mainly had to compete with computers for organizations, from companies such as Digital (which had manufactured VAX computers) and Fujitsu, which had brought to the market minicomputers with strong capabilities and low prices, but it also had to compete on the PC front as well, with other competitors. By the mid-1980s, IBM had become very active in the PC field, as PCs had begun infiltrating business and private markets. Between 1984 and 1989, IBM's profits had grown rapidly, as the market had grown (Austin and Nolan 2000, 5). At the same time, IBM had begun feeling competition from the declining prices of the compatibles, which had reduced IBM's market segment and therefore its profits. Beginning in 1994, IBM saw losses (Thomas and Kanji 2004).

Before the crisis, IBM had operated without paying attention to what had been happening around it, regarding both competitors and customers. Many people in the company had had information, but it never had reached the management level; or, if it had, management had tended not to listen. Important changes had begun occurring, regarding both organizational and PCs, but the company had continued with the same strategy it had been using for years. competitors entered the market, and at the time IBM did not want to enter the minicomputer market, lest it impinge on its main field, the mainframes (Gerstner 2014).

In 1981, IBM launched its own PC, which sold successfully but had been considered a stepchild next to its large, organizational computers. IBM had not sold the PC via its sales force, which had been spread among many companies, but through distributors. By not implementing all of its marketing capabilities to infiltrate the PC market, IBM had lost out, as it could have had a large segment. The CEO of the PC division, O'Sullivan, had claimed that IBM had not supported or helped him and had not exploited its global sales power. He said that he had asked for help, but it had not been forthcoming, as management only had cared about mainframes (Applegate and Collins 2005). Then, Compaq had stolen the PC market from IBM, with an excellent, low-priced computer, and later Dell had done the same to Compaq, ousting it from the market and causing its collapse; Compaq was sold to HP in 2002. At the beginning of the 1990s, Compaq and Dell had been IBM's strong competitors in the PC market, but the market actually had been ruled by Microsoft, with its Windows operating system, and Intel, with its processors. It had taken IBM time to understand that not only had the market changed, but that there were now companies providing services similar to its own at lower prices and that an entirely new PC market had developed and was threatening its core businesses (Slater 1999). It had been important for customers to find word processing software or computer games that were compatible with their machines, fields which had been unknown to IBM, and these customers preferred PCs. The strength of IBM's competitors in both hardware and software soared, while so many new competitors entered the market.

The first signals of trouble for IBM appeared in 1984, following the change in customer habit from purchasing computers to leasing them. That had hampered the company's effectiveness and sales had begun to decline, especially after competitors had appeared on the scene, offering alternatives such as PCs and small and medium-sized computers. The sales of mainframes had comprised between 70% and 80% of the company's business. IBM's sales suffered for years. Its sales representatives had operated in specific fields and no one in the company had had a comprehensive picture of its customers' computing needs (Armstrong et al. 2009, 441-443). That had led to customer dissatisfaction, but nothing changed until a new CEO was appointed; then, IBM began focusing on customer needs, and its sales force became consultants in every field that IBM dealt with and provided solutions for their problems.

The threats had come from new technology and competitors. One of IBM's most famous products, the IBM 9370, was called the "VAX killer" because it was supposed to have competed with Digital's Vax line, which had targeted medium-sized companies (Austin and Nolan 2000). However, costs had increased and customers moved to the competition. Inside IBM, there had been no collaboration between departments. It had had 125 data centers and 128 chief information officers (CIOs), but no information collaboration, and every department had worked alone.

The PC breakthrough at the beginning of the 1980s had changed the structure of the computer market. Within a few years, the market had moved from computer manufacturers, such as IBM, to providers of operating systems, such as Microsoft, and processors, such as Intel. The growth of suppliers and the increase in competition led to a decline in prices, and profits went to those who had improved key products or had created new ones. IBM had not identified the changes in customer preferences nor the value that competitors had placed on customers' needs, including the change that had occurred in business needs for small computer systems, moving away from the systems that IBM had traditionally offered to large and medium-sized businesses (Jacobides and MacDuffie 2013). In addition, a very significant organizational process had occurred in the computer-purchasing departments of the companies. The responsibility for purchasing had moved from the information system departments to the financial departments, which meant that CFOs were examining, more closely, what they were getting in return for their money. CFOs compared IBM with other companies, especially regarding cost. That had put IBM in a relatively inferior position, since its products had been more expensive (and generally also of higher quality). IBM, most of whose contacts in companies had been with computer people and not with financial officers and purchasing decision makers, had been late in understanding the change and its significance, and that had harmed its sales.

IBM's internal compartmentalization and strict hierarchy had meant that the directors had not known what the company's competitive condition had been. The decision-making process was long and inflexible. In 1991, for the first time in the company's history, it downsized. There were waves of layoffs in 1991 and 1992, and by 1993, a total of 40,000 employees had been let go, which had been in direct contradiction to the company's organizational policy. In April 1993, Louis Gerstner was appointed CEO to replace Akers;

for the first time in IBM's history, the CEO was not someone who had risen through the ranks of the company.

The next stage had arrived relatively quickly. PCs had entered the business sector, the sector that IBM had ruled, and the large servers and storage systems, which had been anchors of the company's infrastructure and applications, including data processing for business computing, The new computer companies had convinced businesses that it would be better to integrate PCs into their data processing systems because everyone was using Microsoft and Intel. Sun, HP, Digital, Unisys and Oracle rapidly increased their sales activity. Their prices had been low and they had provided excellent service and, in addition, customers were no longer dependent on IBM, which had made its customers dislike it because of its high prices and poor service.

IBM's assumption had been that the changes—the new computer model and a variety of suppliers which would give services to customers in various fields, could not last long. Companies, IBM had thought, would look to a single source for their computing needs, and that source would be IBM. Another assumption had been that customers would not want to work with many different suppliers and would prefer a focused company. In addition, IBM had believed that technological superiority would be important, which had been its great edge. This had been the concept of IBM's management for a long time, and it had not been concerned about threats from competitors or changes in the market. However, it had become the wrong concept to adhere to. Customers had learned to work with the various suppliers and the market had become more standardized. What had seemed like a significant competitive advantage—working with one supplier—had lost its importance.

Bruce Harreld, who had been senior vice president in charge of strategy for IBM in the 1990s, wrote, with others (Harreld et al. 2007), that a strategic analysis had shown that IBM's collapse had been a case of dynamic capabilities. IBM's exclusive capabilities had developed over the years and had given it a competitive advantage, which had led to its success in the field of mainframes. IBM had not become concerned, in time, that its capabilities were no longer operative. The obstacles to computer market penetration had lessened and new competitors had entered with expanded capabilities (some copied from IBM), at competitive prices. IBM had not been able to find an appropriate response, because its high costs had made it difficult to lower prices, not only for small computers but also for mainframes.

After the great crisis, the company had succeeded in making changes and in recreating the competitive edge it had lost. However, without receiving alerts about its competitors, customers, technology and regulation, IBM, like any company, had not been able to know how to deploy itself, and without that knowledge, its situation had to worsen (Teece 2006). IBM had had no lack of strategists. According to Harreld, IBM had had about 400 strategists, but they had been spread around the various departments and had dealt mainly with keeping management happy, to prove that the company had been on the right track (Harreld et al. 2007, 16).

IBM's management had not identified the rise of minicomputers in time, and new competitors like Digital, Nixdorf, HP, General Data, Prime, and Wang began threatening IBM's business core (Christensen 1997). For example, its short assessment of Digital, which had been a strong competitor, was that it was moving forward like an express train. A company with sales of $7.6 billion ran ahead and left all the competition behind (Business Week 1986). According to the same article, IBM had to be wary of its competitors. The fact that IBM had had excellent developments in various computer fields had not lessened the threat, since its competitors were offering similar products with just as good solutions at competitive prices (Christensen 1997; Nissanson 2013). Many customers had wanted to replace IBM with other suppliers, as IBM's relations with its customers had distanced many of them (Hamel 2000). The companies that had been threatening IBM's hardware were Digital, Fujitsu and Compaq; Andersen Consulting, and EDS, in the field of service integration for computer systems; and Intel and Microsoft, in the field of processors and operating systems for PCs. IBM was being attacked on every side. The introduction of open-source hardware and the standardization of peripherals which could interface with every computer had contributed to breaking IBM's monopoly.

The extent of IBM's divorce from reality and its management's self-confidence had been demonstrated, at the end of the 1980s, at a meeting of the company's approximately 500 directors, in Raleigh, North Carolina. The audience was presented with a graph representing the company's predicted growth for the coming years, which had been prepared by an internal team and two outside consulting firms. According to the information presented, sales, which had stood at $50 billion, in 1990, were expected to soar to $150 million, in 1995. The greatest concern had been that the company was too large, which would deter governments and corporations from working with it, because they would not want one company to have so much power.

Four years later from the end of the 1980s, IBM had been surprised when it began to lose traction (Nissanson 2013). In effect, sales had begun dipping, at the beginning of the 1990s, as shown in table 7.1, below. In 1990, with branches in 44 European countries, the Middle East and Africa, and with 90,000 employees, IBM's earnings had peaked at $27 billion and then began dipping. Its gross marginal profit had fallen from 56% in 1990, to 38% in 1992 (Gerstner 2004). IBM's situation in Europe had been worse. In 1992, its pre-tax marginal profit had fallen from 18% to 6%.

In spite of the falling of earnings and profits, IBM's situation had become apparent only in April 1993, when Gerstner was appointed CEO. When he

Table 7.1 IBM's Financial Data

Year	Earnings (billions)	Profit (billions)	Profit per Share	Shareholder Return	Stock Price ($)	Cash Flow From Activity
1985	50	6.5	–	–	–	12.7
1990	69	6.0	–	–	–	7.4
1992	65.4	−5.0	−2.17	−15.4%	12.72	6.2
1993	62.7	−8.1	−3.55	−35.2%	14.12	–
1994	64.1	3.0	1.24	14.3%	18.37	11.8
1995	71.9	2.4	1.76	18.5%	22.84	–
1996	75.9	5.4	2.50	24.8%	38.87	10.2

Source: Gerstner 2004, 339.

started working at the company, one share of IBM stock sold for $12, having fallen from $43 in 1987, and it continued falling. Gerstner had noted that when he came to IBM, regardless of where he had turned, he had found an identical business message: that the sales of mainframes were falling rapidly, prices were far higher than those of the competition, there was an absence of an upper customer sector (the trend toward PCs), and a worrying decline in the company's image (Ibid, 48). Regarding the place of mainframes in sales, Gerstner said that 90% of the company's profits had come from the sale of mainframes and the software that had run them (Ibid, 49). The company's situation had been so bad that, during the 15 months preceding April 1993, there had been a serious decline in its market share. The reason had been Hitachi, Fujitsu, and Amdahl, whose prices had been 30%–40% lower (Ibid, 50). Gerstner also had said that, at the time, he had come to realize that the company, knowingly or not, "had been milking the System/360 to death" (Ibid). An examination of the data showed him that since the beginning of 1993, the overall decline in the company's earnings had been about $800 million, and the sale of mainframe computers had declined by 43%. The company's other branches—software, maintenance, and funding—had been dependent on mainframe sales, to a large extent (Ibid, 66).

Gerstner called a meeting of senior executives and said that during the three previous years, IBM had lost $16 billion, more than 175,000 employees, and the media and the company's competitors were calling IBM a dinosaur. Customers were not only unhappy, they were angry, and the company was not growing at the same rate as the competition (Ibid, 82). He said that IBM had become blind because of the dizzying success of its mainframe computers, especially the System/360, which led to ignore the threats from competition's being small. The marginal profits had been very large and, from a position of market control, the company had lost its connection to reality, because events in the market had not been, in principle, relevant (Ibid, 121). In 1992, the sale of hardware had been responsible for $33.8 billion; the sale of software, $11.1 billion; and $15 million, from the sale of services, so that there had been a great dependence on mainframes, comprising about 52% of total sales. By way of comparison, in 2001, after the changes that Gerstner had instituted, the picture had changed: most of IBM's earnings (41%), had come from services, and the sale of hardware had declined to about 20%. The company had successfully changed, and its business had stood on three pillars: software, services, and hardware; it had rescued itself from a failure that could have been a disaster (Dixon 2013).

Another prevalent concept had been that PCs were not considered a threat to IBM's core business at a time when competitors had read the map correctly and were going in the right direction. It had become clear that IBM had not understood two things about PCs: the first was that eventually businesses would use them, not just individuals. Gerstner had said that PCs had not been a high corporate priority, because it had never been imagined that they could challenge IBM's business market. Therefore, IBM had given control over valuable PC components to other companies: the operating system to Microsoft, and the microprocessors to Intel. When Gerstner had arrived at IBM, he said that both companies had used the gift they had received from IBM and ridden them straight to the top of the industry (Ibid, 123). IBM had been totally blind, while its competitors had understood the situation. Thus, at the beginning of the 1990s, IBM had found itself irrelevant, assailed on all sides and without a response.

IBM's computer laboratories had been the best and the most productive in the world. For years, they had won every important, relevant prize. Another reason for the fall of IBM had been its inability to bring its scientific discoveries to the market, as had also been the fate of Kodak. Many developments made by IBM had been exploited by its competitors, such as Oracle, EMC, and Cisco. According to Gerstner, the main obstacle had been the fear of harming existing products, especially the mainframes, and of working with other suppliers in the industry to commercialize its new technology (Ibid, 149). For example, by the 1980s, IBM had already developed databases, but they had not been marketed and had remained integrated into IBM systems. Apple had made a similar mistake, at the same time, with an operating system far superior to IBM's and Microsoft's, but Steve Jobs had not been prepared to sell it on non-Apple computers and therefore he had lost the operating system war to Microsoft. Microsoft, on the other hand, had put Windows on the market and had sold it to anyone who had wanted it, which had given Microsoft an enormous market (Beinhocker 2006). Gerstner made changes at IBM, allowing third party licenses to use IBM technology, so that IBM obtained royalties on patents and the sale of intellectual property; this had increased IBM's profits from $500 million, in 1994 to $1.5 billion, in 2001.

In 1984, there had been a total of ninety-two companies in the United States that had made minicomputers; ten years later, in 1994, there were seven (Bell 2012). Most of them had fallen by the wayside because the minicomputer segment of the market had had less need for development. Digital had led the field and had been the second largest computer company in the world. Others threatening IBM had included Data General, Honeywell, Packard Bell, Control Data Corporation, and HP. The threats also had come from companies that had competed with IBM for the mainframe market, mainly Hitachi, Fujitsu, and NEC, which had developed excellent products that matched IBM for both speed and especially, price.

Following its loss of important market segments, at the beginning of the 1990s, IBM had problems in other areas, as well. Mark Loughridge, CFO, was interviewed at that time and said that IBM had been operating in a fog without radar, and that its decentralized structure had made it difficult for its directors to know its financial situation and where it had stood, vis-à-vis its competitors (Leibs and Furman 2011). That was the reason, he said, that it had been impossible to collect internal financial data about its condition, even though they already had felt that they were in freefall. He said that those had been the blackest days in his 34 years with the company, when the financial officers had not been able to put relevant information on the table, which they should have been able to do. According to IBM's financial data, it had been clear that there had been large, rapid losses, and that the directors had been seriously worried about investors' loss of faith in the company.

The large decline in sales had endangered IMB's very existence. Between 1991 and 1993, the company had lost about $14 billion, its shares had dropped by about 70%, and it was on the road to declaring bankruptcy (Applegate and Collins 2005). Its market value had dropped from $105 billion in 1988, to about $32 billion in 1993 (Hamel 2000). The board of directors had ignored changes in the marketplace and had continued to adhere to a strategy that was no longer relevant—that is, focusing on mainframe computers (Austin and Nolan 2000).

THE POSITION OF INTELLIGENCE IN IBM

Before the crisis, no one in the company had seen a need to be competitive, as IBM had ruled the market and had ignored competitors—that is, until they had discovered that IBM was rapidly losing its market segment. Gerstner, who had arrived in 1993, had focused on two issues: competition and customers. When asked why the company had been in such dire straits, he had said that they had been too busy with themselves and had been unaware of what had been going on around them (Behnke and Slayton 1998, 4-9). When referring to "around them," Gerstner had meant not only customers, but competitors, as well. Only with Gerstner did IBM establish a good competitive intelligence unit (Behnke and Slayton 1998). One of the most notable competitive intelligence analysts, John Prescott, of the University of Pittsburgh, said that IBM, after its crisis, had turned into a company with one of the best competitive intelligence units in the business (Prescott and Williams 2003), which had not been the situation beforehand.

IBM'S LOSSES IN COMPETITION WITH MICROSOFT

The roots of IBM's failure had been a lack of understanding of the situation, as it had been developing, and overfocusing on mainframe computers. At the beginning of the 1980s, IBM had begun collaborating with Microsoft to develop the disk operating system, or "DOS," which had been created for IBM's PCs. At that time, IBM had estimated that it would not sell more than 200,000 units; it had not understood the threat that had been posed to the company, by Bill Gates and Microsoft. The heads of IBM had believed that the market would continue to trend toward mainframes. Bill Gates had decided to increase the use of MS DOS for other PC manufacturers. Instead of becoming part of an IBM PC, MS DOS became independent, and within a decade, it was on a par with IBM. This had made it very difficult for IBM to compete in the PC market, since it had lost one of its advantages. At the same time, Microsoft had given IBM's competitors a terrific incentive for successful competition (Baker 1998).

During the second half of the 1980s, Microsoft had made one of the most important moves in the computer market, weakening IBM and marking the rise of PCs over mainframes. Microsoft's success had been the result of its correct assessment of the direction that computing was going and its decision to lead the field, while IBM, on the other hand, had not been able to preserve its advantages. Microsoft's victory had changed the computing field; it has held its lead for the past thirty years (Beinhocker 2006).

After deciding that MS DOS had run its course, the heads of Microsoft had thought about how to develop the next generation of its operation system (Beinhocker 2007). Microsoft's competitors, IBM, with its OS/2 operating system, a collaboration between HP and Digital, Xerox with Unix (Sun Microsystems) and Apple's operating system. Bill Gates had planned his move very carefully with each of those companies, and at the same time he had continued investing in MS DOS, which had had a large customer base, thus fooling his competition regarding his true intentions. To prepare for the possibility that Unix would lead the market, he simply bought the company. He sent his people to the various companies to see how collaboration with them might be possible, but his real objective had been to learn where they were in developing a better operating system. He had begun developing Windows and had thought about a partnership with both IBM and Apple; sensing the new directions that Windows would take, he had decided that MS DOS had outlived its usefulness.

At the end of a process that had lasted several months, Gates had prepared several strategic options for his company by learning, firsthand, what the competition had, what they had been planning to do, and where he was, in comparison. He had focused on studying and collecting information, accompanied by competitive intelligence units and by Gates himself. His teams had not known which direction he would choose, which had made it very difficult for his competitors to block Microsoft's next development. When he had decided to develop Windows and put it on the market in 1987 (the previous version, marketed in 1985, had not been a success), it had been a strategic surprise for his competitors. It had been a winning solution and had surprised the market, especially IBM, with which Microsoft had partnered in MS DOS. Windows was better than MS DOS: despite the fact that version 3.0 had been launched only in 1990, it enjoyed an immense success and swept the operating system market after it.

IBM would have seemed to have had an advantage because it manufactured computers, an operating system, and peripherals. IBM, which had been Microsoft's strongest competitor, had made the strategic decision to focus only on developing and marketing software. Microsoft's success had been so impressive that eventually IBM PCs started running Windows with Intel processors, which had been better than its own. For a few years, IBM had tried to work with its own operating system, but it was forced to stop because Microsoft's products had been much better. IBM's PC competitors—HP, Gateway, Dell, Apple, Compaq and others—had done the same, especially since organizations were rapidly moving toward the use of PCs (Rivkin 1999).

Those had been IBM's difficulties in dealing with competition. It had adhered to its software and had incorrectly assessed the capabilities of Microsoft, which had been a far smaller but a more opportunistic company. It had taught IBM a lesson in PCs and had proved the power of strategic thinking, as Microsoft had correctly assessed the growth of the computing market. That had given Microsoft an edge that its competitors had found hard to overcome (Beinhocker 1999, 95-106).

THE GERSTNER REVOLUTION

The first thing that Gerstner did as IBM's new CEO was to improve customer relations, especially with the CIOs of large American companies. They had demanded that IBM also deal with information systems and not only provide hardware, as it had, until then, especially since the market had been full of better and cheaper products. Gerstner had done much to keep employees from leaving the company for the competition. His strategy had been called, "One IBM," meaning that the company would be run differently: it would now be one company enlisting all of its capabilities to provide a broad, integrated response for its clients.

One of the most important things that had to be done was to lower IBM's costs, in order to make it more competitive. Gerstner had come to the conclusion that its expenses were far greater than necessary. Therefore, at the beginning of 1993, a total of 75,000 employees were laid off. The IBM Services department, which had managed the units of outsourcing information systems, was greatly reinforced, and between 1994 and 2006, its earnings increased fourfold (Sperger 2008).

IBM's PC department had undergone an overhaul with the appointment of a new director, who had created the ThinkPad PC, for anyone who had wanted a quality product and had been prepared to pay more. The department's business activity was reorganized, and its earnings increased. All IBM's other trademarks were discarded. There also had been a revolution in information centers, which had been reduced from 155 to three; additionally, the entire company now had been connected to one communications network, instead of the many that had been in operation in the past. In the first quarter of 1993, for the first time in years, the company showed a profit of $382 million. At the end of 1994, profits had reached $5 billion and its total earnings were $69 billion.

In the middle of the 1990s, IBM had understood the significance of the Internet differently from others. It had regarded it as a tool for conducting business between companies (B to B) in the field of ecommerce, and the use of the Internet for marketing to individuals had seemed less relevant. Gary Hamel claimed IBM had once again been in error and had not understood the importance of the Internet revolution, and therefore had entered the field late (Hamel 2001). After IBM went in the opposite direction from the Internet, eventually it found its place and integrated. The Internet had been an extremely important field, but IBM had not invested enough in it to become a leader, leaving that to other companies.

IBM AND THE INTELLIGENCE FAILURE

In 1993, IBM had been strategically surprised by measures taken by its competitors and their new technologies, which it had been aware of but had not prepared for. The explanation for its intelligence failure, which had been a concentrated surprise, was that IBM had focused on preserving its leadership and had not sufficiently dealt with development and responding to the needs of consumers; it had not correctly assessed the importance of the fundamental changes taking place in the competitive environment. Its key intelligence topic had been to find a correct focus and it had received the relevant information, but its error had come from its assessment of its competitors' capabilities and intentions, especially—although not only—from Microsoft and Intel. Its intelligence unit had been unfocused and had operated without a complete picture of what had been done around it, a situation which had changed only when Gerstner was appointed and had made changes. Gerstner's revolution, with the aid of the development of improved intelligence capabilities, has been considered to be one of the greatest turnaround-success stories, and has been studied in business schools all over the world.

Therefore, it is important to take a closer look at IBM. Before the crisis, IBM had held a multifaceted concept: first, the new computing model of its competitors would not harm its status, because its customers would not want to work with many suppliers and would prefer solutions from one source, an IBM specialization. Second, the market leader would be determined by technological superiority, which had been IBM's great advantage. Third and final, the demand for mainframe computers would continue, and PCs would not become a threat to IBM's core business.

The company that had ruled the computer market and had followed the above concept thought that the market would not change and that IBM would continue to lead it. The company had been caught unawares and unprepared even though it had had significant computing and technological capabilities. It simply had not known how to respond to the threat. A case such as IBM's has been described in the literature dealing with business surprises, in monitoring and analyzing a competitive environment when a company has not used such tools to prepare a strategic plan based on events, generally in the wake of (erroneous) self-confidence that its strength is greater than the competitors.

IBM should have identified the significance of the threats earlier, as well as the opportunities to have dealt with these threats, especially because of its great technological strength and enormous client base; it should have prepared itself in time. However, it did not. The new CEO had made changes within a few short years, doing things that could have been done before the crisis. Management had made two mistakes, in underestimating the strength of the competition and in assuming itself to have been stronger than it was when faced with competition.

Gerstner's strategy of One IBM had opposed the previous intentions of Aker, the previous CEO, to divide the company into several subsidiaries. At the same time, Gerstner's strategy had favored the rapid entrance into new fields of consultation and information services, and it had caused a fundamental, rapid change in the company's revenue. At a later stage, at the end of the 1990s, the company made another great leap forward, when Gerstner had identified eighteen areas in which it could expand its activities. As a result, IBM then gained capabilities in those areas and provided responses to the special needs of its customers.

Rivkin (Frick 2013) had regarded Gerstner's activities as an example of the organization's strategic change in direction. He had called it "the golden recipe" for rescuing companies in the computing industry (Applegate and Collins 2005). Rivkin's observations are still applicable; in fact, he recently referred to them in relation to the slippage of Dell.

REASONS FOR THE INTELLIGENCE FAILURE

Collection Capabilities

IBM had not had a problem of a lack of information. It had developed the branch of organizational computing and had led it for years. It had had information about its competition but had not used it, since it had had no fear of competitors. Although during the relevant era, there had been no Internet or open information collecting from the Web, IBM had had information from its customers about its competitors, and there had been open-source information as well. The information from customers had been exclusive because of their large number and the fact that they had been spread out in various branches of the business world. IBM had known not only what their needs were but also what their competitors had been offering them. In organizational computing, it always had been relatively easy to collect information, because information usually has been shared by customers with customer management, to get the most attractive offer. IBM's competitive information had been spread throughout the company, but its importance had not been assessed. Once Gerstner had made his changes and had constructed internal and external intelligence collecting networks, it became clear that the necessary information had been almost immediately accessible. Using that information, decisions were then made which were important for the company's functioning.

While IBM had had important information about its competitive environment, the heads of the company had not used it before the crisis, because they had believed that their situation had been good and that the information would not contribute to advancing the company's business results. There had been competitive intelligence functions in the business branches, but no central view. However, the lack of information had not been the main cause of the intelligence failure, nor had it been the reason for the lack of an alert regarding market changes.

Noisy Work Environment

In the mid-1980s, many companies had entered the market offering alternatives to IBM's products, especially in the field of minicomputers. A new market had developed for PCs, to which IBM had given a low sales priority. IBM had known about events but had not thought that the PC branch would develop; rather, it had believed that organizations would continue to rely on mainframes. As a world leader in the computer market, IBM had ignored its connection to market events and had not been worried by them. It had believed that the determining factor would be technological superiority, which had been IBM's great advantage. It had been of the opinion that the demand for mainframes would continue; it had not seen the threat from PCs to their core business. It had had the information that its competitors had correctly read the market map and quickly had taken a bite out of IBM's market, but the company directors had not related to the information because they had been focused on running their business.

By the 1990s, there had been a great deal of open-source information that had indicated the enormous advance of IBM's competitors and that IBM had been gradually losing its technological edge. On the other hand, the company had been well-rooted in large organizations and its systems had been of higher quality than those of its competitors. Therefore, the directors had not seemed to be concerned about the competition. The comparisons that they had made had indicated that while the competition had been making progress, IBM still led the field. They had not understood that often such discrepancies in favor of IBM capabilities were not so important to its customers. The general feeling had been that IBM had been too big to fail. Its competitors had exploited IMB's overconfidence and some of them had chosen a direct attack. Others had chosen flank attacks: Honeywell, for instance, had manufactured mainframes and had had branches in small and medium-sized cities that had been ignored by IBM and thereby had increased its market segment (Kotler, Clarke, and Hornig 2012, 106-108). IBM had ignored the analysis of the strategic direction of development in computing because it had felt it had been superior to its competition.

The conclusion to be drawn is that the large amount of information that had been in IBM's possession had been partially contradictory: on the one hand, it had shown that the company continued to lead the market, and on the other hand, it had shown that there had been a developing threat from its competitors. In addition, the information that customer satisfaction had been high was incorrect, because that information had come from biased sales personnel and not from a professional analytical firm. There had been a contradiction between the information that the company had possessed and what actually had been happening in the environment. As a result, the directors had not taken the possible consequences into consideration.

Human Failures

IBM's directors had been wrong in their assessment and had failed to understand that the market had been changing and rapidly turning to smaller machines. That market had been growing very rapidly, turning into a market for both personal and business customers—not, as it had been previously, a mainframe market. The main reason behind the directors' mistake had been the confidence that IBM had had no competition in providing mainframes for businesses.

That faith had been a significant edge and cannot be underestimated because it had helped them reduce the strength of the threat. In addition, the internal reports that management had received from the field had not told the real story. IBM's sheer size and its technological might have seemed to have made it competition-proof. The company had been ruled by a conservative business culture and managers had tended not to contradict their superiors. There had been no culture that had fostered critical thinking or positive conflict (Roberto, Bohmer, and Edmondson 2006). In addition, there also had been a culture of internal compartmentalization, in which every branch had to take care of itself. That had been how IBM had always operated and how it had grown, successfully, from year to year, until its competitive environment had begun to change. Senior management had had no experience in dealing with a competitive market and, as market rulers, it had been easy to believe that the threat was temporary. Further, they had believed that, by virtue of its technological edge and global distribution, the company would not be harmed and, if it were to be harmed, the harm would be temporary. IBM had not invested effort in a strategic analysis of the directions that computerizing had been taking, in order to prepare itself for the future; rather, it had designed developments according to what it had thought was correct. Generally speaking, the company heads had had only a partial picture and a personal viewpoint, not an overall organizational view. Tellis, who had analyzed 770 companies in fifteen countries, had claimed that the one important reason for IBM's failure had been its inability to identify changes in the competitive environment and to adapt to the new situation (Tellis 2013).

The conclusion to be drawn is that both senior management and the intelligence units in the various branches of IBM had found it hard to assess the company's genuine situation, and other information had never been brought to their attention. In a culture that had lacked development and information-sharing, there had not been a chance that bad news would be brought to the attention of the company's management. Thus, the picture of the allegedly positive situation had remained in place, almost until the crisis began. For that reason, no assessment had been made of the size of the threat from competitors, and existing assessments had been adhered to, as had previously been done.

Organizational Difficulties and Faulty Cooperation

For years, IBM had been ruled by an organizational culture of compartmentalization and a lack of cooperation among its various branches. Senior management had been distant from the employees and had not known what had been happening, either inside or outside of the company. Thus, sales personnel from the various departments had gone to customers without having coordinated with one another or with competitors, regarding whom the customer would buy from. That had not been the result of a lack of information systems, because in that field IBM had led the market and its systems had been deeply ingrained. There also had been no sharing of competitive information; intelligence units that had operated within the various branches had not shared information about the activities of competitors with internal customers. IBM's competitors had known about the lack of coordination and sharing and about IBM's slow reaction time and had exploited it for their own benefit. IBM also had not cooperated with outside experts. Its organizational structure had been very complex, and in such a situation it had been hard for the various business units to cooperate. The company's CFO said that at the beginning of the 1990s, IBM had been working in a fog without radar—a radar which would have alerted it to changes; also, the decentralized structure had made it very difficult for the heads of the company to know what its financial situation was (Leibs and Furman 2011). Later, after changes had been made, an organizational culture of information-sharing and relevant information systems was formulated.

The conclusion to be drawn is that IBM had been isolated, within itself, and had paid no attention to its employees or external factors. The company's size and its culture of lack of sharing of information had made it extremely difficult to know what its real situation had been— and IBM also had been a culture of not bearing bad news. No use had been made of its information systems, and employees had not brought to the attention of management information from the field about the situation of the company, or the progress of the competition.

Interaction of the Decision Makers

According to IMB's organizational culture, management had been fully aware of what had occurred in the company and their authority could not be challenged. Therefore, they had not listened to the assessments of the analysts that had surveyed the market and had criticized IBM for not having successfully dealt with the competition. Senior management had not accepted external opinions of what could have helped it correctly assess the company's situation. The lack of influence of external factors had been one of the things that had been troubling the company. Its close-mindedness to what had been going on beyond its walls had kept it from understanding the significance of the developments taking place around it and from assessing the situation correctly and in time.

Regarding the reasons that had brought the company to its situation, Gerstner said that they had been too busy with themselves and unaware of what had been going on around them. The directors had not listened to the employees and had received only reports that had been filtered through rose-colored glasses—a view that had been erroneous, as had been made clear later. The board of directors had been far away and had received partial reports, from management only.

The conclusion to be drawn is that senior management had been divorced from events and had disregarded the assessment of threats, out of a sense that the situation had been good and would remain so. Others in the company, who had formed different assessments, had not thought it proper to bring them to the board of directors because they had assumed that they would be rejected. The directors' faith in the company's strength had been so firm that lower echelons had not seen any chance of changing their position. Senior management had influenced those beneath them to continue in the same direction—that is, they were not to make changes or adaptations to events in the competitive environment.

QUESTIONS EXAMINED IN THIS TEST CASE

1. What had been the assessments before the crisis, regarding the possibility that one would occur?

   The accepted assessment in IBM had been that the company would continue to rule the market for mainframe computers for organizations, even if its market segment declined, and that its competitors could not endanger that rule because there had been no alternative products of equally high quality and, in any case, IBM had had a technological edge. The comprehensive solution that IBM had offered its customers could not be beat, and that had been one of its most important competitive edges.
2. What signs had there been of a coming crisis?

   The signs had been a loss of customers in the business market; the rapid development and growth of competing companies, in the wake of the fact that they could offer alternatives to the products IBM had offered the business market; and the continuing decline in IBM's earnings and profits. IBM's customers had expressed dissatisfaction with its prices and service, and they had felt that they were being taken for granted—that no special effort was being made to ensure that they would be satisfied.

3. Despite the fact that for a long while there had been signs of a coming crisis, why hadn't the company not correctly assessed its development or possible significance?

   IBM had had no comprehensive picture of the threat. The company had been constructed of departments which had had no contact with one another and had not collaborated with each other. Some of the departments had had their own intelligence units, but there had been no central unit at the corporate level that had put together a comprehensive picture. No one in IBM had thought that there had been a need for business intelligence from outside the organization. There had been a thought about dismantling the company into independent subsidiaries, but Gerstner had rejected this idea. He had understood the potential of One IBM and its ability to enter new fields in service and software.

4. Nevertheless, had there been other significant assessments regarding the possibility of a crisis? What had led to the failure of the established assessors and the success of the competitors?

   IBM had suffered from its strict hierarchy, divisions, and size, and had not been deployed for criticism or for sharing of ideas that had pictured the company in a negative light. Therefore, there had been no one of importance who had expressed opinions different from those of management and the board of directors. The fostering of positive conflict and other ways of thinking had not been part of the company's organizational culture. IBM had never encountered genuine competition, and therefore when such competition began to appear, it had not understood the importance of the threat it had posed.

5. Had there been an intelligence failure, and if so, what had been its nature?

   IBM strongly had believed that it would continue leading the organizational computing market and while there might be some competition, it would be marginal. The assumption had been that the company was strong, its products firmly established at the heart of the business activity of large businesses, which were dependent on IBM and could not leave it. The heads of the company had believed that IBM had had no competitors whose products were better and that there had been no real threat to this market dominance. IBM had exaggerated its own capabilities and had not correctly assessed its competitors.

6. What had been the reason for the business failure?

   IBM's great failure had been in not understanding its competitive environment and the significance of the changes in the prices of computers around the world. That had prevented the company from changing its strategy, as it should have begun to compete or to enter the new fields, to increase its earnings, but it had not done so. The board of directors had not understood what had been happening and had not correctly assessed the growing power of its competitors or of its customers' extensive criticism of the services that they had been receiving. Customers had been happy when IBM's competitors had offered them products that had been just as good, at competitive prices, and with good service. IBM had conducted surveys and had collected information about customer satisfaction, but had not internalized the information nor had it made the necessary changes. That had meant a rapid decline in earnings without alternative growth engines, and IBM quickly lost a market segment.
7. What had been the reasons for the intelligence failure?

   The reasons for the intelligence failure had included the rapid changes in the computing world, the entrance of new competitors, new technical developments, the rapid lowering of prices resulting from competition, a decline in dependence on IBM, and a feeling among its customers that it had been no longer necessary to rely only on IBM. Customers had realized that it had become possible to obtain better service from competitors and they also had obtained a high degree of satisfaction from these competitors; this had stood in contrast to IBM's high-handedness in dealing with its customers, whom they had taken for granted. There had been IBM's divorce from reality and its exaggerated self-confidence, which had damaged its ability to read the competition map. Monitoring the competition and formulating a strategy for the coming years that had been supported by realistic assessments regarding the directions that computing would take had been given a low priority at IBM. Instead, IBM had looked mainly to itself, to events inside the company, but not at the competitive environment.
8. What is the main explanation for IBM's intelligence failure?

   The main explanation for the failure is that it had been a concentrated surprise, caused by an incorrect assessment of the capabilities of the competition and of the strength of the threat that they had posed. The rise of competitors and the changes in the competitive environment had not been secret. IBM's board of directors had been aware of them, but they had not correctly assessed the speed of their market penetration and the influence that they would have on IBM's earnings. It had been a concentrated surprise because the competition had learned a great deal from IBM, including its capabilities and weaknesses and had found solutions for successfully overcoming the difficulties. IBM, on the other hand, had not focused on its competitors nor on trying to find suitable responses to their threat.

9. Which factors had influenced the intelligence failure?

   As can be seen from table 7.2, the attack on IBM had been a concentrated surprise by known competitors; they had not been considered serious competitors, yet they had made fundamental changes in the computing world that IBM had been unprepared for. Theoretically, it would have seemed easier to have identified a concentrated surprise: an intelligence system is supposed to focus on its intelligence collecting efforts, from the direction of approaching threats and to focus on opportunities, as well, but that had not happened, because IBM's competitors had been underestimated.

10. Which tools had been used to try to prevent the failure?

    At the time of the crisis, IBM's board of directors had done nothing to prevent it. They had been thinking about breaking the company into independent subsidiaries and had assumed that, in this way, they would be able to better deal with their competitors. Only after Gerstner had been appointed CEO did IBM develop a business strategy based on leveraging the company's strengths and on an understanding of the needs of the computing market, supported by competitive intelligence, which Gerstner had considered to be very important.

11. Which tools could have been used to prevent the intelligence failure?

    IBM should have identified the threats earlier, should have understood their importance, and then should have monitored them as they had developed. Then IBM should have decided what to do to overcome the threats, including developing new products, improving service, adapting prices to the competitive market, providing better solutions for its customers' needs, and entering new fields. It should have started thinking outside of the box to understand which fields it could enter, focusing on complementary fields, which had been their main strength. They also

Table 7.2 Factors Influencing the Intelligence Failure

Number	*Issue*	*Response*
1	Had the event been routine?	No
2	Had it been familiar from the past?	No
3	Had the threatening factors been known?	Yes
4	Had the modus operandi been familiar?	No
5	Had the event been directed?	No
6	Was the information that had been received clear?	Yes
7	Had it been clear what had been intended?	Yes

Source: Avner Barnea 2020.

should have increased their intelligence capabilities and given the strategic unit a higher status to provide the board of directors with an ongoing, integrated picture of the company's situation.

INTELLIGENCE LESSONS THAT HAD BEEN IMPLEMENTED LATER

IBM fundamentally improved the way it read the competitive map and learned how to monitor it. A corporate intelligence unit was established, and the strategic unit was made stronger; unlike beforehand, when there had been a certain amount of intelligence activity in the business units, but the issue had only had a low priority and no professional authority. The lessons learned and the changes that were made are that IBM now monitors the computing technological world, develops new products, and purchases the companies whose products are suitable for its needs. IBM operates in various computing spheres, including products, services, and consulting, which reduces the danger of its continuing success. It has significantly improved its internal cooperation and has given priority to service and to providing responses to the needs of its customers. It monitors developments in fields relevant to its activity, such as developing tools to monitor social media, after having learned of its importance to its customers; it also monitors the big data field. If IBM cannot find a solution on its own, it purchases a company that can.

Chapter 8

Mutual Learning

Discussion

OVERVIEW

While there has been extensive national intelligence research for the past fifty years, competitive business intelligence research is at a stage where it is trying to establish its status. Mutual learning between the national and business fields is only beginning and is not yet the product of a systematic approach.

National intelligence began as military intelligence, was used on the battlefield to provide commanders with tactical and strategic information about the enemy's intentions and capabilities, and it developed other functions to give a country's decision makers information about security and foreign relations. Business/competitive intelligence learns from national intelligence and applies some of its principles.

After years, during which strategic national intelligence had not been open to learning from business experience, a change has gradually occurred in recent years. Various topics have trickled into national intelligence from business intelligence and vice versa (table 8.1). The failure of national intelligence to predict the so-called "Arab spring," in 2011, had led intelligence agencies in the United States, Britain, Canada, and Israel to recognize the need for deploying methods, such as monitoring the public, to prevent diffused surprises. They had noted that global corporations, such as Intel, HP, Dell, Google, Eli Lilly, Amazon, and Procter and Gamble, had accumulated a great deal of experience in these methods, by employing competitive business intelligence and market research.

Despite the use of national intelligence in business, intelligence failures have occurred in large conglomerates, such as Motorola, Xerox, Lucent, General Electric, Johnson & Johnson, Kodak, IBM, Erikson, and Nokia. Generally, they occurred because the intentions and activities of their

Table 8.1 Mutual National Intelligence and Business Intelligence Learning

Intelligence Activity	*From Business Intelligence to National Intelligence*	*From National Intelligence to Business Intelligence*
Methodology	Sharing internal information using known management tools	Implementing intelligence using the intelligence cycle
Plan and Direction		Defining intelligence needs (Key Intelligence Topics)
Collection	OSINT (Open-Source Intelligence) and social media to analyze large audience positions and using crowd sourcing and prediction markets	Identifying threats and formulating early warning strategies
Analysis	Using prediction markets and scenario analysis	Analysis Competing Hypothesis (ACH)
Distribution	Information sharing (see Methodology, above)	
Other	Measuring information values	

Source: Avner Barnea 2020.

competitors, as well as market directions, had not been correctly assessed, resulting in serious commercial and financial damage. Since intelligence in business uses intelligence disciplines with marketing research topics that focus on recent years for understanding large number of consumers, the chance of a business surprise, especially of a diffused surprise, is smaller. Similarities have been noted between the dilemmas facing competitive intelligence analysts, who are expected to indicate business threats, and the dilemmas facing national intelligence analysts (Skipper 2012).

This book has presented a research picture of both the fields. There is a difficulty in the methodology, resulting from the fact that the national intelligence communities are not open. However, in recent years there has been an increase in the flow of its published information which can be studied, mostly reports issued by investigatory committees after intelligence failures, in the wake of strategic surprises, but also research papers and memoirs, and even classified material has been released for study. The business field is far more open to researchers. However, business failures are often not discussed, in general, and business intelligence failures, in particular. Nevertheless, information is made public, which makes it possible to analyze what happened.

The importance of mutual learning is the contribution that can be made to enrich comparative knowledge between the failures that have occurred in national intelligence and those in business intelligence. This could help improve the preparedness of states and businesses in dealing with strategic surprises. The possible contribution of the intelligence discipline is its ability to help in assessing complex situations and in preventing failures, by issuing alerts, and therefore helping to prevent both national and business surprises.

Thus, the conclusions of this study can be used as the foundation for further studies, which will be better able to distinguish between intelligence failures, in both fields, in situations of concentrated surprises and diffused surprises. The conclusions formulated here also can be used as a model for analyzing the two types of intelligence failures.

APPLYING POSSIBILITIES FROM COMPETITIVE BUSINESS INTELLIGENCE TO NATIONAL INTELLIGENCE, AND VICE VERSA, ACCORDING TO TEST CASES

This book examines four test cases according to four types of surprise (chart 2), two in the field of national intelligence and two in intelligence in business. Each field examines a concentrated surprise and a diffused surprise.

An analysis of the test cases indicates that, to assess the threat in each field, there are no important differences between the factors leading to a surprise and an intelligence failure. In other words, the test cases show that the reasons for failure in concentrated surprises and diffused surprises had been similar. For example, there had been no lack of information; there also had been equivocal and sometimes contradictory information, human failures, a tendency to adhere to previous assessments, a lack of internal cooperation, and external factors had influenced intelligence assessments. Therefore, for both national and business intelligence, learning from the other field could help prevent future intelligence failures. Not every topic that appears in table 1.2 is relevant for mutual learning, as some had not been present in the test cases examined. For example, social media, which contributes a great deal to business and marketing intelligence (Bughin and Chui 2013; Ament 2013), and which in recent years has been used by national intelligence (Wheaton and Richey 2014) had not yet existed, when the test case occurred.

Following the new division that I have presented, between the two types of surprises—that is, "concentrated" versus "diffused" —it becomes clear that there is a greater chance that intelligence would provide a warning of a concentrated surprise, rather than of a diffused surprise. A diffused surprise has been difficult to detect early, because ordinary intelligence analysts have been monitoring events according to the criteria of concentrated surprises, such as changes in the routine of intelligence targets and in the assessment of the intentions and capabilities of known targets. In diffused surprises, the targets often have been unknown, so the key intelligence topic has not been correct and the information received and the potential, indicative signs have not been suitable. Table 1.2 does not include collecting and analyzing cases referring to covert operations, which are central to national intelligence, as they are not relevant to business. However, the use of covert information has not necessarily increased the chances of correctly assessing the importance of a strategic threat.

TEST CASES DIVIDED ACCORDING TO TYPE OF SURPRISE

Based on an analysis of four test cases, six questions have been raised (table 8.2), regarding the information received about a possible surprise. The answers indicate that there is a notable difference between a concentrated surprise and a diffused surprise, in all elements associated with the ability to assess the threat and prevent an error in prediction.

The conclusion to be drawn from table 8.2 is that in test cases of concentrated surprises, it would have seemed easier to identify the threat, but that did not happen in many instances, the most important having been mentioned in the survey of the literature. It can be assumed that, in many other instances of successful intelligence, the threat assessment was correct and the surprise was prevented or prepared for successfully, but accessibility to these cases of successful intelligence, in the national field, is very limited. The number of instances of diffused surprise has been smaller, but the possibility of a mistake in prediction has been higher in the national field because, among other reasons, there has been a problem in focusing on key intelligence topics, as

Table 8.2 Questions Regarding the Test Cases According to the Type of Surprise

Concentrated			*Diffused*	
9/11	*IBM*	*Question*	*2008 Financial Crisis*	*Intifada*
+	+	Was it Known from the Past? (Routine/ not Routine)	–	–
+	+	Were the Threatening Factors Known? (Difficulty in Determining the Leader)	–	–
+	+	Was the Method Familiar?	–	–
+	+	Was there Direction (+) or was it a Spontaneous Development (–)?	–	–
+	+	Was Clear, Unequivocal Information Available?	–	–
+	+	Was it Clear what was Intended/What the Targets were?	–	–

Source: Avner Barnea 2020.

preparations have been made for a concentrated surprise. When mistakes are made in identifying key intelligence topics, the information collected is liable to be irrelevant and the chance of error increases. However, in business, intelligence that has been used for preventing a concentrated surprise (e.g, from competitors) has been combined with intelligence for preventing a diffused surprise (e.g., understanding large audiences), and also has been combined with other analysis tools from the business world, with the result that there have been fewer chances for prediction error. One possible conclusion is that the use of business tools in national intelligence and national intelligence tools in business could increase the chances of preventing both concentrated and diffused surprises.

MUTUAL LEARNING: POSSIBLE TOOLS FROM BUSINESS INTELLIGENCE FOR NATIONAL INTELLIGENCE, AND VICE VERSA, ACCORDING TO THE TEST CASES

The similarity between the factors for intelligence failures and the need to enrich intelligence theory, especially in national intelligence, raises the possibility of examining the contribution of mutual learning between the national and business environments. In the past, this was not done methodically, although it was mentioned from time to time, as noted in the survey of the literature, generally by analysts outside the intelligence organizations. For business intelligence, it clearly has been important to learn from national intelligence, but for national intelligence, learning from business intelligence has not been an obvious path to take. National intelligence analysts have been sure of their abilities, despite a long series of failures.

This book has proposed improvements to the theoretical side of intelligence, largely in its presentation of the types of surprises, concentrated and diffused, and in the discussion of key intelligence topics, which are assessed routinely, and not only by assessors. For a concentrated surprise, the factors are generally linked to the assessor's capabilities; however, there is a new factor for an intelligence failure—the difficulty in identifying the key intelligence topic, which has not received attention. In such instances, the key intelligence topic often has been incorrect and the information collected has been liable to be irrelevant, causing difficulties for the assessor, who has been unaware of the fact. A very possible result has been and could be failure to identify the threat.

A comparative analysis between national and competitive business intelligences shows that there has been a great deal of similarity between the approaches of intelligence in both environments. Each could potentially aid the other.

Table 8.3 Business Intelligence Tools for Possible Use in National Intelligence, According to the Test Cases

Tool Number	*Business Intelligence Tool*	*Test Case*	*Surprise Type*	*What might have happened if the Business Tool had been used*
1	Information Management, Information Sharing	2008 Financial Crisis	Diffused	By using Information Sharing, it would have been possible to have improved the picture of the developing strategic threat to the financial system.
		IBM	Concentrated	It would have been possible to have issued an early warning about the developing threat to the company.
		Intifada	Diffused	There had been a tendency to see things as "concentrated," and therefore the chance of error of misdiagnosing the type of surprise was greater.
		9/11	Concentrated	There had been no sharing of information among the security and intelligence agencies. Otherwise it could be prevented before the attack.
2	OSINT (Open-Source Intelligence)	2008 Financial Crisis	Diffused	According to a scenario of open- source information collection, it would have been possible to indicate threatening developments and to have raised doubts about the Fed's assessment of the situation.
		IBM	Concentrated	According to a scenario of open- source information collection, an early alert could have been received about the developing threat.
		Intifada	Diffused	According to the scenario, its use as the tool—along with focusing on the key intelligence topic with open-source information collection could have improved the assessment of the developing threat.
		9/11	Concentrated	According to the scenario, the use of the tool could have helped assess the threat, and its contribution was apparently high since there had been erroneous concrete intelligence.

3	Social Media and Crowd Sourcing	2008 Financial Crisis	Diffused	According to the scenario, the use of the tool and focusing on the key intelligence topic in objectives which were not covered could have supplied additional information that would have presented a different picture.
		IBM	Concentrated	According to the scenario, using the tool could have provided addition information, which would have shown a different picture of the threat to the company.
		Intifada	Diffused	According to the scenario, the use of the tool and focusing the key intelligence topic differently would have shown the extent of the anger and frustration before and immediately after the outbreak of the Intifada.
		9/11	Concentrated	According to the scenario, the use of the tool apparently would not have helped, because of al-Qaeda's high level of compartmentalization.
4	Scenario Analysis	2008 Financial Crisis	Diffused	According to the scenario, the use of the tool could have helped to correctly assess the situation and thus make preparations in time to prevent the financial crisis.
		IBM	Concentrated	According to the scenario, use of the tool could have influenced the company to have acted in a way that would have lessened its chance of collapse.
		Intifada	Diffused	According to the scenario, the use of the tool could have raised doubt about the current assessment and could have helped to better predict the developments and to make preparations earlier.
		9/11	Concentrated	According to the scenario, the use of the tool could have led to preparations that would have prevented the planes from being hijacked.

(Continued)

Table 8.3 Business Intelligence Tools for Possible Use in National Intelligence, According to the Test Cases (*Continued*)

Tool Number	*Business Intelligence Tool*	*Test Case*	*Surprise Type*	*What might have happened if the Business Tool had been used*
5	Prediction Markets	2008 Financial Crisis	Diffused	According to the scenario, the use of the tool by employees of the large banks, government institutions, and other financial institutions could have shown that the threat had been greater than it had seemed to have been to the Fed.
		IBM	Concentrated	According to the scenario, the timely use of the tool could have helped provide a correct assessment of the threat.
		Intifada	Diffused	According to the scenario, using the tool could have contributed to the receipt of indications, before the uprising, and to the assessment of its significance and strength, after it broke out.
		9/11	Concentrated	According to the scenario, the use of the tool could have raised doubts about the current assessments and could have contributed to assessing the strength of the threat, since opinions had been held that an attack was upcoming.
6	Measuring Information Value	2008 Financial Crisis	Diffused	According to the scenario, the use of the tool could have indicated the discrepancy in information and strengthened the need to have examined what had been occurring.
		IBM	Concentrated	According to the scenario, the use of the tool could have indicated discrepancies in information and strengthened the need to have examined events.
		Intifada	Diffused	According to the scenario, the use of the tool could have indicated discrepancies in all the information related to trends in the civilian population.
		9/11	Concentrated	According to the scenario, an examination of the information could have indicated the discrepancies between the high quality of the information and the erroneous assessments which had minimized its importance without providing a convincing reason.

Source: Avner Barnea 2020.

Tables 8.3 and 8.4 are based on the four test cases of strategic surprise, which have been described in the chapters, above, according to division into types (i.e., concentrated and diffused) and environments (i.e., national and business intelligences). Based on an analysis of failures in predicting surprises in each environment, several subjects have been identified in which, by my assessment, intelligence could have improved its capabilities, if it would have used the tools of the other environment (see table 8.1). The tools that I am referring to have been used in business intelligence and may be adapted to national intelligence, some of which national intelligence has begun using, although too late. Tools from national intelligence also could be adapted to business intelligence, but that has not yet happened in an efficient fashion.

In particular, I have used a system of scenario analysis familiar from business intelligence that deals with what would happen if use were made of a specific test case and how it could improve prediction capabilities (Schoemaker 1995). Schoemaker's article shows the way for using scenario analysis as a tool for business planning by combining theoretical and practical aspects.

Based on a reasonable scenario which, in turn, is based on a serious study of each of the test cases above, I have attempted to discover if intelligence assessment for a specific event, whose results are known today, could have been different if tools from the other environment had been used.

The examination is based on the fact that there is solid experience in the use of scenario analysis in both the business and national fields. My intention has been to assess how an erroneous identification of an intelligence target in a concentrated surprise versus a diffused surprise (independent variable) could cause an incorrect assessment (intervening variable), whose result would be an error in threat prediction (dependent variable). Based on the analysis of each of the four test cases examined in this book, I have reached the conclusion that mutual learning would have positive results.

BUSINESS INTELLIGENCE TOOLS THAT COULD BE USED FOR NATIONAL INTELLIGENCE

Based on the test cases, table 8.3 examines business intelligence tools which seem suitable for improving national intelligence capabilities. The table shows what happened in each of the test cases of diffused surprise and concentrated surprise in a business environment, and assesses, based on a possible scenario, what might have happened if those tools had been used in the terrorist attack cases of concentrated surprise and diffused surprise in the national field. The results indicate the possibility for improvement in national

Table 8.4 National Intelligence Tools for Possible Use in Business Intelligence, According to the Test Cases

Tool Number	*National Intelligence Tool*	*Test Case*	*Surprise Type*	*What might have happened, if the National Intelligence Tool had been Used*
7	Implementing the Intelligence Cycle	Intifada	Diffused	According to the Scenario, the use of the tool could have indicated a mistake in mapping the threat, and improving the mapping of it would have raised the chance for an alert.
		9/11	Concentrated	A systematic mapping of the threat could have prevented the attack.
		2008 Financial Crisis	Diffused	The Fed had been familiar with the banks but had not assessed the extent of the threat, and no organized assessment had been carried out by any financial institution.
		IBM	Concentrated	According to the scenario, the use of the tool and improving collection and assessment could have given an alert in time.
8	Designating Key Intelligence Topics	Intifada	Diffused	According to the scenario, the use of the tool could have indicated an error in predicting the assessed target, and thus raised the chance of an alert.
		9/11	Concentrated	According to the scenario, the use of the tool could have indicated the error in mapping the threat, and an improvement in mapping could have raised the chance of receiving an alert.
		2008 Financial Crisis	Diffused	According to the scenario, the use of the tool could have indicated an error in the key intelligence topic; identifying it correctly could have increased the chances of receiving an alert.
9	Early Warning and Tools for Analyzing Information	Intifada	Diffused	According to the scenario, the use of the tool could have raised the need to alert the system to the fields of political subversion, and the chance of an alert would have increased.
		9/11	Concentrated	There had been no orderly assessment of the threat, which had been one of the reasons for the strategic concentrated surprise.
		2008 Financial Crisis	Diffused	According to the scenario, the use of the tool could have created a warning system for financial stability, and the chances of having received an alert would have increased.
		IBM	Concentrated	According to the scenario, the use of the tool could have given an early warning regarding the loss of the company's competitive edge.

Source: Avner Barnea 2020.

intelligence performance, especially in better threat prediction, by learning from the field of business.

POSSIBLE NATIONAL INTELLIGENCE TOOLS FOR USE IN BUSINESS INTELLIGENCE

Based on the test cases, table 8.4 examines possible tools from the national arena suitable for business. The table shows what happened in the various test cases of diffused and concentrated national surprise and what could have happened if the tools had been used. Thus, it indicates the possibility for improving business intelligence performance, mainly in predicting a threat by learning from national intelligence.

Chapter 9

Conclusion

This book has drawn attention to two issues: one, the type of strategic surprise in the national and business fields, and two, the division of strategic surprise into four main dimensions, according to the type of surprise and the environment in which it occurs, business or national.

In addition, the book has shown that concentrated surprise and diffused surprise appear to occur in both fields, national and business. In each field, there is established activity whose role is to predict a threat. As noted in the review of the literature, most of the intelligence failures have been concentrated surprises, while only a few were diffused surprises. However, in some of the instances, a diffused surprise had been mistaken for a concentrated surprise. This was due to a lack of awareness of the distinction between the two types of surprise and a lack of knowledge that this second type of surprise—diffused surprise—even had existed. The errors that had arisen had resulted from the fact that diffused surprise requires a different kind of response.

This book has drawn another important inference, namely that when a diffused surprise has occurred, the assessed key intelligence topic often has not focused on the correct target. The reason is that intelligence analysts intuitively have been thinking in terms of concentrated surprise, with the result that the key intelligence topic—the foundation for collecting information, analysis, and the distribution of intelligence reports—has been incorrectly assessed. Intelligence usually has focused on known targets and has examined how to improve the analysts' capabilities, but it has not paid enough attention to whether it has correctly identified the key intelligence topic. When a mistake has been made in identifying the key intelligence topic, the results are errors caused by the irrelevant information collected and not by a lack of information. The damage to the national interest can be great, from loss of life to endangering the country's existence. In business, the damage has been more focused, resulting in loss of money, investments, and sometimes the collapse of the company.

To enrich our understanding of the reasons for intelligence failures, in each of the types of surprises, a comparative analysis has been conducted of intelligence failures in concentrated surprises and diffused surprises. Four test cases have been examined. The comparative analysis has shown that there was great similarity among the reasons for intelligence failures, in each of the categories, and discrepancies have been found in the literature, which the definition of diffused surprise helps resolve. The definition of diffused surprise was presented and then discussed in the section on the literature review, and it was significantly reinforced by the analysis of the test cases.

The comparative analysis of the test cases of strategic concentrated and diffused surprises has indicated that in a concentrated surprise, the failure generally has been in one or all stages of the intelligence cycle, especially in the activity of the assessors. This often has resulted in difficulties in the intelligence cycle, which then influenced the quality of the intelligence product.

The comparative analysis of intelligence failures in both fields, and in the pattern of concentrated surprises and diffused surprises that have been presented in this book could not only contribute to the theory of strategic surprise and intelligence failure, but could actually help prevent intelligence failures, in reality. From the lessons derived from the comparative analysis, attention could be focused on the correct key intelligence topic and, with awareness of the possibility of a diffused surprise, it would be possible for mutual learning to occur between national intelligence and business intelligence. Intelligence work could be improved, thus improving the satisfaction of the heads of government with the intelligence product.

The following are the main understandings reached by the discussion in this book:

1. The Chance of Intelligence Failure

   The more that the key intelligence topic is diffused and the less it is defined, the greater the chance of an intelligence failure. This hypothesis was found to be correct, based on the analysis of the two test cases of diffused surprise presented in this book: the First Intifada, which was in the field of national intelligence, and the Financial Crisis of 2008, in the field of business-economic intelligence. The hypothesis also was proven by other cases that were mentioned but not fully analyzed in this book, in chapters 2 and 3. For the First Intifada and the Financial Crisis of 2008, the surprise had been diffused, the error had been an incorrect identification carried out by the assessor, which only became clear after the strategic surprise took place; further, the error had been appropriate for intuitive thinking about the intention to prevent a concentrated surprise.

2. The Contribution of Mutual Learning

   The accumulated experience in business and the nature of the intelligence activities used in the business field could lessen, relatively, the chance of a diffused surprise in the national field. A review of the literature of the nature of business intelligence has indicated that what has helped prevent diffused surprises is when business intelligence has been combined with national intelligence, as well as when it has maintained an openness to influence from analytic and other tools in the business field. In the test case of the Financial Crisis of 2008, The Fed had had sufficient tools to prevent the surprise, which occurred when the financial system collapsed, but because of the dismissal of important information, including indicators of the development of a significant threat to financial stability, it had erred in its predictions and had not given the decision makers a timely warning. As noted in other cases of diffused surprise, accumulated experience and information from assessors have not been sufficient. A mistake had been made in predicting the assessed intelligence target about factors in the financial system, which had then increased the chances for intelligence failure. This is also what had occurred in the diffused surprise, described in the test case of the First Intifada.

3. The Chance for Intelligence Failure in a Diffused Surprise

   When it has been a question of national assessors, the intuitive tendency is to regard the situation as concentrated, and thus the chance of error is larger when the surprise is diffused. That is what had happened in the case of the First Intifada, where the focus had been on preventing organized terrorist activity, mainly by the PLO. This had been the situation in the past, but in reality, what had occurred was a diffused surprise of a popular uprising without organizational affiliation, for which no preparations had been made; as a result, the error in the key intelligence topic had become important. Despite correctly focusing on the key intelligence topic, the failure had been the result of factors known from other intelligence failures, especially in the implementation of the intelligence cycle. Thus, important information, mainly from indicators that a threat had been developing, had been ignored. That being the situation, a prediction error was made and the terrorist attack was not prevented. In other words, even when the key intelligence topic has been correctly identified, an error can occur in threat prediction when other aspects of the intelligence cycle have not operated as required. This is also what had happened in the collapse of IBM. Intelligence had been focused correctly, but because of complacency and excessive self-confidence, the indicators had not been interpreted correctly and the threat was not identified in time.

SURPRISES AND ERRORS OF PREDICTION: THE BOTTOM LINE

The chance for error in threat prediction grows when an error occurs in defining the characteristics of the key intelligence topic, which leads to an error in assessing the importance of developments in national or business arenas—it is an error in prediction. One of the reasons behind it is that the information that has been collected is irrelevant to the threat. Thus, when the development of a concentrated or diffused surprise has been correctly identified, the chance that a prediction error will occur is smaller. When an error in identifying the key intelligence topic has been made, the chance of an error in threat prediction is greater in cases of concentrated surprises than in cases of diffused surprises.

What Comes Next?

Based on this book, it will now be possible to continue studying diffused surprises in the national arena and to examine additional cases to further refine the distinction between diffused surprise and concentrated surprise. In every instance of a strategic surprise, business or national, what has to be determined is whether the surprise is concentrated or diffused. It is advisable to continue examining what develops in terms of the learning that will be acquired by national intelligence from business intelligence. National intelligence needs these strategic business intelligence tools to improve its capabilities, so we also should study what occurs when national intelligence adapts these tools, to see if it develops the necessary new capabilities and improve based on what it learns.

Bibliography

"Meet the Press" *NBC News*, Transcript for August 10, 2008.

A. Willoughby's Role in the United Nations Command's Defeat in November, 1950", *U.S. Army Command and General Staff College.*

ABC News, Sept. 19.

Ablan, J. (2007). "PIMCO's Gross Says 'Subprime Crisis' not ISOLATED", *Reuters*, June 26.

Ahikam, A. (2013). "The Intifada and the Arab Spring, Comparative View of the Intelligence Aspect", *Israel Intelligence Heritage and Commemoration Center*, No. 65, February. In Hebrew.

Ahir, H., and Loungani, P. (2014). "Can Economists Forecast Recessions? Some Evidence from the Great Recession", *George Washington University Research Program in Forecasting Seminar*, January 30.

Aid, M., and Burr, W. (2013). "Secret Cold War Documents Reveal NSA Spied on Senators", Foreign Policy, September, 25.

Allan, R. (2001). *A History of the Personal Computer: The People and the Technology*, Allan Publishing.

Allen, L. (2013). *The Global Economic Crisis, A Chronology*, UK: Reaktion Books.

Ament, L. (2013). "Social Intelligence: A Time to Listen, A Time to Engage". Hypatia Research Group.

Amit, R., Domowitz, I., and Fershtman, C. (1988). "Thinking One Step Ahead: The Use of Conjectures in Competitive Analysis", *Strategic Management Journal*, Vol. 9.

Analysis, Center for the Study of Intelligence, Washington, DC.

and the Work Ahead, Penguin Press HC.

Appelbaum, B. (2012). "Inside the Fed in 2006: A Coming Crisis, and Banter", New York Times, January 13.

Applegate, L., and Collins, E. (2005). *IBM's Decade of Transformation: Turnaround to Growth*, Harvard Business School Prod. #: 805130.

Argaman, Y. (1987). "Interview with Ephraim Sneh", *Bamahaneh*, November 4. In Hebrew.

Erlich, Y. (2008). "From Whom the Bells Toll, International and the First Intifada", *Israel Intelligence Heritage and Commemoration Center*, No. 51. In Hebrew.

Armstrong, G., Kotler, P., Harker, M., and Brennan, R. (2009). *Marketing an Introduction*, Pearson Education Inc.

Armstrong, A. (1989). "Bridging the Gap: Intelligence and Policy", *The Washington Quarterly, Winter* 1989.

Aspin-Brown Commission. (1996). "Preparing for the 21st Century: An Appraisal of U.S. Intelligence", *Commission on the Roles and Capabilities of the United States Intelligence Community*, United States Publishing Office. March 1.

Austin, R., and Nolan, R. (2000). "IBM Corporation: Turnaround 1991–1995", HBS Case No. 600–098.

Awad, Mubarak E. (1984). "Non-Violent Resistance: A Strategy for the Occupied Territories", *Journal of Palestine Studies*, University of California Press, Vol. 13, No. 4. Summer.

Baer, R. (2002). *See No Evil: The True Story of a Ground Soldier in the CIA's War on Terrorism*, Crown Books.

Baker, S. (1998). "What Every Business Should Learn from Microsoft", *The Journal of Business Strategy*, Boston: Sep/Oct 1998.Vol.19, No. 5.

Balzli, B., and Schiessl, M. (2009). "The Man Nobody Wanted to Hear".

Bar-Joseph, U. (1995). "Israel's Intelligence Failure of 1973: New Evidence, A New Interpretation and Theoretical Implications", *Security Studies*, Vol. 4, No. 3.

Bar-Joseph, U. (2004). *Intelligence and Politics, Intelligence and the Decision Makers*, Tel Aviv: The Broadcast University of the Ministry of Defense. In Hebrew.

Bar-Joseph, U. (2013). "Forecasting a Hurricane: Israeli and American Estimations of the Khomeini Revolution", *Journal of Strategic Studies*, 15 February.

Bar-Joseph, U., and McDermott, R. (2017). *Intelligence Success and Failure, The Human Factor*, Oxford University Press.

Bar-Joseph, U., and Kruglanski, A. (2003). "Intelligence Failures and the Need for Cognitive Closure: On the Psychology of the Yom Kippur Surprise", *Political Psychology* 24.

Bar-Joseph, U., and McDermott, R. (2008). "Change the Analyst and Not the System: A Different Approach to Intelligence Reform", *Foreign Policy Analysis*, Vol. 4.

Barnea, A. (2010). "Creating More Value to the Competitive Intelligence Function", *Competitive Intelligence Magazine*, Vol. 13, No. 1, January/ March.

Barnea, A. (2015). "Comparative Analysis of National and Business Intelligence Failures", PhD thesis, Haifa University, Department of Political Science, August. In Hebrew.

Baron, J. (2000). *Thinking and Deciding*, Cambridge University Press.

Barr, C. (2008). "Europe: The New Wall Street?" *Fortune*, October 7.

Baumfeld, M. (2014). "Sadat Initiative from February 1971: Was It Really a Missed Opportunity?" *Israel Intelligence Heritage and Commemoration Center*.

Bazerman, M., and Chugh, D. (2006). "Decision-Making without Blinders", *Harvard Business Review*, Vol. 84, No. 1.

Bazerman, M., and Watkins, M. (2003). "Predictable Surprises: The Disasters You Should Have Seen Coming", *Harvard Business Review*, OnPoint, Product 337x.

Also in Bazerman, M., and Watkins, M. (2004). *Predictable Surprises: The Disasters You Should Have Seen Coming and How to Prevent Them*, Harvard Business Press.

Behnke, L., and Slayton, P. (1998). "Shaping a Corporate Competitive Intelligence Function at IBM", *Competitive Intelligence Review*, Vol. 9.

Beinhocker, E. (1999). "Robust Adaptive Strategy", *Sloan Management Review*, Spring.

Beinhocker, E. (2006). "Creating Strategy in an Unknowable Universe".

Beinhocker, E. (2007). *The Origin of Wealth, The Radical Remaking of Economics and What it Means for Business and Society*, Harvard Business Review Press.

Bell, G. (2012). "Stars: Rise and Fall of Minicomputers", *IEEE Global History Network*.

Belvedere, M. (2013). "Bubbles and Leverage Cause Crisis: Alan Greenspan", https://www.cnbc.com/2013/10/23/something-fundamentally-wrong-with-the-way-i-look-at-the-economy-alan-greenspan.html.

Ben-Ishai, R. (1988). "A Blow from the Territories", *Yedioth Ahronot*, April 1, 1988. In Hebrew.

Ben-Porat, Y. (1988). "The Surprise of the Intifada – How Did This Happen To Us Again?" *Hamanit, the Israeli Intelligence Corps*, No. 9, September 1988. In Hebrew.

Bensoussan, B., and Fleisher, C. (2008). *Analysis without Paralysis*, Upper Saddle River, NJ: FT Press.

Bergman, R. (2013). "How To Prevent The Next Crisis", *Mammon*, October 11.

Berkowitz, B. (2003). "The DI and 'IT': Failing TO KEEP UP with the Information Revolution", *Studies in Intelligence* 47, No. 1.

Bernanke, B. (2007). "The Subprime Mortgage Market", At the *Federal Reserve Bank of Chicago's 43rd Annual Conference on Bank Structure and Competition*, Chicago, Illinois, May 17.

Bernanke, B. (2007). "To the 2007 International Monetary Conference, Cape Town, South Africa" (via satellite), June 5, 2007.

Bernanke, B. (2012). "The Absence of Regulation Worsened the Crisis of 2008", *The Marker*, April 13. In Hebrew.

Bernanke, B. (2012). "The Federal Reserve's Response to the Financial Crisis, Lecture 3, The Chairman of the Federal Reserve Lectures at George Washington University".

Bernanke, B. (2013). "Bernanke Speech at 49th Annual Conference on Bank Structure and Competition", May 10.

Bernanke, B. (2013). *The Federal Reserve and the Financial Crisis*, Princeton University Press.

Best Jr., R. (2004). Proposals *for Intelligence Reorganization, 1949–2004*, Washington, DC: Congressional Research Service, 2004.

Betts, R. (1980). "Surprise Despite Warning: Why Sudden Attacks Succeed".

Betts, R. (2003). "Politicization of Intelligence: Costs and Benefits", In Betts.

Betts, R. (2004). "Analysis, War, and Decision: Why Intelligence Failures Are Inevitable?", In Lock, J. Johnson and James, J. Wirtz (Eds.), *Strategic Intelligence: Windows into a Secret World,* Los Angeles: Roxbury Publishing Company.

Betts, R. (2004). "Politization of Intelligence: Costs and Benefits", in Richard Betts and Thomas Mahnken (Eds.), *Paradoxes of Strategic Intelligence*, London: Frank Cass Publishers.

Betts, R. (2004). "The New Politics of Intelligence: Will Reforms Work This Time", *Foreign Affairs*, 83, No. 3, June.

Betts, R. (2007). *Enemies of Intelligence: Knowledge and Power in American National Security*, New York: Columbia University Press.

Binder, A. (2008). "Two Bubbles, Two Paths", *The New York Times*, June 15.

Blanchard, O., Romer, D., Spence, M., and Stiglitz, J. (2012). *In the Wake of the.*

Blinder, A. (2013). *After the Music Stopped: The Financial Crisis, the Response.*

Bloomberg Businessweek Global Economics. (2013). "Hank Paulson: This Is What It Was Like to Face the Financial Crisis", *Bloomberg Businessweek Global Economics*, September 12.

Borio, C., and White, W. (2003). "Whither Monetary and Financial Stability: the Implications of Evolving Policy Regimes".

Bossie, D. (2004). *Intelligence Failure: How Clinton's National Security Policy Set The Stage for 9/11*, Nashville, TN: WorldNetDaily Books.

Brady, D. (2012). "Is Wells Fargo Another Bad Actor in the Housing Crisis?", *Bloomberg Businessweek*, Oct. 9.

Bughin, J., and Chui, M. (2013). "Evolution of the Networked Enterprise", *McKinsey and Company.*

Cabinet Office, *The National Security Strategy of the United Kingdom, Update 2009, Security of the Next Generation*, The Stationary Office, London, June 9, 2009.

Calof, J. (2008). "Selling Competitive Intelligence", *Competitive Intelligence Magazine*, Vol. 11, No. 1.

Calof, J., and Wright, S. (2008). "Competitive Intelligence: A Practitioner, Academic and Inter-Disciplinary Perspective", *European Journal of Marketing*, Vol. 42, No. 7/8.

Carroll, R. (2001). "Missiles to Protect Summit Leaders", *The Guardian*, July 11.

Carton, R., and Hofer, C. (2008). *Measuring Organizational Performance*, Edward Elgar Publishing.

Case-Shiller Home Price Indices, Understanding the Case-Shiller Housing Index. *Investopedia.*

Cavelty, M., and Mauer, V. (2009). "Postmodern Intelligence: Strategic Warning in an Age of Reflexive Intelligence", *Security Dialogue*, Vol. 40, No. 2.

Chan, S. (2010). "US Faults Regulators Over a Bank", The New York Times, April 12.

CBS, "Face the3 Nation with Bob Schieffer", December 8, 2002, https://www.cbs news.com/news/ftn-12-8-02/.

Central Intelligence Agency. (2007). "OIG Report on CIA Accountability with Respect to the 9/11 Attacks".

Chan Kim, W., and Mauborgne, R. (2007). *Blue Ocean Strategy*, Tel Aviv: Matar. In Hebrew.

Charan, R., and Colvin, G. (1999). "Why CEOs Fail", Fortune, June 21.
Chernev, A., and Kotler, P. (2012). *Strategic Marketing Management*, Cerebellum Press.
Childers, G., and DePippo, H. (1998). "Foreign Terrorists in America: Five Years After the World Trade Center", *Prepared Testimony before the Senate before Judiciary Committee, Subcommittee on Technology, Terrorism and Government Information.*
Chossudovsky, M. (2002). "Political Deception: The Missing Link behind 9–11", *Global Research*, June, 2002.
Christensen, C. (1997). *The Innovator's Dilemma: When New Technologies Cause Great Firms to Fail*, Boston, MA: Harvard Business School Press.
Church Committee Reports. (1976). *U.S. Senate Selected Committee on Intelligence.*
Chussil, M. (2005). "With All This Intelligence, Why Don't We Have Better Strategies?" *Journal of Business Strategy*, Vol. 26, No. 1.
Clark, A., and Treanor, J. (2008). "Greenspan: I Was Wrong About the Economy, Sort of", *The Guardian*, October 24, 2008.
Clarke, R. (2004). *Against All Enemies, Inside America's War on Terror*, Free Press, a subsidiary of Simon and Schuster.
Colander, D., Föllmer, D., Haas, A., Goldberg, M., Juselius, K., Kirman, A., Lux, T., and Sloth, B. (2009). "The Financial Crisis and the Systemic Failure of Academic Economics", *University of Copenhagen Dept. of Economics Discussion Paper, No. 09-03*, March 11.
Colby, W. (1978). *Honorable Men: Life in the CIA*, New York: Simon and Schuster.
Colby, W. (1980). "Recruitment, Training and Incentives for Better Analysis".
Coll, S. (2004). *Ghost Wars*, New York: Penguin.
Collins, J. (2009). *How The Mighty Fall: And Why Some Companies Never Give In*, Collins Business Essentials.
Cooper, J. (2005). "Curing Analytical Pathologists to Improved Intelligence Analysis", Langley, VA, *Central Intelligence Agency, Center for the Study of Intelligence.*
Copeland, T. (2006). "Surprise, Intelligence Failure, and Mass Casualty Terrorism", PhD thesis, The Graduate Faculty of the Graduate School of Public and International Affairs, University of Pittsburgh.
Cordesman, A. (2002). *Terrorism, Asymmetric Warfare and Weapons of Mass Destruction, Defending the US Homeland*, Center for Strategic and International Studies, Washington, D.C.
Courtney, H., Horn, J., and Kar, J. (2009). "Getting into Your Competitors Head", *The McKinsey Quarterly*, November.
Coyne, K., and Horn, J. (2009). "Predicting Your Competitor's Reaction", *Harvard Business Review*, April, 2009.
Crisis: Leading Economists Reassess Economic Policy, The MIT Press.
Crutsinger, M. (2014). "Bernanke Likens '08 Financial Crisis to Car Crash", ABC News, January 16.
Cumming, A., and Masse, T. (2004). "FBI Intelligence Reform Since September 11 2001: Issues and Options for Congress", *Congressional Research Service*, Report No. RL32336, April 6.

Dahl, E. (2010). "Missing the Wake-Up Call: Why Intelligence Failures Rarely Inspire Improved Performance", *Intelligence and National Security*, Vol. 25, No. 6.

Dahl, E. (2013). *Intelligence and Surprise Attack: Failure and Success from Pearl Harbor to 9/11 and Beyond,* Washington DC: Georgetown University Press.

Damon, A. (2013). "Top US Officials Vastly Underestimated 2008 Economic and Financial Crisis Federal Reserve Transcripts", *Global Research*, January 27.

Davis, J. (2002). "Improving CIA Analytic Performance: Strategic Warning", *Occasional Papers:* Volume 1, Number 1, September, Sherman Kent Center.

Davis, J. (2003). "Strategic Warning: If Surprise is Inevitable, What Role for Analysis?", The Sherman Kent Center for International Analysis, *Occasional Papers*, Vol. 2, No. 1 Jan.

Davis, J. (2006). "Intelligence Analysts and Policymakers: Benefits and Dangers of Tensions in the Relationship", *Intelligence and National Security*, Vol. 21, No. 6.

Davis, J. (2007). "Intelligence Analysts and Policy Makers: Benefits and Dangers of Tensions in Relationships", in Johnson, L. (Ed.), *Strategic Intelligence: The Intelligence Cycle*, New York: Praeger Security International.

Day, G., and Reibstein, D. (1997). "Introduction: The Dynamic Challenges for Theory and Practice", in Day, G., and Reibstein, D. (Eds.), *Wharton on Dynamic Competitive Strategy*, New York: John Wiley and Sons, Inc.

de Franco, C., and Meyer, C. (2011). "Introduction: The Challenges of Prevention", in Chiara de Franco, and Christoph O. Meyer (Eds.), *Forecasting, Warning and Responding to Transnational Risks*, Palgrave Macmillan.

DeRosa, M. (2004). *Data Mining and Data Analysis for Counterterrorism*, Washington, DC: CSIS Press.

Diamond, J. (2008). *The CIA and the Culture of Failure: U.S. Intelligence from the End of the Cold War to the Invasion of Iraq*, Stanford Security Studies.

Dikova, D., Smeets, R., Garretsen, H., and Van Ees, H. (2013). "How Multinational Corporations are Buffered from Financial Crises", *International Business Review*, Vol. 22, No. 1, February.

Dishman, P., and Calof, J. (2008). "Competitive Intelligence: A Multiphasic Precedent to Marketing Strategy", *European Journal of Marketing*, Vol. 42, No. 7/8.

Dixon, S. (2013). "Failure, Survival or Success in a Turbulent Environment: The Dynamic Capabilities Lifecycle", Management Articles of the Year, *CMI, Cartered Management Institute*, UK, January.

Drori, Y. (2004). *Dealing with Vague Reports, Intelligence and the Decision Makers*, Tel Aviv: Ministry of Defense, the Broadcast University.

Drucker, P. (1993). *Post-Capitalist Society*, New York: Harper Business.

DW staff (2008). "German Finance Minister Blames US for Financial Crisis", September 25.

Dwyer, J. (1994). *Two Seconds Under the World*, New York: Crown Publishing.

Eaves, E. (2007). "Don't Buy That House", *Forbes*, June 26.

Eichenwald, K. (2013). *500 Days: Secrets and Lies in the Terror Wars*, New York: Touchstone; Reprint edition.

Eichenwald, K. (2012). "The Deafness Before the Storm", New York Times, September 10, 2012.

Ekstein, T, Fisher, S and Flug, K. (2011). *Israel and the Global Crisis, 2007–2009.* Jerusalem, Bank of Israel. In Hebrew

Eldar, A. (2009). "Operation Cast Lead: Israeli Military Intelligence Did Not Expect a Hamas Victory in the 2006 Elections or Its Takeover of the Gaza Strip. Intelligence Failure? Not Necessarily", *Haaretz*, January 9. In Hebrew.

European Union, "A Secure Europe in a Better World", *European Security Strategy*, December 12, 2003, Brussels.

Evangelista, E. (2005). "Pairing up", *Pharmaceutical Executive*, Vol. 25, No. 10.

Evans, M. (2013). *Algeria: France's Undeclared War*, Oxford University Press.

Evgeniou, T., Gaba, V., and Niessing, J. (2013). "Does Bigger Data Lead to Better Decisions?", *HBR Blog Network*, October 21.

Fahey, L. (1998). *Competitors: Outwitting, Outmaneuvering, and Outperforming*, John Wiley & Sons.

Farkash, Z., and Tamari, D. (2011). *To the Best of Our Knowledge, Intelligence, Operations and Policy*, Tel Aviv, Yedioth Ahronoht. In Hebrew.

Farmer, J. (2009). *The Ground Truth: The Untold Story of America Under Attack on 9/11*, New York, Riverhead Books.

Farrall, J. (1993). "Suddenly, Questions of Security Jolt American the Invulnerable: Explosion in New York", *The Boston Globe*, February 28.

Feder, S. (2001). "Overcoming "Mindsets": What Corporations Can Learn from Government Intelligence Failures", *Competitive Intelligence Review*, Vol. 11, No. 3.

Federal Bureau of Investigation. FBI. (2004). "The FBI's Counterterrorism Program Since September 2001", *Report to the National Commission on Terrorist Attacks Upon the US*, April 14.

Fellman, P., and Post, J. (2010). "Complexity, Competitive Intelligence and the First Mover Advantage", *Unifying Themes in Complex Systems: Vol. VI: Proceedings of the Sixth International Conference on Complex Systems*, In Minai, A., and Braha, D.

Ferguson, N. (2008). *The Ascent of Money: A Financial History of the World*, London: Allen Lane.

Ferguson, N. (2011). *Civilization: The West and Everything Else*, Tel Aviv: Am Oved. In Hebrew.

Ferris, J., and Handel, M. (1995). "Clauzewitz Intelligence Uncertainty and the Art of Command in Military Operations", *Intelligence Journal and National Security*, Vol. 10, No. 1.

Fingar, T. (2011) *Reducing Uncertainty: Intelligence Analysis and National Security*, California: Stanford University Press.

Finkelstein, S. (2004). *Why Smart Executives Fail: And What You Can Learn from Their Mistakes*, New York: Portfolio Penguin Group.

Fischhoff, B. (2011). "Communicating about Analysis", *Intelligence Analysis, Behavioral and Social Scientific Foundations*, Baruch Fischoof and Cherie Chauvin (Eds.), Washington, DC: National Research Council of the National Academics, the National Academic Press.

Fleisher, C., and Wright, S. (2010). "Competitive Intelligence Analysis Failure: Diagnosing Individual Level Causes and Implementing Organizational Level Remedies", *Journal of Strategic Marketing*, London, Vol. 18, No. 7.

FOMC (2006). "Transcripts and Other Historical Materials".

Foreign and Military Intelligence (Church Committee), *Select Committee to Study Governmental Operations, US Senate*, April 26, 1976, Book 1, Report No. 94–755.

Fox, J. (2014). "What Alan Greenspan Has Learned Since 2008", Harvard Business Review, HBR Blog Network, January 7.

Freeh, L. (2005). *My FBI: Bringing Down the Mafia, Investigating Bill Clinton and Fighting the War on Terror*, New York: St. Martin's Press.

Freeman, C. (2012). "Change Without Progress in the Middle East", *Middle East Policy Council*, October 25.

Frey, D. (1982). "Different Levels of Cognitive Dissonance, Information Seeking and Information Avoidance", *Journal of Personality and Social Psychology*, Vol. 43.

Friedman, G. (2005). *America's Secret War: Inside the Hidden Worldwide Struggle Between America and Its Enemies*, Broadway Books.

Friedman, H. (2012). *The Measure of a Nation: How to Regain America's Competitive Edge and Boost Our Global Standing*, New York: Prometheus Books.

Friedman, T. (1990). *From Beirut to Jerusalem*, Tel Aviv: Ma'ariv Books. In Hebrew.

Frish, H. (1992). "From Armed Struggle to Political Enlistment: Changes in PLO Strategy In the Territories", in Sasser, A., Gilber, G. *In the Eye of the Conflict: the Intifada*, Tel Aviv: Hakibbutz Hameuhad, Red Line. In Hebrew.

Fuld, L. (1995). *The New Competitor Intelligence*, New York: John Wiley and Sons.

Fuld, L. (2013). "Competitive Intelligence Global Benchmarking Project Update", *Fuld Insights*, March.

Fuld, L., and Chodnowsky, M. (2010). "The Art of Anticipating Disruptions". *Fuld and Company White Papers*.

Gainor, R., and Bouthillier, F. (2014). "Competitive Intelligence Insights for Intelligence Measurement", *International Journal of Intelligence and Counter Intelligence*, No. 27.

Ganagher, A. (2008). "Hedge Funds' Growth Prospects Hit by Lehman's Demise", *Financial Times*, September 17.

GAO, U.S. Government Accountability Office, "Financial Crisis Losses and Potential Impacts of the Dodd-Frank Act", February 14, 2013.

Gates, R. (1987). "The CIA and Foreign Policy", *Foreign Affairs* 66. Winter.

Gates, R. (1989). "An Opportunity, Unfulfilled: The Use and Perceptions of".

Gazit, S. (1999). Fools in a Trap: 30 Years of Israeli Policy in the Territories, Tel Aviv: Zamora Bitan. In Hebrew.

Gelbar, Y. (1992). *The Roots of the Lily: Intelligence in the Yishuv, 1918–1947*, Tel Aviv: Ministry of Defense Publication. In Hebrew.

George, R., and Bruce, J. (2008). *Analyzing Intelligence: Origins, Obstacles, and Innovations*, Georgetown University Press.

Gerstner, L. (1973). "Can Strategic Planning Pay Off?", *McKinsey Quarterly*, December.

Gerstner, L. (2014). "Lou Gerstner on Corporate Reinvention and Values", *McKinsey Quarterly*, September.

Gerstner, L. (2004). *Who Says Elephants Can't Dance*, Tel Aviv: Modan. In Hebrew.

Gertz, B. (2002). *Breakdown: How America's Intelligence Failures led to September 11*, Washington, DC: Regnery Publishing Inc.

Gibson, S. (2014). "Exploring the Role and Value of Open Source Intelligence", in Christopher Hobbs, Matthew Moran, Daniel Salisbury (Eds.), *Open Source Intelligence in the Twenty-First Century: New Approaches and Opportunities*, Palgrave Macmillan, UK.

Gilad, B. (1989). "The Role of Organized Competitive Intelligence in Corporate Strategy", *Columbia Journal of World Business*, Vol. 24, No. 4.

Gilad, B. (1998). *Business Blindspots*, UK: Infonortics.

Gilad, B. (2004). *Early Warning: Using Competitive Intelligence to Anticipate Market Shifts, Control Risks and Create Powerful Strategies*, New York: Amacom Books.

Gilad, B. (2011). "Strategy without Intelligence, Intelligence without Strategy", *Business Strategy Series*, Vol. 12, No.1.

Gilboa, A. (2012) "The Surprise of the Yom Kippur War – Broad Outlook", *Israel Intelligence Heritage and Commemoration Center*, No. 64, October. In Hebrew.

Giraldi, P. (2005). "Deep Background", *American Conservative*, April 1.

Glaser, B., and Strauss, A. (1967). *The Discovery of Grounded Theory*, Hawthorne, NY: Aldine Publishing Company.

Glees, A., and Davies, P. (2008). "Intelligence, Iraq and the Limits of Legislative Accountability during Political Crisis", in Scott, L., and Hughes, R. (Eds.), *Intelligence, Crises and Security*, New York: Routledge.

Global Banking Economist Warned of Coming Crisis", *Spiegel Online*, August 7.

Baram, M. (2008). "Who's Whining Now? Gramm Slammed by Economists".

Goldberg, J. (2007). "Letters From Washington: Woodward Vs. Tenet", *New Yorker*, May 21.

Goldfarb, Z. (2012). "Fed's Image Tarnished by Newly Released Documents", *Washington Post*, January 12.

Goodman, M. (2003). "9/11: The Failure of Strategic Intelligence", *Intelligence and National Security* 18/4.

Goodwin, J., and Skocpol, T. (1989). "Explaining Revolutions in the Contemporary Third World", *Politics and Society*, December 17.

Gordon, M., and Trainer, B. (2006). *Cobra II: The Inside Story of the Invasion and Occupation of Iraq*, New York: Pantheon.

Gorton, G. (2012). *Misunderstanding Financial Crises: Why We Don't See Them Coming*, Oxford University Press.

Graham, B., and Nussbaum, J. (2008). *Intelligence Matters: The CIA the FBI Saudi Arabia and Failure of America's War on Terror*, University Press of Kansas.

Grant, R. (2005). *Contemporary Strategy Analysis*, Oxford, UK: Blackwell Publishing.

Greeley, B. (2012). "The Fed Takes a Crash Course in Finance", *Bloomberg Businessweek*, August 20.

Green, J. (2013). "Where Is Dick Fuld Now? Finding Lehman Brothers' Last CEO", *Bloomberg Businessweek*, September 12.

Greenspan, A. (1997). "The Evolution of Banking in a Market Economy", Remarks by Chairman Alan Greenspan At the Annual Conference of the Association of

Private Enterprise Education, Arlington, Virginia April 12. *The Federal Reserve Board*, Washington, DC.
Greenspan, A. (2002). "Remarks by Chairman Alan Greenspan, Before the Council on Foreign Relations, International Financial Risk Management", *The Federal Reserve Board*, Washington, DC. November 19, 2002. Retrieved from http://www.federalreserve.gov/boarddocs/speeches/2002/20021119/.
Greenspan, A. (2005). "Remarks by Chairman Alan Greenspan: Economic Flexibility", *The Federal Reserve Board*, Washington, DC. October 12.
Greenspan, A. (2009). *The Age of Turbulence*, Tel Aviv: Matar. In Hebrew.
Greenspan, A. (2010). "The Crisis", Brookings Papers on Economic Activity, Brookings Institution Washington Press, DC.
Grove, A. (1997). *Only Paranoids Survive*, Tel Aviv: Matar. In Hebrew.
Gulcin Ozkan, F., and Filiz Unsal, D. (2012). "Global Financial Crisis, Financial Contagion, and Emerging Markets", *IMF Working Paper*, WP/12/293.
Gurr, R. (1970). *Why Men Rebel*, Princeton: Princeton University Press.
Hackman, R. (2011). *Collaborative Intelligence: Using Teams to Solve Hard Problems*, Berrett-Koehler Publishers.
Hacham, D. (2006). "And the Land Will Be Filled with Hamas", *Haikin Geostrategy Chair*, Haifa University. In Hebrew.
Halberstam, D. (2007). *The Coldest Winter: America and the Korean War*, New York: Hyperion.
Hamel, G. (2000). "Waking Up IBM: How a Gang of Unlikely Rebels Transformed Big Blue", *Harvard Business Review*, Vol. 78, July–August.
Hamel, G. (2001). "Waking up IBM: How a Gang of Unlikely Rebels Transformed Big Blue", *Harvard Business Review OnPoint.*
Handel, M. (1987). "The Politics of Intelligence", *Intelligence and National Security*, Vol. 2, No. 4.
Handel, M. (2003). "Intelligence and the Problem of Strategic Surprise", in Richard.
Harkabi, Y. (1984). "The Intelligence-Policymaker Tangle", *The Jerusalem Quarterly*.
Harkabi, Y. (1987). "Between Intelligence and the Decision Makers", Tsvi Ofer and Avi Kober (Eds.), *Intelligence and National Security*, Tel Aviv: Maarchot. In Hebrew.
Harreld, B., O'Reilly, C., and Tushman, M. (2007). "Dynamic Capabilities at IBM: Driving Strategy into Action", *California Management Review*, Vol. 49, No. 4, Summer.
Harris, S. (2013). "NSA Hype Machine", *Foreign Policy*, July 31.
Harvard Business School - Working Knowledge, June.
Haynes, J. (2009). "Intelligence Failure in Korea: Major General Charles".
Hedin, H., Hirvensalo, I., and Vaarnas, M. (2011). *The Handbook of Market Intelligence: Understand, Compete and Grow in Global Markets*, Wiley.
Hendel, M. (1987). "Intelligence and Deception", in Tsvi Ofer and Avi Kober (Eds.), *Intelligence and National Security*, Tel Aviv: Maarchot. In Hebrew.
Herman, M. (1996). *Intelligence Power in Peace and War*, Cambridge University Press.

Herring, J. (1990). "Senior Management Must Champion Business Intelligence Program", *Journal of Business Strategy*, September-October.

Herring, J. (1995). "Producing Actionable and Effective Intelligence", *Competitive Intelligence Review*, Vol. 6, No. 1.

Herring, J. (1999). "Identify and Define Intelligence Needs", *Competitive Intelligence Review*, Vol. 10, No. 2.

Herring, J. (2008). "Defining Competitive Intelligence Needs: The Role of Key Intelligence Topics" in Sawka, K., and Hohhof, B. (Eds.), *Staring a Competitive Intelligence Function*, Competitive Intelligence Foundation, Alexandra, Virginia.

Herring, R., and Wachter, S. (2002). "Bubbles in Real Estate Markets", in Hunter, W., Kaufman, G., and Pomerleano, M. (Eds.), *Asset Price Bubbles: The Implications for Monetary, Regulatory, and International Policies*, Massachusetts: The MIT Press Cambridge.

Hertz, N. (2013). "Every Leader Needs a Challenger in Chief", *HBR Blog Network, Harvard Business Review*, September 11.

Heuer, R. (1980). "Strategies of Analytical Judgment", *Analytical Methods Review*, November.

Heuer, R. (1999). *Psychology of Intelligence Analysis*, Washington, DC: CIA Center for the Study of Intelligence.

Hiam, M. (2006). *Who the Hell Are We Fighting? The Story of Sam Adams and the Vietnam Intelligence Wars*, Steerforth Press, Hanover, New Hampshire.

Hill, E. (2002). "The Intelligence Community's Knowledge of the September 11 Hijackers Prior to September 11, 2001", *Testimony before the Senate Select Committee on Intelligence [SSCI] and House Permanent Select Committee on Intelligence [HPSCI], 107th Cong., 2nd sess.*, September 20.

Hilsman, R. (1956). *Strategic Intelligence and National Decisions*, Chicago: Free Press.

Hollister Hedley, J. (2005). "Learning from Intelligence Failures", *International Journal of Intelligence and Counter Intelligence*, Vol. 18, No. 3, Fall.

Hollywood, J., Snyder, K., McKay, and Boon. J. (2004). *Out of the Ordinary: Finding Hidden Threats by Analyzing Unusual Behavior*, Santa Monica, CA: RAND Corporation.

Holtzman, J. (2005). "Competitive Intelligence Blindspots", *Competitive Intelligence Magazine*, Vol.8, No. 4 July-August.

Horn, J., Lovallo, D., and Viguerie, P. (2005). "Beating the Odds in Market Entry How to Avoid the Cognitive Biases that Undermine Market Entry Decision", *McKinsey Quarterly*, November.

Hudson, J. (2014). "In Reversal, FBI Now Emphasizes Role in Law Enforcement", *Foreign Policy*, January 17.

Hudson, R. (1999). "The Sociology and Psychology of Terrorism: Who Becomes a Terrorist and Why?" *Federal Research Division Library of Congress*, September.

Hughes, D., Le Bon, J., and Rapp, A. (2013). "Gaining and Leveraging Customer-Based Competitive Intelligence: The Pivotal Role of Social Capital and Salesperson Adaptive Selling Skills", *Journal of the Academy of Marketing Science*, Vol. 41, No. 1, January.

Hughes, T. (1976). "The Fate and Facts in World of Men-Foreign Policy and Intelligence Making", *Headline Series, No. 233*, New York: Foreign Policy Association.
Hughes-Wilson, J. (1999). *Military Intelligence Blunders*, London: Robinson.
Hulnick, A. (2006). "What's Wrong with the Intelligence Cycle?", *Intelligence and National Security*, Vol. 21.
Huntington, S. (1957). *The Soldier and the State, The Theory and Politics of Civil-Military Relations*, Harvard University Press.
Hypatia Research Group.
Inbari, P. (1994). *Broken Swords: the Palestinians in the Peace Process*, Tel Aviv: Ministry of Defense. In Hebrew.
Intelligence and National Security, 22/2, April.
"Intelligence at White House", *The Washington Quarterly*, Winter 1989.
George, A., and Smoke, R. (1974). *Deterrence in American Foreign Policy: Theory and Practice*, New York: Columbia University Press.
Intelligence", *E-International Relations*, January.
Israeli Military Intelligence, Defining the Role of Intelligence August 1956, IDF Archive (400/765/2004).
Jacobides, M., and MacDuffie, J. (2013). "How to Drive Value Your Way", *Harvard Business Review*, July-August.
Janis, I. (1972). V*ictims of Groupthink*, New York: Houghton Mifflin.
Janis, I. (1982). Gr*oupthink*, New York: Houghton, Mifflin.
Janis, I., and Mann, L. (1977). *Decision Making*, New York: Free Press.
Jeffries-Jones, R. (2009). *FBI, The History of the FBI in the United Sta*tes, Tel Aviv: Resling. In Hebrew:
Jenis, L. A., and Mann, L. (1980). *The Decision-Making Process*, Tel Aviv: Ministry of Defense Publication. In Hebrew.
Jenkins, P. (2013). "Lehman Legacy", *Financial Times*, September 9.
Jervis, J. (1986). "What's Wrong with the Intelligence Process, *International Journal of Intelligence and CounterIntelligence*, Vol. 1 No. 1.
Jervis, R. (1976). *Perception and Misperception in International Politics*, Princeton, NJ: Princeton University Press.
Jervis, R. (1985). "Perceiving and Coping with Threat", in Jervis, R., Ned Lobow, R., and Gross Stein, J., *Psychology and Deterrence*, pp. 24–25, Baltimore: Johns Hopkins University Press, 1985.
Jervis, R. (2006). "Reports, Politics and Intelligence Failures: The Case of Iraq", *The Journal of Strategic Studies*, Vol. 29, No. 1.
Jervis, R. (2011). *Why Intelligence Fails: Lessons from the Iranian Revolution and the Iraq War*, Ithaca, NY: Cornell University Press.
Johansson, A., Roos, D., and Kirchgeorge, V. (2010). "The Art of Systematic Surveillance", *Arthur B. Little.*
Johnson, C. (2008). "Guidelines Expand FBI's Surveillance Powers", *The Washington Post*, October 4.
Johnson, L. (1985). *A Season of Inquiry: The Senate Intelligence Investigation*, University Press of Kentucky.

Jones, M., and Silberzahn, P. (2013). *Constructing Cassandra: Reframing Intelligence Failure at the CIA, 1947–2001*, Stanford University Press.

Kabha, M. (2010). *The Palestinians: A Dispersed People*, Tel Aviv: Open University. In Hebrew

Kahaneman, D. (2013). *Thinking Fast and Slow*, Tel Aviv: Matar. In Hebrew.

Kahaner, L. (1996). *Competitive Intelligence: How to Gather Analyze and Use Information to Move Your Business to the Top*, Simon and Schuster.

Kahn, D. (1991). "The Intelligence Failure of Pearl Harbor", *Foreign Affairs*, Vol. 70, No. 5, Winter.

Kahn, D. (2006). "The Rise of Intelligence", *Foreign Affairs*, Sep/Oct, Vol. 85, No. 5.

Kahn, D. (2009). "An Historical Theory of Intelligence", in Gill, P., Marrin, S., and Pythian, M. (Eds.), *Intelligence Theory: Key Questions and Debates*, New York: Routledge, Taylor and Francis Group.

Kam, E. (1987). "Surprise Attack – Failures and Prevention", in Tsvi Ofer and Avi Kober (Eds.), *National Security and Intelligence*, Maarachot. In Hebrew.

Kam, E. (1990). *Surprise Attack*, Tel Aviv: Maarachot. In Hebrew.

Kaplan, R., and Mikes, A. (2012). "Managing Risks: A New Framework", *Harvard* Business *Review*, June.

Kaspit, B., and Kfir, A. (1998). *Barak, Soldier Number One*, Tel Aviv: Alfa Communications Publishing. In Hebrew.

Kean, T., and Hamilton, L. (2005). "9/11 Panel's Report Must Not Go Unheeded", *Baltimore Sun*, June 12.

Keidar-Levi, H. (2013). *The Great Financial Crises of the Past Hundred Years*, Tel Aviv: Broadcast University, Modan. In Hebrew.

Kennan, G. (1997). "Spy and Counterspy", *New York Times*, May 18.

Kent, S. (1949). *Strategic Intelligence for American Foreign Policy*, Princeton, NJ: Princeton University Press.

Kindleberger, C., Aliber, R., and Solow, R. (2012). *Manias, Panics and Crashes: A History of Financial Crises*, Sixth Edition, New York: Palgrave Macmillan.

Klein, M. (1991). *The PLO and the Intifada*, Tel Aviv University, Dayan Center. In Hebrew.

Kotler, P., and Hornik, Y. (2000). *Market Management,* Vol. 1, Tel Aviv: Open University. In Hebrew.

Kotler, P., Keller, K., and Hornik, Y. (2012). *Market Management*, Vol. 1, Tel Aviv: Open University. In Hebrew.

Kruglanski, A., Bar-Tal, D., and Klar, Y. (1993). "A Social Cognitive Theory of Conflict", in Larsen, K. (Ed.), *Conflict and Social Psychology*, London: Sage.

Krugmam, P. (2009). "How Did Economists Get It So Wrong?" *New York Times*, September 2.

Krugman, P. (2009). *Economics in Days of Crisis*, Tel Aviv: Yedioth Ahronoth. In Hebrew.

Krugman, P. (2008). "The Gramm Connection", *New York Times*, March 29.

Krugman, P. (2009). "How Did Economists Get It So Wrong?" *New York Times*, September 6.

Kulikowski, L. (2007). "Lehman Brothers Amputates Mortgage Arm", *TheStreet.com.*
Kunda, Z. (1990). "The Case of Motivated Reasoning", *Psychological Bulletin*, Vol. 108.
Kurtz, A. (2008). "A Struggle on Two Fronts: The Palestinian Uprising Between Internal War and War against Israel", *The Institute of National Strategic Studies*, Tel Aviv, Memorandum 95. In Hebrew.
Lahart, J. (2009). "Mr. Rajan Was Unpopular (But Prescient) at Greenspan Party", *The Wall Street Journal*, January 2, 2009.
Lahav, S. (2005). *Go to Gaza*, Tel Aviv: Ma'ariv. In Hebrew.
Lance, P. (2003). *1000 Years for Revenge: International Terrorism and the FBI—The Untold Story*, New York: Regan Books.
Lanir, T. (1983). *The Basic Surprise: Intelligence in Crisis*. Tel Aviv, Hakibutz Hameochad. In Hebrew.
Laqueur, W. (2009). *The Uses and Limits of Intelligence*, London: Transactions Publishers.
Latimer, T. (1979). "US Intelligence and the Congress", *Strategic Review*, Summer.
Lavi, A. (2008). "Intelligence Work in the Palestinian Arena, Critical Assessment", *Israel Intelligence Heritage and Commemoration Center*, No. 52, December. In Hebrew.
Lawson, S. (2003) I*nternational Relations*, London: Polity Press.
Ledeen, M. (2005). "Intelligence Failures, Virtues and Sins of Commission", *National Review*, April 7.
Leibs, S., and Furman. M. (2011). "Think (again)", *CFO*, July/August.
Levenberg, H. (2011). "Developments in the Intifada during the First Stage", Lecture at the "Intifada 1987–1992" Seminar held on July 7, 2011, at the *Center for Defensive Studies*, Ramat Efal. In Hebrew.
Levine, R. (2010). "An Autopsy of the US Financial System: Accident, Suicide, or Negligent Homicide", *Journal of Financial Economic Policy*, Vol. 2, No. 3.
Levy, D., and Weizer, S. (1985). "System Error: How the IBM Antitrust Suit Raised Computer Prices", AEI, *Journal on Government and Society*, September/October.
Lewis, M. (2010). *The Money Machine*, Tel Aviv: Yedioth Books. In Hebrew.
Lichtblau, E. (2005). "FAA Alerted on Qaeda on 98, 9/11 Panel Said", New York Times, September 14.
Lichtblau, E., and Piller, C. (2002). "Without a Clue: How the FBI Lost Its Way", *Milwaukee Journal Sentinel*, August 11.
Lichtblau, E., and Sanger, D. (2004). "August '01 Brief is Said to Warn of Attack Plans", *The New York Times*, April 10.
Litani, Y. (1998). "Where Did We Go Wrong – We Didn't Listen to Our Inner Voice", *The Seventh Eye*, No. 16, September. In Hebrew.
Lohr, S. (1994). "On the Road with Chairman Lou", *New York Times*, June 26.
Lohr, S. (2008). "Betting to Improve the Odds", *New York Times*, April 9.
Lovallo, D., and Sibony, O. (2010). "The Case for Behavioral Strategy", *McKinsey Quarterly*.
Lowenthal, M. (2013). "A Disputation on Intelligence Reform and Analysis: My18 Theses", I*nternational Journal of Intelligence and Counter Intelligence*, Vol. 26, No. 1, Spring.

Lundberg, K. (2002). "Credible Warnings or False Alarms? What the US Knew on September 10, 2001", *Harvard Kennedy School*, Harvard Business Publishing.

Lustick, I. (1993). "Writing the Intifada: Collective Action in the Occupied Territories", *World Politics*, Vol. 45, July.

Maddrell, P. (2016). "Introduction", in Paul Maddrell (Ed.), *The Image of the Enemy*, Washington, DC: Georgetown University Press.

Malfatto, P. (2007). "A Diagnosis of the Failure of American Intelligence Community before 9/11: Organizational and Perceptual Explanations", *Paper presented at the annual meeting of the International Studies Association 48th Annual Convention, Hilton Chicago*, Chicago, USA, February 28, 2007.

Marcus, Y. (2013). "Living on the Knife-Edge", *Haaretz*, December 27. In Hebrew.

Marlin Tepper, J. (1991). "Bills for Gulf War Are Higher Than You Think", *Newsday*, March 8.

Marrin, S. (2011). "The 9/11 Terrorist Attacks: A Failure of Policy Not Strategic Intelligence Analysis", Intelligence and National Security, Vol. 26, 2–3.

Martin, A. (2002). *Harnessing the Power of Intelligence, Counterintelligence and Surprise Events, the Professional Development Institute/Executive.Org.*

McCarthy, A. (2005). "It's Time to Investigate Able Danger, and the 9/11 Commission", N*ational Review*, December 8.

McCubbins, M. (1985). "The Legislative Design of Regulatory Structure", *American Journal of Political Science*, Vol. 29, No. 4, November.

McGovern, R. (2011). "Did Tenet Hide Key 9/11 info?", 911Truth.Org, August 17.

McGonagle, J., and Vella, C. (2003). *The Manager's Guide to Competitive Intelligence*, Westport, CT: Praeger.

McGravey, P. (1973). "DIA: Intelligence to Please", in Halperin, M., and Kanter, A. (Eds.), *Readings in American Foreign Policy*, Boston: Little Brown.

McHenry, C., and Fleisher, C. (2012). "How to Measure Strategic Market and Competitive Intelligence Performance", *Aurora WDC.*

McQueen, M.P. (1993). "Prevented Defense; Experts: US Can't Stop Them", *Newsday*, New York, March 10.

Medina, C., and Fisher, R. (2009). "What the World Economic Crisis Should Teach Us", *Studies in Intelligence*, Vol. 53, No. 3, September.

Mellers, B., Erev, R., Fessler, d., Hemelrijk, C., Hertwig, G., Laland, k., Schereere, K., Seeley, T., Selten, R., and Tetlock, P. (2001). "Group Report: Effects of Emotions and Social Processes on Bounded Rationality", in Gigerenzer, G., and Selten, R. (Eds.), *Bounded Rationality: The Adoptive Toolbox*, Cambridge, MA: MIT Press.

Melman, Y., and Raviv, D. (2012). *The Shadow War, the Mossad and the Intelligence Community*, Tel Aviv: Yedioth Ahronoth. In Hebrew.

Meridor, D. (2013). "Does Intelligence Need a Reform?" "Intelligence 2013, What has Changed?" Conference, Tel Aviv: *The Institute for National Security Studies*, No. 26, May. In Hebrew.

Miller, S. (2002). "Competitive Intelligence—An Overview", *Competitive Intelligence Magazine*, Vol. 4, No. 2.

Ministry of Defense. (2001). *Quadrennial Defense Review Report*, September 30.

Miniter, R. (2003). *Losing Ben Laden: How Bill Clinton's Failures Unleashed Global Terrorism*, Washington, DC: Regnery Publishing.

Minsky, H. (1986). *Stabilizing an Unstable Economy*, McGraw-Hill Professional.

Mintz, A., and DeRouen, K. (2010). *Understanding Foreign Policy Decision Making*, Cambridge University Press.

Mintzberg, H. (2009). *Managing*, California: Berrett-Koehler Publishers.

Mishkin, F. (1999). "Lessons from the Asian Crisis", *Journal of International Money and Finance*, Vol. 18.

Mishal, S., and Aharoni, R. (1989). *Stones Aren't Everything*, Tel Aviv: Hakibbutz Hameuhad. In Hebrew.

Missal, M. (2011). "United States Bankruptcy Court for the District Delaware New Century TRS Holdings Inc", February 29.

Montegomry, D. B., and Weinberg, C. (1979). "Toward Strategic Intelligence Systems", *Journal of Marketing*, Vol. 43.

Montgomery, D., Moore, M., and Urbany, J. (2005). "Reasoning About Competitive Reactions: Evidence from Executives", *Marketing Science*, Vol. 24, No. 1, Winter.

Moran, P. (2005). "Structural vs. Relational Embeddedness: Social Capital and Managerial Performance", *Strategic Management Journal*, Vol. 26.

Moreh, D. (2014). *Guardians at the Gate*, Tel Aviv: Yedioth Books. In Hebrew.

Morgan, I. (2009). *The Age of Deficits: Presidents and Unbalanced Budgets from Jimmy Carter to George W. Bush*, University Press of Kansas.

Morgenson, G., and Rosner, J. (2011). *Reckless Endangerment: How Outsized Ambitions, Greed and Corruption Led Economic Armagenddon*. New York: Times Books.

Mouton, Troy, M. (2002). "Organizational Culture's Contributions to Security Failures within the United States Intelligence Community". *Louisiana State University, LSU Master's Theses*.

Mullen, M. (2010). "Admiral Mullen Speech on Military Strategy", Kansas University, March 3.

Myers, L. (2004). "The Missed Opportunities of 9/11: Could the Attacks on America have been Disrupted or Delayed?", July 26.

MyLroie, L. (2000). *Study the Revenge: Saddam Hussein's Unfinished War with America*, Washington, DC, The AEI Press.

Na, M. (2008). "Three Paradoxes of the Financial Crisis", *Foreign Policy*, February.

Naftali, T. (2005). *Blind Spot*, New York: Basic Books.

Nakashima, E. (2010). "Former NSA Executive Thomas A. Drake May Pay High Price for Media Leak", *The Washington Post*, July 14.

Nassar, J., and Heacoock, R. (Eds.). (1990). *Intifada: Palestine at the Crossroads*, New York: Praeger Publishers.

National Intelligence Council (2008). "Global Trends 2025". *Foresight for Development*.

National Security Agency (2001). "The Pyramid of Excellence for Intelligence Analysis and Production: A Maturity Model", *Criptologic Quarterly*.

Neilson, G., Martin, K., and Powers, E. (2008). "The Secrets to Successful Strategy Execution", *Harvard Business Review*, June.

Neumann, P. (2009). *Old and New Terrorism*, Polity Press.
Nicolaci Da Costa, P. (2014). "N.Y. Fed Staff Afraid to Speak Up, Secret Review Found", *Wall Street Journal*, September 26.
Nir, A. (1987). "The IDF Will Take a Firm Hand", *Haaretz*, December 11. In Hebrew.
Nir, A. (1987). "The Trouble in the Territories: A Civil Revolt", Haaretz, December 13. In Hebrew.
Nir, A. (1987). Editorial. *Haaretz*, December 14. In Hebrew.
Nisbett, R., and Ross, L. (1980). *Human Inference: Strategies and Shortcomings of Social Judgment*, Englewood Cliffs, NJ.
Nonaka, I. (1991). "The Knowledge Creating Company", *Harvard Business Review*, Vol. 69, No. 6.
NSC 68: "United States Objectives and Programs for National Security", April 15, 1950.
Nunes, P., and Breene, T. (2011). *Jumping the S-Curve: How to Beat the Growth Cycle, Get on Top, and Stay There*, Harvard Business Review Press.
Oberdorfer, D. (2001). *Tet! The Turning Point in the Vietnam War*, Johns Hopkins University Press.
O'Malley, J. (2006). "September 11 Intelligence Failures Problems Prior to 9–11", Yahoo Voices, November 21.
Parker, C., and Stern, E. (2002). "Blindspots? September 11 and the Origins of Strategic Surprise", *Political Psychology*, Vol. 23, No. 3.
Pascale, R. (1984). "Perspectives on Strategy: The Real Story Behind Honda's Success", *California Management Review*, Vol. 26.
Pasternak, J. (2001). "FAA, Airlines Stalled Major Security Plans", *Los Angeles Times*, October 6.
Paulson, M. (2011). *On the Brink: Inside the Race to Stop the Collapse of the Global Financial*, New York: Grand Central Publishing.
Peri, Y. (1999). *He Who Comes to Kill You*, Tel Aviv: Keshet. In Hebrew.
Petersen, M. (2011). "What I Learned in 40 Years of Doing Intelligence Analysis for US Foreign Policymakers", *Studies in Intelligence*, Vol. 55, No. 1, March.
Pike Papers. (1976). *The US Congress, House, Selected Committee on Intelligence, CIA Report*, January 29, Published in a Special Supplement of The Village.
Pillar, P. (2004). "A Scapegoat Is Not a Solution", *New York Time*, June 4.
Pillar, P. (2006). "Good Literature and Bad History: The 9/11 Commission's Tale of Strategic Intelligence", *Intelligence and National Security*, Vol. 21, No. 6.
Pointer, J. (2007). "UPDATE 2-Top Five US Subprime Lenders Asked to Testify-Dodd", *Reuters*, March 19. *Political Science Quarterly*, Vol. 95, No. 4.
Porter, M. (1991). *Competitive Strategy*, Herzliya: Ateret. In Hebrew.
Porter, M. (2000). On *Competition*. Tel Aviv: Matar. In Hebrew.
Posner, G. (2004). *Why America Slept: The Failure to Prevent 9/11*, New York: Ballantine Books.
Posner, R. (2004). "The 9/11 Report: A Dissent", *New York Times Book Review*, August 29.
Posner, R. (2005). *Preventing Surprise Attacks: Intelligence Reform in the Wake of 9–11*, Lanham, MD: Rowman and Littlefield Publishing.

Posner, R. (2009). *A Failure of Capitalism: The Crisis of '08 and the Descent into Depression*, Cambridge, MA: Harvard University Press.

Prescott, J. (2001). "Competitive Intelligence: Lessons from the Trenches", *Competitive Intelligence Review*, Vol. 12, No. 2.

Prescott, J., and Williams, R. (2003). "The User-Driven Competitive Intelligence Model", *Competitive Intelligence Magazine*, Vol. 6, No. 5, September-October.

Prunckun, H. (2014). "Extending the Theoretical Structure of Intelligence and Counterintelligence", *Salus Journal*, Vol. 2, No. 2.

Pundak, R. (2013). *Secret Channel, Oslo, the Full Story*, Tel Aviv: Yedioth Ahronoth, Hemed Books. In Hebrew.

R., and Mahnker, T. (Eds.), *Paradoxes of Intelligence: Essays in Memory of Michael Handel*, Portland, OR: Frank Cass.

Rajan, R. (2005). "Has Financial Development Made the World Riskier?", NBER Working Paper No. 11728, Issued in November.

Rajan. R. (2008). "Bankers' Pay Is Deeply Flawed", *Financial Times*, January 8.

Reeve, S. (1999). *The Jackals: Ramzi Yousef, Osama Bin Laden and the Future of Terrorism*, Boston: Northeastern University Press.

Reger, R. (1990). "Managerial Thought Structure and Competitive Positioning". In A. S. Huff (Ed.), *Mapping Strategic Thoughts,* pp. 71–88. Chichester, UK: Wiley.

Reimer, J. (2009). "Personal Computer Market Share: 1975–2004", November 2.

Reinhart, C., and Rogoff, K. (2008). "Is the 2007 U.S. Sub-Prime Financial Crisis So Different? An International Historical Comparison", *National Bureau of Economic Research Working Paper*, No. 13761, Issued in January 2008.

RepoWatch (2008). "Geithner: At Heart of Crisis Were Repos and Shadows", *The Economic Club of New York,* June 9.

Riebling, M. (1994). *Wedge: The Secret WAR Between the FBI and CIA*, New York, Alfred Knopf.

Riley, M. (2013). "How the U.S. Government Hacks the World", *Bloomberg Businessweek*, May 23.

Roberto, M., Bohmer, R., and Edmondson, E. (2006). "Facing Ambiguous Threats", *Harvard Business Review*, November.

Robinson, W., and Johnson, G. (2001). "Airlines Fought Security Changes Despite Warnings, Companies Wanted to Avoid Delays", *Boston Globe*, September 20.

Rose, A., and Spiegel, M. (2010). "The Causes and Consequences of the 2008 Crisis: Early Warning", *Global Journal of Economics*, Vol. 1, No. 1.

Rosen, J. (2005). "General Confirms al Qaida Hunt", *Sacramento Bee*, December 7.

Rotemberg, J. (2014). "The Federal Reserve's Abandonment of Its 1923 Principals", *NBER* Working Paper No. 20507, September.

Roth-Meyer, Y. (2007). *The Binding—The Intifada Trial.* Tel Aviv: Efi Melzer Publications. In Hebrew.

Roubini, N. (2006). "Why Central Banks Should Burst Bubbles", *International Finance*, Vol. 9, No. 1, pp. 87–107, Spring.

Roubini, N., and Meihm, S. (2011). *Crisis Economics*, Tel Aviv: Modan. In Hebrew.

Rowley, C. (2002). "Coleen Rowley's 9/11 Memo to FBI Director Mueller", *Time Magazine.*

Rubinstein, D. (2001). *Arafat, a Portrait,* Tel Aviv: Zamora Bitan. In Hebrew.
Sageman, M. (2008). *Leaderless Jihad: Terror Networks in the Twenty First Century*, Philadelphia: University of Pennsylvania Press.
Sawka, K. (2010). "The Death of the Competitive Intelligence Professional", *Competitive Intelligence Magazine*, Vol. 13. No. 2, March/April 2010.
Schmitt, G. (2005). "Truth to power: Rethinking Intelligence Analysis", in Peter Schoemaker, P. (1995). "Scenario Planning: A Tool for Strategic Thinking", *Sloan Management Review*, Winter.
Schiff, Z. (1987). "The Worse Extent of the Riots since '67", *Haaretz*, December 20. In Hebrew.
Schiff, Z., and Yaari, E. (1990). *Intifada*. Tel Aviv: Shoken. In Hebrew.
Schiffer, S. (2011) *Yedioth Ahronoth*, June 10. In Hebrew.
Schroen, G. (2006). "Schroen Interview", *The Dark Side*, January 20.
Senator Charles, E., and Schumer (2007). Latest News, September 10.
Sela, A. (2012). "The First Intifada, History of Violence", *Haaretz supplement*, December 7. In Hebrew.
Setser, B. (2009). "Debating the Global Roots of the Current Crisis", *Council on Foreign Relations*, January 29.
Shalev, A. (1990). Intifada: The Causes, the Characteristics and the Consequences. Papirus. In Hebrew.
Shiller, R. (2005). *Irrational Exuberance (2d ed.)*, Princeton University Press.
Shulsky, A., and Scmitt, G. (2002). *Silent Warfare: Understanding the World of Intelligence*, Potomac Books Inc.
Siegel, E. (2013). P*redictive Analytics: The Power to Predict Who Will Click, Buy, Lie, or Die*, New Jersey: John Wiley and Sons Inc.
Siegel, E., and Davenport, T. (2013). *Predictive Analytics: The Power to Predict Who Will Click, Buy, Lie, or Die*, Wiley and Sons, Inc.
Simmons, W. (1988). *Inside IBM: The Watson Years, a Personal Memoir*, Dorrance & Co.
Simon, H. (2000). "Public Administration in Today's World of Organizations and Markets", John Gaus lecture, Annual Meeting of the American Political Science Association, Washington, DC, September 1, 2000, reprinted in *PS: Political Science and Politics*, Vol. 33, No. 4, December.
Sinclair, R. (2010). *Thinking and Writing: Cognitive Science and Intelligence.*
Singer, D. (1958). "Threat -Perception and the Armament—Tension Dilemma", *Journal of Conflict Resolution*, March, No. 2.
Sivan, A. (2004). "Quod licet imperatori", *Haaretz*, June 14. In Hebrew.
Skipper, S. (2012). "Future Proofing Competitive Intelligence: Macro Trends in the Strategic Landscape", *SCIP. Insight*, January, Vol. 4, No. 1.
Slater, R. (1999). *Saving Big Blue: Leadership Lessons and Turnaround Tactics of IBM's Lou Gerstner*, New York: McGraw-Hill.
Solomon, J. (2002). "1999 Report Warned of Possible Suicide Hijackings into Federal Buildings", *The Associated Press*, May 18.
Sperger, M. (2008). "Starting an Intelligence Function in the Information Technology Industry", in Sawka, K., and Hohhof, B. (Eds.), *Starting a*

Competitive Intelligence Function, Alexandra, VA: Competitive Intelligence Foundation.

Steele, D. (2003). "On Intelligence", *OSS. Net*, October 11.

Stein, M. (2013). "When Does Narcissistic Leadership Become Problematic? Dick Fuld at Lehman Brothers", *Journal of Management Inquiry*, July.

Steinberg, M. (2008). *Their Fate: Palestinian National Awareness, 1967–2007*, Tel Aviv: Yedioth Books. In Hebrew.

Stiglitz, J. (2010). *Freefall: America, Free Markets, and the Sinking of the World Economy*, W. W. Norton and Company.

Stockman, D. (2013). *The Great Deformation: The Corruption of Capitalism in America*, Public Affairs.

Strasser, S. (2004). *House-Senate Joint Inquiry Report on 9/11*, New York: Public Affairs.

Strauss, A. C., and du Toit. A. (2010). "Competitive Intelligence Skills Needed to Enhance South Africa's Competitiveness", *Aslib Proceedings*, Vol. 62, No. 3.

Summary of Commentary on Current Economic Conditions, By Federal Reserve Districts, February 2008.

Szanton, P., and Allison, G. (1976). "Intelligence: Seizing the Opportunity", Foreign Policy, No. 22.

Tal, N. (1995) "Sheikh Izz al-Din Qassam", MA thesis, Department of Political Science, Haifa University. In Hebrew.

Tal, N. (1998). "The Tenth Anniversary of the Intifada", *Israel Intelligence Heritage and Commemoration Center*, No. 17, January. In Hebrew.

Tal, N. (2004). "The Intifada, 1987–1992", Seminar Held on July 11, 2011, *at the Center for Defensive Studies*, Ramat Efal. In Hebrew.

Taylor, A. (1995). "BANKING: Committee Approves 'Narrow' Glass-Steagall Rewrite", *CQ Weekly*, Washington, DC, May 13.

Teece, D. (2007). "Explicating Dynamic Capabilities: The Future and Microfoundations of Sustainable Enterprise Performance", *Strategic Management Journal*, Vol. 28.

Tellis, G. (2013). *Unrelenting Innovation: How to Build a Culture for Market Dominance*, San Francisco, CA: John Wiley and Sons, Jossey-Bass books.

Tett, G. (2009). *Fools's Gold: How the Bold Dream of Small Tribe at J.P/Morgan Was Corrupted by Wall Street Greed and Unleashed a Catastrophe*, New York: Free Press.

The 9/11 Commission Report Final Report of the National Commission on Terrorist Attacks Upon the United States, Executive Summary.

The Economist. (2008). "What Went Wrong", *The Economist*, Mar 19th.

The Financial Crisis Inquiry Report, Final Report of the National Commission on the Causes of the Financial and Economic Crisis in the United States (2011). *US Government Publishing Office*, February.

The House of Commons. (2004). "Review of Intelligence On Weapons of Mass Destruction", Chairman: The Rt. Hon The Lord Butler of Brockwell, July 14.

The Intelligence Reform and Terrorism Prevention Act of 2004, Public Law 108–458, December 17, 2004, Title 50 United States Code, §401. Referenced as the IRTPA, 2004.

The Jerusalem Center of Public Affairs (1997). "The Palestinians Mark the Tenth Anniversary of the First Intifada", December 10. In Hebrew.

The National Archives, Intifida- The Palestinian Uprising. (1989). *The National Archives*, April 1, Ref: FO 973/579/C568863

The National Commission on Terrorist Attacks Upon the United States. 2004). (known as "the 9–11 Commission Report"), *Government Printing Office*.

Thomas, D., and Kanji, A. (2004). "IBM's Diversity Strategy: Bridging the Workplace and the Marketplace", *Harvard Business School*, November 17, 9-405-044.

Thompson, P. (2004). *The Terror Timeline*. New York: HarperCollins.

Travers, R. (1997). "The Coming Intelligence Failure", *Studies in Intelligence*, Vol. 1, CIA/CSI.

Treverton, G. (2005). "Terrorism, Intelligence and Law Enforcement: Learning the Right Lessons", in Wesley K. Wark (Ed.), *Twenty-First Century Intelligence, Studies in Intelligence*, Routledge.

Treverton, G. (2011). *Intelligence for the Age of Terror*, Cambridge University Press.

Tsitoura, N., and Stephens, D. (2012). "Development and Evaluation of a Framework to Explain Causes of Competitive Intelligence Failures", *Information Research*, Vol. 17, No. 2, paper 521.

Turbiville, G. (2005). "Future Trends in Low Intensity Conflict", in Bunker, R. (Ed.), *Networks, Terrorism and Global Insurgency*, New York: Routledge, Taylor and Francis Group.

Tversky, A., and Kahanman, D. (1974). "Judgment under Uncertainty Heuristics and Biases", *Science*, Vol. 185.

Tversky, A., and Kahneman, D. (1982). "Evidential Impact of Base Rates", in D., United States Congress (1997). "Report on the Permanent Select Committee on Intelligence of House Permanent Select Committee on Intelligence", Representative Porter Goss, Chairman, June 18, 1997.

United States Select Committee on Intelligence and U.S House Permanent Committee on Intelligence. (2002). "Report of the Joint Inquiry into the Terrorist Attacks of September 11, 2001 by the House Permanent Select Committee on Intelligence and the Senate Select Committee on Intelligence", December, 2002.

United States Senate Permanent Subcommittee on Investigations (2011). "Wall Street and the Financial Crisis: Anatomy of a Financial Collapse", *Committee on Homeland Security and Governmental Affairs Carl Levin, Chairman Tom Coburn, Ranking Minority Member*, April 13.

United States Senate Select Committee on Intelligence. (2002). "Congressional Joint Inquiry into Intelligence Community Activities Before and After the Terrorist Attacks of September 11, 2001", December.

US Senate Committee on Banking, Housing and Urban Affairs (2006). Hearings.

US Senate Select Committee on Intelligence (2009). "Annual Threats Assess of the US Intelligence Community".

US Senate Select Committee on Intelligence (2010). "Annual Threats Assess of the US Intelligence Community".

Utterback , J. (2007). "Dominant Designs and the Survival of Firms", Excerpted from *Mastering the Dynamics of Innovation*, pp. 2–33, Harvard Business School Publishing Corporation.

Valukas, A. R. (2010). "Lehman Brothers Holdings Inc. Chapter 11 Proceedings Examiner's Report", *United States Bankruptcy Court Southern District, New York*, NY.

Waller, D. (1998). "Inside the Hunt for Osama", Time, December 21.

Walton, T. (2010). *Challenges in Intelligence Analysis: Lessons from 1300BCE to the Present*, New York: Cambridge University Press.

Walton, T. (2012). *The 2007–2009 Financial Crisis as a Way to Better Understand Intelligence Failure*, presented in ISA conference, April 2012.

Warsh, K. (2007). "Financial Stability and the Federal Reserve", At the *New York State Economics Association 60th Annual Conference*, Loudonville, New York, October 5.

Wasserman, B. (1960). "The Failure of Intelligence Predictions", *Political Studies*, June 8.

Watermam, H. (1981). "Reasons and Reason: Collective Political Activity in Comparative and Historical Perspective", *World Politics*, Vol. 33, July.

Waters, T. (2010). *Hyperformance, Using Competitive Intelligence for Better Strategy and Execution*, John Wiley and Sons.

Weiner, T. (2009). *Legacy of Ashes*, Tel Aviv: Resling. In Hebrew.

Weiner, T. (2012). *Enemies: A History of the FBI*, New York: Random House.

Wheaton, K., and Richey, M. (2014). "The Potential of Social Networks in".

Werner, E. (2013). "Intelligence Failure: Officials Brief Congress on Boston Bombing", *AP*, April 24.

Wheaton, K. (2001). *The Warning Solution: Intelligent Analysis in the Age of Information Overload*, AFCEA International Press.

White House Committee on Aviation Safety and Security Final Report, February 12, 1997.

White, W. (2012). "Credit Crises and the Shortcomings of Traditional Policy Responses", *Second International Research Conference, Reserve Bank of India*, Mumbai, February 1–2.

Wilensky, H. (1967). *Organizational Intelligence*, New York: Basic Books.

Wilson, T. (2008). "Working with Information Professionals, in Sawka, K., and Hohhof, B. (Eds.), S*tarting a Competitive Intelligence Function*, Alexandra, VA: Competitive Intelligence Foundation.

Wiltz, T. (2005). "TV's Hot Properties: Real Estate Reality Shows", *The Washington Post*, December 28.

Wohlstetter, R. (1962). *Pearl Harbor: Warning and Decision*, Stanford: Stanford University Press.

Wray, R. (2013). "Bernanke's Obfuscation Continues: The Fed's $29 Trillion Bail-Out Of Wall Street", *The Huffington Post*, December 14.

Wright, L. (2006). *The Looming Tower: Al-Qaeda and the Road to 9/11*, New York: Vintage Books.

Yoaz, Y. (2014). "When the Court Authorized the Sale of Lehmann, Everyone Present Rose and Applauded", *Globes*, January 28–29. In Hebrew.

Zajac, E., and Bazerman, M. 1991. "Blind Spots in Industry and Competitor Analysis: Implications of Interfirm (mis) Perception to Strategic Decisions", *Academy of Management Review*, Vol. 16.

Zandi, M. (2009). *Financial Shock: A 360 Look at the Subprime Mortgage Implosion and How to Avoid the Next Financial Crisis*, Upper Saddle River, NJ: FT Press.

Zegart, A. (2005). "September 11 and the Adaptation Failure of U.S. Intelligence Agencies", *International Security*, Vol. 29, No. 4, Spring.

Zegart, A. (2007). "9/11 and the FBI: The Organizational Roots of Failure".

Zegart, A. (2009). *Spying Blind: The CIA, The FBI and the Origins of 9–11*, Princeton University Press.

Zohar, G. (2008). "Better a Good Neighbor, How the Intelligence Community Copes in the Palestinian Arena", in Gilboa, A., and Lapid, *Israel's Silent Defender*, Tel Aviv: Yedioth Ahronoth. In Hebrew.

Zohar, G. (2013). "Chief of Staff General David Elazar and the General Staff in the Yom Kippur War", *Armored Corps Website*, July 9. In Hebrew.

Index

About the Author

Dr. Avner Barnea is a research fellow at the National Security Study Center (NSSC), at the University of Haifa, in Israel. He is also a lecturer in the School of Business Administration at Netanya Academic College, and at the School of Management and Economics, The Academic College of Tel Aviv-Yaffo, in Israel. He is a former senior member of the Israeli Security Agency (ISA). He received a PhD in International Relations from the University of Haifa. Barnea is the author of the book *We Did Not Anticipate That: Comparative Analysis of Intelligence Failures in the National Field and the Business Field* (2019—Hebrew).

www.ingramcontent.com/pod-product-compliance
Ingram Content Group UK Ltd.
Pitfield, Milton Keynes, MK11 3LW, UK
UKHW040910190926
475560UK00009B/179

9 781793 619884